Igniting Collective Goodness

Igniting Collective Goodness

Mann Ki Baat @100

BlueKraft Digital Foundation

First published by Westland Books, a division of Nasadiya Technologies Private Limited, in 2023

No. 269/2B, First Floor, 'Irai Arul', Vimalraj Street, Nethaji Nagar, Alapakkam Main Road, Maduravoyal, Chennai 600095

Westland and the Westland logo are the trademarks of Nasadiya Technologies Private Limited, or its affiliates.

ISBN: 9789357766555

10 9 8 7 6 5 4 3 2 1

Typeset by Jojy Philip, New Delhi

Printed at Thomson Press (India) Ltd

Contents

SECTION III: India's Civilisational Unity in Its Splendid Diversity

SECTION IV: Statistics and Number

Foreword

I am glad that a book is being penned on *Mann Ki Baat,* in light of this programme having completed 100 episodes in April 2023. *Mann Ki Baat* is a journey that we collectively began on the auspicious day of Vijaya Dashami, back in 2014. Today, over a hundred episodes later, I am filled with gratitude and joy as I reflect on our remarkable journey together.

Mann Ki Baat started as a small experiment, an endeavour to bring to light the inspiring life stories that often remain overshadowed in the daily hustle of politics and governance. Life stories of collective good and societal transformation are happening across India's length and breadth. The radio show created a direct channel of communication with the people, a channel where we could listen to each other, learn from each other, and grow together as a nation. As I said during Episode 100, *Mann Ki Baat* is about Guno Ki Pooja or worshipping the collective goodness of the people. Over the years, it has evolved into much more than just a radio program. It has become a platform for the voices of our nation, particularly those from the grassroots, whose stories of perseverance, courage and innovation continue to inspire us all.

It is heartening to see that the topics we discuss on *Mann Ki Baat* have a multiplier effect—it inspires several other people to initiate similar efforts or embark on something totally new and transformative. This ignites collective goodness, as the title suggests.

Throughout these 100 episodes, we have traversed across our diverse nation. We have celebrated the unsung heroes, acknowledged the relentless efforts of our farmers, appreciated the creativity of our artists, and admired the spirit of our young innovators. Each episode of *Mann Ki Baat* is a testament to the indomitable will and strength of our people, and their relentless pursuit of progress and development.

I am particularly glad to note the positive impact that *Mann Ki Baat* has had in stimulating thoughtful discussions and research around the topics we have covered. These topics, ranging from environmental conservation to technological innovation, and cultural preservation to social welfare, are crucial for our collective progress and prosperity. It is indeed heartwarming to see that *Mann Ki Baat* has inspired intellectual curiosity and scholarly study. I hope this trend continues in the times to come.

I am confident that the analysis of *Mann Ki Baat* episodes, in this book, will inspire many more to contribute to the making of a New India.

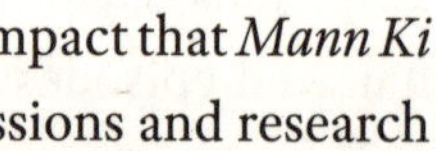

Narendra Modi
New Delhi

Introduction

BlueKraft Digital Foundation has had the privilege of chronicling the journey of Mann Ki Baat, through the years. *Igniting Collective Goodness: MKB@100* is the third book in the series. Each of the three books captures the extraordinary journey to a distinct milestone of *Mann Ki Baat*—an ongoing dialogue, which has kept the nation engaged once a month since 3 October 2014.

The first book was published following the culmination of 26 episodes and was released in May 2017 by the then President of India. The completion of 50 episodes marked the second milestone. The ensuing book delved into an analysis of the various facets of the initial 50 episodes. It was launched in March 2019 by the then Finance Minister of India.

As the title suggests, *Igniting Collective Goodness* celebrates the collective impact of individual goodness, on the landmark occasion of *Mann Ki Baat* completing 100 glorious episodes.

Mann Ki Baat is intricately intertwined with Prime Minister Narendra Modi's innate characteristics and personal ethos. His life is a lesson in the transformative power of dedicated and honest effort. No other leader in the history of Independent India has displayed such unwavering consistency in pursuing the right actions, no matter how small, which has, over time, compounded into substantial and previously unimaginable changes. Several of these changes have fundamentally transformed our nation. *Mann Ki Baat* stands as a prominent testament to this work ethos. The compounding effect of the collective goodness that each episode has individually ignited has made it the fulcrum of numerous transformative shifts within society. Beyond the rough and tumble of day-to-day politics, *Mann Ki Baat* has evolved into a monthly festival of identifying, encouraging and celebrating the goodness of our people. Its influence has transcended boundaries, leaving no household untouched and no barrier unbreached.

In a nation as diverse as ours, *Mann Ki Baat* has established a profound connection between Prime Minister Modi and every household in India. This connection is nurtured by the fact that the issues addressed by the PM resonate deeply within each home. From a heartfelt focus on every state of India—from the Northeast to Jammu & Kashmir—to the diversity of topics covered—from Digital India or Made in India Toys—to the inspirational conversations with various groups—from empowered women to entrepreneurial youth—every episode of *Mann ki Baat* has contributed to a collective discourse that unites our vast national family.

This book is, therefore, uniquely placed to analyse the impact of *Maan Ki Baat,* not only in terms of its far-reaching influence but also in its extensive scope. It presents a comprehensive, holistic and historical account, making it a standalone work that offers a fresh perspective on the phenomenon of *Mann Ki Baat.*

The book is divided into four segments with nineteen chapters, and traverses the entire gamut of the *Mann Ki Baat* phenomenon.

Section I, aptly titled 'Speaking to the Nation', comprises four insightful chapters. The chapters essentially document the two-way dialogue that the nation indulges in every month and the macro, cross-sectoral impact made by such an effort. The conversations with students appearing for the board exam in 2016 and 2017, which then inspired the standalone Pariksha Pe Charcha with *Exam Warriors* in subsequent years; the Jan Bhagidari that the nation exhibited during the fight against COVID-19 pandemic and the subsequent vaccination phase; the inspirational stories of unsung Padma Award winners, reaching every home in India, thereby inspiring thousands of others to understate similar selfless efforts; the process that is followed to ensure that *Mann Ki Baat* reaches the people of India in the language of their day-to-day conversations—such small anecdotes from various episodes, that together had a big impact, are the highlight of this section.

Section II, titled 'Enabling Social Change', comprises nine chapters. Each chapter focuses on a particular domain and documents how Prime Minister Narendra Modi's persistent and consistent focus has had a transformative impact on each domain. If Swachh Bharat is now a mass movement, then in large parts, it is due to the personal capital that the Prime Minister deployed in almost every episode of *Mann Ki Baat*, to spread awareness about the topic. Similarly, other issues related to women empowerment, youth, farmers, health and fitness, Aatmnirbhar Bharat, water conservation, drugs-free India, dangers of single-use plastic, mainstreaming every part of the Northeast by making it part of the routine conversation, promoting both awareness and inquisitiveness about science and technology, and various such topics are covered in this section. One chapter is especially dedicated to how Prime Minister Modi has used *Mann Ki Baat* to inculcate a national culture about sports.

Section III, named 'India's Civilisational Unity in Its Splendid Diversity' has five chapters and is about the simple and the small, the big and the beautiful, the different and the diverse, and yet the common and the connected facets of our nation that make us the unique civilisation that we are. A consistent theme over the 100 episodes of *Mann Ki Baat*, is about educating the citizen about the nation's fabulous diversity, yet celebrating our essential unity. The chapters in this section chronicle the monumental effort that Prime Minister Modi has undertaken in the nine years since he first started the monthly radio dialogue—from promoting the tourism potential of Incredible India to making it a regular feature to honour our unsung heroes. And from promoting local short stories, lullabies and folk songs of each state to highlighting the festivals, dances forms and music that may be unique to a particular geography.

The concluding section, Section IV, titled 'Statastics and Strategies', has a single chapter that presents a multifaceted view of *Mann Ki Baat* through the lens of both quantitative and qualitative analysis. One analysis and three surveys, done by four reputed individuals or institutions, are discussed in this chapter. A reputable data science professor from the Indian Institute of Management, Bangalore conducted the first analysis exclusively for this book. The other three studies, discussed in this chapter, were released in the public domain upon completing 100 episodes of *Mann Ki Baat* in April 2023. However, their incorporation within this chapter provides a comprehensive and all-encompassing analysis within a singular framework. These are respective studies done by Indian Institute of Management

Rohtak; a study done by Institute for Competitiveness (IFC) and supported by Axis My India and Bill and Melinda Gates Foundation; and lastly, a study undertaken by Indian Institute of Mass Communication, New Delhi.

Ideating the book's title was one of the relatively easy tasks while conceptualising this book. Consider some of these interesting examples. In one episode, Prime Minister Modi gave a national voice to a young girl who talks of her novel experiments in conserving rainwater. Soon it became a national character and even spurred concerted government action towards conserving rainwater in our lakes and ponds across every district. In another episode, the PM proudly cited the accumen of a young woman entrepreneur who took a small Mudra loan to start her own leather goods business. Soon enough, millions of such young women and men were inspired to become not just job seekers, but job givers and livelihood creators. As of 15 August 2023, over 80 million such new entrepreneurs have become part of the New India growth engine. In yet another episode, Prime Minister Narendra Modi recounted the exemplary voluntary efforts of a young girl from Nagaland cleaning the ghats in Kashi. The inspirational impact of this story spurred hundreds of other voluntary efforts for Swachh Bharat. One such story was of a man who was so inspired that he started an on-ground movement to clean the Juhu beach in Mumbai. His ability to build a movement also found a mention in a subsequent episode.

So, what is the common thread that unites these disparate examples that constitute the central essence of Prime Minister Narendra Modi's endeavours and accomplishments throughout the episodes of *Mann Ki Baa*t? When the Prime Minister of India, the most popular democratically elected leader in the world, becomes the broadcaster of an act of individual goodness, it perforce inspires millions of other people to follow suit, replicate and multiply that goodness in their own little ways. And thus, the title of the book—*Igniting Collective Goodness*. The power of this collective is more than the sum of the individual parts and this book demonstrates, through ample evidence, that this is indeed what has happened.

Finally, we are deeply indebted and honoured that Hon'ble Prime Minister Narendra Modi has himself penned the foreword of this book. Rarely do books have this unique honour. Hence, the book, in a sense becomes a historical document for future researchers and authors. We are also grateful to the Prime Minister for providing us the occasion to personally interact with him, while we were researching this book. We have had the occasion to quote him in many chapters, as and where relevant.

We are also deeply thankful to the many other domain experts and national and international experts who have enlightened us with their insights and have been appropriately quoted in the book. We are thankful to the publishers Westland Books for being very professional and thoughtful in helping us structure this book while simultaneously understanding the nuances that differentiate this book from others.

Last, but not the least, we would like to thank the readers. We have made every effort possible to encapsulate the entirety of the experience that *Mann Ki Baat* has been for India. Any shortcomings or errors are entirely our responsibility. Happy reading!

SECTION I

Speaking to the Nation

1

The World's Largest Democracy in Conversation

> 'We should not forget that our strength lies in our democracy. Our strength lies in the people's power. Our strength lies in each and every citizen of our country.'
>
> – Prime Minister Narendra Modi

Mann Ki Baat, Prime Minister Narendra Modi's popular monthly radio address has transformed into an example of how a living democracy celebrates its citizens. It is a resounding testament to the power of collaboration, simplicity and authenticity when it comes to leadership, in word and, indeed, in deed. The Prime Minister has said in one of the episodes of the programme, '*Where there is a soul, there is a story.*' Each episode is the story of the universal soul that connects Prime Minister Modi directly, distinctly and palpably with every citizen of India.

Mann Ki Baat, the programme is a dialogue and, therefore, it is as organic as the nuanced conversations of our leader. It is not a manifesto; it is a direction. It is not a collection of policies; it is a mosaic of experiences. Above all, it is not a political treatise, it is a heart-to-heart conversation that is beyond mundane politics, and some may even say, beyond boundaries. Through the powerful style of his expression, he gives a voice to the sincere efforts of the common woman and man.

Acknowledging the invaluable impact of the show, eminent spiritual leader **Sri Sri Ravi Shankar** says, '*Mann Ki Baat* is such a wonderful idea, such a great project for the leader of the country to be connecting with the common man on the ground. It is the best use of electronic media. One benefit is that people are getting the information that they would usually get through the news and the other is they are getting inspired. Our Prime Minister is inspiring millions, especially the youth and workers ... Sunday morning has come to be a time for the young and the old to sit together in front of the radio and listen to what our Prime Minister has to say. It is an inspirational idea worth being emulated by every leader on the planet.

If the leader only sits in an ivory tower, surrounded by just a few people and the information of what is happening in the world doesn't reach him, progress doesn't happen and happiness cannot blossom. The biggest sign of the progress of a country is when people's voices are heard and answered.'

In keeping with this spirit of natural conversation, the show consists of relevant insights and naturally endearing anecdotes about *Mann Ki Baat*, as it relates to preserving the democratic principles of a nation as vast and diverse as India. Another synergy that continues to imbue every conversation the PM has on or off the camera with the citizens is the fact that the programme has proven to be an invaluable tool that reiterates the actionable social and policy changes that have come into being as a result of the Prime Minister's conversations with the many, many ordinary citizens of India over the course of the last 100 episodes.

Having been successfully incubated, deployed, experimented with and, finally, vehemently validated by a billion-strong nation, *Mann Ki Baat* has created a veritable legacy—of being the only, one-of-its-kind national broadcast—steered by the sitting head of the world's largest democracy, who is in conversation, often real-time, always unbiased, with the most powerful democratic entity: the Indian citizen.

Speaking of the powerful impact of the programme, former director general of AIR, and the man responsible for its genesis, former director general (AIR), **Fayyaz Shehryar** elaborates: 'As the year 2014 witnessed a change in the ruling government of India, the All India Radio (AIR) also thought of a programme—a programme with a difference. The plan was to take the Prime Minister of India, who is the Prime Minister of the world's largest democracy directly to his electors, in a way that the electors and the elected could remain connected on a definite frequency each month. What the Prime Minister chose to do was amazing, that is, he made his discussions very apolitical. There was no politics involved, no political axe to grind. He just focused on the children, women and sportspersons of India, on the industrial revolution and development in India, on the system of examinations conducted by various educational institutions in India. He used a tone that was totally different from the tone that he would generally use in his election rallies, or which other national and world leaders would use. His tone, demeanour and manner were affectionate, and that attracted the attention of all people across the world, not just those in India.

Indians felt empowered because it was a broadcast with a difference. India had never seen any Prime Minister coming to them so openly on the radio, on the television, or through such a simple mode of communication. What the Prime Minister of India has been doing from October 2014 till date, is becoming the people's Prime Minister. He invites letters and video messages from Indian citizens, and gets them in abundance.

The PM's broadcast has had an impact on the administrative structure at the Central government level, the state level and the district level. He has received a huge response. We have translated the programme; we have created regional versions not only in the regional languages enshrined in the eighth schedule of the Indian Constitution, but also in some of the major dialects spoken by millions and millions of Indian people.

In the historic 100th episode of the programme, Prime Minister Modi expressed his emotions by saying,

> 'Every month I read thousands of messages from the people of the country, every month I get to view one or the other wonderful manifestation of my countrymen. I see and feel the extremities of the penance and sacrifice of my countrymen. I don't feel as if I am even a little far away from you. For me *Mann Ki Baat* is not a programme, for me it is a matter of faith, of worship, a type of vrat. Like when people go to worship God, they bring along a thaal of prasad. For me, *Mann Ki Baat* is like a thaal of prasad I offer at the feet of God in the form of the janata janardan, the people. *Mann Ki Baat* has become a spiritual journey of my being.
>
> *Mann Ki Baat* is a journey from the self to the collective.
> *Mann Ki Baat* is a journey from myself to ourselves.
> It is not about me; but you are its sanskar sadhana.'

Once the format and the modus operandi of the programme were final, the substance part of it was set into motion. The Prime Minister believes in the power of a democracy and that no country can, in today's time, progress without the active participation of its people. His faith, that the majority of the problems in society can be solved by the people themselves through debates and deliberation, has been a leading leitmotif of *Mann Ki Baat*. This practice of deliberation and active citizen participation in the decision-making process dates back to his time as the Chief Minister of Gujarat. In Episode 21, PM Modi said:

> 'As I talk to you all on 26 June, we should not forget that our strength lies in our democracy. Our strength lies in the people's power. Our strength lies in each and every citizen of our country. We have to carry forward this commitment and make it stronger. And it is this people's power that has sustained democracy as its living embodiment. At one time, there might have been locks placed on newspaper houses, the radio might have been speaking just one kind of language, and yet, given the opportune moment, the citizens gave an example of the power of democracy ... And the more the governments get connected with the people, the stronger they become. The chasm between the government and the people leads to ruin. My endeavour has always been to ensure that the nation moves forward on the strength of people's participation.'

The Prime Minister, whose rich experience of serving people and being involved at every stage of development, has always involved himself with the common concerns of the general masses. Back in the 1970s and '80s, as a karyakarta serving in different districts of Gujarat, he would interact with people on a routine basis, listen to their problems and challenges, and take note of their concerns.

As the Chief Minister of Gujarat, he still didn't lose touch with the people. And this was not just restricted to ordinary citizens, but also the officers and ministers working for him. He provided platforms like Chintan Shivir for them to openly deliberate. Narendra Modi also broke the silos between different departments for better productivity, overall growth and development. Even after becoming the Prime Minister, he has continued with this tradition and has tried to follow this method, building upon already existing practices and implementing newer ones. In his *Mann Ki Baat* broadcasts, he often cites examples of goodness, kindness, self-realisation and working for the greater good in the most relatable manner.

In one episode of the show, he referred to the Mutthi Bhar Dhaanya initiative that has turned into a big movement in Nashik. Under this novel scheme, during the harvest period, Anganwadi workers collect a handful of rice from people. This grain is used to make piping hot food for children and women. In this way, each and every person who contributes a handful of grain transmutes into a conscientious civil social worker dedicated to this cause, becoming a soldier for the movement in the process. All of us have heard about the annaprashana sanskar that takes place in families all across India, where the first morsel of solid food is given to toddlers. This initiative carries forward that very same thought.

Similarly, in Episode 60 of the show, encouraging people to believe in their own democratic strength, the Prime Minister said,

> 'Come, we will buy only local products, emphasise the use of local products, which carry the fragrance of the sweat of our

> countrymen. That will be the most exultant moment for my free India. Let these be the dreams with which we proceed.'

Time and again he has said that it is imperative for the citizens of our country to become self-reliant and to live their lives with dignity. He reiterated,

> 'I would like to discuss one such initiative that has caught my attention, and that is the Himayat Programme of Jammu & Kashmir and Ladakh. In the Himayat programme, teenagers and youth from 15 to 35 years of age, those denizens of Jammu and Kashmir whose studies could not be completed for some reason or those who have had to leave school and college midstream are introduced to skill development and employment. My dear countrymen, it would gladden you to know that under the aegis of this programme, during the last two years, 18,000 youths, have been trained in 77 different trades. Out of these, around 5,000 people are now working somewhere or the other, and many have moved towards self-employment. The success stories of lives which have changed under the aegis of the Himayat programme truly touch the heart!'

Continuing his journey towards strengthening democratic tools, and involving larger and larger sections of the population, Narendra Modi has, since his election in 2014, been devising new methods and initiatives to engage more people more often. In Episode 8, he spoke of the Padma Awards. Referencing a video that had become the centre of attention in the media, in which a 107-year-old elderly motherly figure had broken with protocol to bless the President, the Prime Minister spoke of the honour and pride that all Indians must feel on hearing of such down-to-earth, rooted individuals. The lady was Saalumarada Thimmakka, who is famous in Karnataka as the Vriksha Mata (Tree Mother), and the ceremony was the Padma Awards distribution. The country was recognising and honouring the extraordinary contribution of Thimmakka who came from an ordinary background. She was decorated with the Padma Shri award.

Prime Minister Modi praised ordinary citizens receiving these awards, saying that today India feels proud of such great personalities. He urged listeners to read up about each of the Padma awardees and to discuss their contribution to society with their families. In 2020 alone, over 46,000 nominations were received for the Padma Awards. This number is more than 20 times the number of nominations received in 2014. This statistic reveals the faith of every one of us in the authenticity of these awards and tells us that the Padma Awards have now become the people's awards. The entire process of the Padma Awards is now completed online. Earlier, the decision had been taken by a select few, but it is now completely people-driven. We could even say that there is now a newfound faith and respect for these awards in the country.

In Episode 97, the PM spoke of how the Padma Awards reflected the love for music that is deeply ingrained in all. He said, 'Everyone's choice of music may differ, but music is a part of everyone's life. This time, among the Padma awardees are those with expertise in spreading the melody of our traditional musical instruments like Santoor, Bamhum and Dwitara. Ghulam Mohammad Zaz, Moa Su-Pong, Ri-Singhbor Kurka-Long, Muni-Venkatappa and Mangal Kanti Rai are just a few of the names being felicitated.'

He reiterated that the unique quality of all Padma awardees. He said the award rightfully belongs to those who always kept the country paramount, dedicating their lives to the principle of 'Nation first'. He reminded the future generation that just working for the country is an award for these silent warriors.

Praising this recognition given to the common citizen, famous Kathak dancer **Shovana Narayan** says, 'Recently there was the Padma Puraskar ceremony. The way the PM urged the people of this country to be forthcoming with their contribution to the development of society is inspiring. People from villages, and from every corner of the country, at every level are contributing to the development of the country. In the development of our society lies the development of our economy. The most important point is that such people are working for the development of all people of India. The PM has made us aware of such people and has given them recognition through the Padma Awards. So, he has made us aware of a lot of things and we have gained knowledge from them. I want to congratulate the PM again for *Mann Ki Baat*.'

Indeed, many Padma awardees are those who have risen to the top from the bottom of the pyramid by dint of sheer hard work. They have overcome the limitations of their resources and the terrible atmosphere of despair around them, and have forged ahead. In fact, their strong resolve and spirit of selfless service inspires us all. All these extraordinary stories would have remained unearthed had it not been for *Mann Ki Baat* and the PM's reference to them. Similarly, Episode 59 of the show began with a shout-out to the young people of our young nation, to their enthusiasm, patriotism and the sense of selfless service that envelops them. Celebrating NCC Day in that episode, the Prime

Minister said, in a warm jovial tone, that generally the young generations were more likely to remember Friendship Day, but there were still many people who remembered and celebrated NCC Day with equal fervour:

> 'So, let's talk about the NCC today. I, too, will get an opportunity to refresh a few memories. At the outset, on the occasion of NCC Day, I extend my best wishes to all NCC Cadets, both former and present. More so, since I was a cadet once too, I consider myself to be a cadet even today. All of us know that India's National Cadet Corps [NCC] is one of the largest uniformed youth organisations in the world. It is a tri-services organisation comprising the Army, the Navy and the Air Force. NCC means cultivating the qualities of leadership, patriotism, selfless service, discipline and hard work as an integral part of one's character, and imbibing them into one's habits.'

On the programme, he often reminds us of the greatness in the goodness of ordinary everyday actions. In one episode, he praised a divyang brother (a person living with disabilities).

> 'I have seen another piece news from Kerala that can make us realise our responsibilities. In Kottayam of Kerala, there is an elderly divyang person, N.S. Rajappan sahab. Due to paralysis, Rajappan is incapable of walking, but this has not affected his commitment towards cleanliness. For the past several years, he has been going out to the Vembanad lake in a boat and removing plastic bottles thrown into the lake. Think, how great is Rajappan's thought! Taking inspiration from Rajappan, we should also, wherever possible, make our contribution to cleanliness.'

Mann Ki Baat has become the platform through which Prime Minister Modi explicitly conveys this message to the world—India was, is and will always believe in a government 'of the people, by the people, for the people'. Urging his listeners to become active participants in the democratic functioning and awareness of everyday life, the Prime Minister cited the example of Mohammad Aslam, in Episode 68. A man from Baran district in Rajasthan, he was working to increase awareness among farmers. He would call himself the CEO of a farmer-producer organisation:

> 'I hope this is heart-warming news for the CEOs of major companies—that farmers from far-flung areas of the country are also becoming CEOs of farmer organisations now! Friends, Mohammad Aslam has made a WhatsApp group comprising several farmers from his area. On this group, every day he shares updates with the farmers on the prevalent prices at the neighbouring mandis in the area. His own FPO [Farmer Producer Organisation] also buys produce from the farmers, hence, this effort of his also helps farmers in taking a decision. Whichever be the field, accurate knowledge, free from misconceptions and rumours, can act as a force multiplier for every individual.'

It wouldn't be misplaced to say that whatever topic the Prime Minister touches upon, resonates heartily with the audience. In Episode 21, he had expressed his happiness at the active involvement of the nation in the various journeys of growth and self-actualisation that the people were undertaking.

> '*Mann Ki Baat* has become a platform to express the power of society. I had just casually mentioned "Selfie with Daughter" here and what a movement it became. The whole world was

amazed. Lakhs of people, perhaps from all the countries of the world, posted a selfie with their daughters. What great dignity it lent to our daughters! Anyone who clicked this selfie not only boosted their daughter's confidence, but also made a commitment to them. Whosoever saw these selfies realised that they will now have to give up their indifferent attitude towards daughters. This was a kind of a silent revolution.'

Praising the show for its candour and courage, veteran journalist **Smita Prakash** says, 'There will always be people who will make fun of anything to do with the government or governance in India. *Mann Ki Baat* (MKB), when it began in 2014, also faced this kind of sceptical non-belief, especially among the elite who said Mr Modi was probably trying to do what PM Nehru did with the AIR broadcast to the people of the country. They were convinced, that he would not be able to match Nehru's oratorial skill, and that was even before MKB had finished two or three episodes. But then, nobody had any doubts about Mr Modi's skill as a communicator. He is self-taught and has a unique flair to be a mass communicator.

'Right from the first episode to the 100th, Mr Modi has made the people of India his core focus group. He talks to those who want the demystification of government schemes and functioning. He praises success stories; he is empathetic to failure and he encourages achievers. He lays out his game plan for the week, month, year and even longer-term than that. The thing is, he keeps on communicating with the only people who matter—those who want to log on to listen to their PM, those who want to benefit from government schemes, those who want to be part of nation-building and those who want to be better informed.

'MKB has worked for the Prime Minister. He does not need his message to be interpreted by a third party. He speaks directly to the people, it is an idea that has worked for the party, leader and the government.'

Indeed, this radio programme has strengthened the bonds between the people of India and their representatives in its truest sense. It has diminished the artificial boundary that had existed between the people and their government, and has instilled trust in the choice India made in 2014. In September 2021, Prime Minister Modi paid a glowing compliment to a team of eight divyang citizens who hoisted the flag atop the Siachen Glacier:

> 'The cold there is so terrible that it is beyond the capacity of a common person to live there. With snow spread far and wide, there is no sign of any vegetation anywhere. The temperature here dips to even minus 60 degrees. The feat that was performed in this inaccessible region of Siachen a few days ago is a matter of pride for every countryman. This team created a world record by hoisting its flag on the Kumar Post situated at an altitude of more than 15,000 feet at the Siachen glacier.'

In Episode 52, the Prime Minister lauded the enormous contribution of our Armed Forces, Police and Paramilitary forces in the strides made by the country. He also praised Atish Mukhopadhyay who had written to him about the courage and patriotism of a 25-year-old youth, Birsa Munda. Coincidentally, 3 March is also the birth anniversary of Jamsetji Tata. Prime Minister Modi paid tributes to Birsa Munda and Jamsetji Tata, who despite hailing from very different family backgrounds, had both enriched the legacy and history of Jharkhand. It is because of the PM that these two distinguished personalities who have brought glory and honour not just to Jharkhand, but to the entire country, were venerated yet again.

He also drew our attention to the fact that, on a voyage to America, Jamsetji Tata met Swami Vivekananda on the ship, and an important topic of their discussion was the outreach and spread of science and technology in India. It is said that this very discussion led to the founding of the Indian Institute of Science.

The PM has ensured on many occasions that *Mann Ki Baat* becomes the platform through which he not only creates awareness about the significant changes happening within and outside India, but that it also becomes a medium through which one region of India gets to know about the rich culture and tradition of another region of India. Suggestions and recommendations on pertinent issues are always welcomed by him and applied as and when the situation requires.

In Episode 10, Akhilesh Vajpayee, a resident of Kanpur suggested the provision of a separate quota for the disabled for booking tickets on the IRCTC website. In the conversation taken forward by the Prime Minister, Vajpayee had described how unfair it was that disabled citizens had to go through the same tiring procedure as everyone else to buy tickets at the railway station. The government had never taken note of this issue or thought about it previously. This novel thought was now taken seriously by the government, and changes were introduced in the IRCTC system for disabled travellers.

In another such episode in 2019, while highlighting the great contributions of people towards the overall growth of the country, the Prime Minister shared the story of our quintessential Indian brave heart, Sardar Vallabhbhai Patel. He related an incident in which Sardar Patel had been informed about a conspiracy against the Lakshadweep islands, and he had wasted no time in initiating stern action. He had urged the Mudaliar brothers, Arcot Ramaswami Mudaliar and Arcot Laxmanaswami Mudaliar to immediately undertake a mission with the people of Travancore to Lakshadweep, and to take the lead in unfurling the Indian tricolour there.

Following his orders, the Indian tricolour was promptly unfurled there, and the nefarious plans of a neighbouring country of annexing Lakshadweep were thwarted in no time. After this incident, Sardar Patel asked the Mudaliar brothers to personally ensure all assistance for the development of Lakshadweep. Today, Lakshadweep is contributing significantly to India's progress. It is an attractive tourist destination too!

Praising Narendra Modi's leadership of our democracy, the first woman IPS officer, **Dr Kiran Bedi** said, '*Mann Ki Baat* over the course of the years has inadvertently become a democratic yardstick. It said what needed to be said and repeated what deserved praise.'

Take the instance of bringing the nation together for Jal Shakti and Jan Shakti. The Prime Minister had stated:

> 'I was reading about a collective endeavour in Vellore of Tamil Nadu where 20,000 women came together to revive the Nag river. I have also read about the women of Garhwal who are working together on the good work of implementing rainwater harvesting. I believe that many such attempts are being made and we can turn the impossible into the possible when we are together and strive with collective resolve. When people join hands, water will be conserved. Today, through the *Mann Ki Baat* programme, I am entreating my fellow countrymen and putting forward three requests. My first

> request is that, just like the cleanliness drive has been given the shape of a mass movement by the countrymen, let's also start a mass movement for water conservation. We should all resolve to save every drop of water and I believe that water is God's prasad to us, water is like a philosopher's stone! It used to be said that, by the touch of a philosopher's stone, iron could be transmuted into gold. I tell you—water is like the philosopher's stone and its mere touch creates and regenerates life!'

By saying this, Prime Minister Modi started an awareness campaign to save every single drop of water. He mentioned the contributions of the women of Vellore yet again in Episode 100, praising them and their self-help group.

Stories like this form the basis of the programme. To normalise it for the general masses and to ensure that the citizens of India know that they are the real warriors is what the radio programme has tried to convey. Issues like stubble burning and the Beti Bachao Beti Padhao movement are known to the entire population in every nook and cranny of the country. The power to drive change through the people for the overall development of the country has finally emerged.

Today, if the people of this country take an oath to bring about change, it will surely happen, and this is the message that has been conveyed across all the episodes of *Mann Ki Baat*. In Episode 50, Prime Minister Modi said that this programme proved to be one of the strongest pillars for the citizens of India when the entire country grappled with the ravages of COVID-19. Through this platform, the Prime Minister not only created awareness about the situation and discussed the safety precautions to be taken but also went on to share some extraordinary stories of yoddhas who were fighting against the tide and providing support to the population in whichever capacity they could.

In Episode 76, he spoke about how the country's personnel from the medical field and all the frontline workers were engaged 24×7 in service work. Other Indians were not lagging behind either. The one-and-a-half years since the initial outbreak COVID-19 saw the general public delivering medicines, food and other essentials to families that were quarantined, while others were seen offering free ambulance services to patients. Even in such challenging times, voluntary organisations came forward and extended support to people in different corners of the country. He ended the episode by saying,

> 'This resolve gives us so much strength, so much confidence. Whatever efforts are being made are of great service to society. They strengthen the power of society.'

The example above and many others like this only point to the fact that, when today the world over democracy and its tools are being largely ignored, the PM has only tried to enhance the power of the people and democracy, and has brought it to the forefront through *Mann Ki Baat*. Initiatives enumerated in the show have not only instilled a sense of trust within the hearts of the 130 crore population that forms the largest democracy, but have also strengthened its pillars by moving in the direction of growth and development. Every small thing matters in a democracy and this is what Prime Minister Modi reiterates. Eminent industrialist **Anand Mahindra** tweeted: 'You'd never expect to hear a leader in a national address advise small acts of kindness in the summer heat. @PMOIndia redefining leadership.'

In unmistakably potent and apt words, spiritual guru **Sadhguru Jaggi Vasudev** too talks about the phenomenon that *Mann Ki Baat* has become and says, 'For a divided humanity, *Mann Ki Baat* is a spectacular effort to communicate the policies and intentions of the elected government led by a never-before head-of-state. This has definitely been a tool to make many welfare schemes of the government become people's movements. One earth, one family, one future is a spiritual ethos. One of the many achievements of our beloved Prime Minster is to formally internationalise yoga as a science of well-being. This is yoga, this is the way forward. Let us make it happen.'

The language of *Mann Ki Baat* is the language of the common man—All India Radio (AIR) broadcasts *Mann Ki Baat* in 23 languages, 29 Indian dialects, 11 foreign languages and in English. It is broadcast in the 22 languages mentioned in the eighth schedule of the Constitution. The 29 dialects in which it is broadcast include Chhattisgarhi, Gondi, Halbi, Sargujia, Pahari, Sheena, Gojri, Balti, Ladakhi, Karbi, Khasi, Jaintia, Garo, Nagamese, Hmar, Paite, Thadou, Kabui, Mao, Tangkhul, Nyishi, Adi, Monpa, Ao, Angami, Kokborok, Mizo, Lepcha and Sikkimese (Bhutia).

The eleven foreign languages that *Mann Ki Baat* is also broadcast in are French, Chinese, Indonesian, Tibetan, Burmese, Baluchi, Arabic, Pashtu, Persian, Dari and Swahili.

Mann Ki Baat is, in its simplicity and brevity, the most direct heart-to-heart conversation between an overwhelmingly popular leader and ordinary citizens. In its expansiveness and incisiveness, however, it is also a potent tool that establishes, negotiates and resolves the most relevant issues facing a democracy like India, a country that is as diverse and variegated as it is animated. Using radio as the primary medium for *Mann Ki Baat* is a very carefully considered communications strategy in our democracy.

In an age where visuals dominate, Prime Minister Narendra Modi has injected a new lease of life into a medium that has the longest-standing history of being contextually resonant and ubiquitously available to all citizens. In a way, by using that one hour on the radio, at 11 a.m. on a Sunday each month, he has catalysed the transition from the conventionally institutional to the unconventionally conversational!

2

Strengthening the Future of GenNext

> 'The youth of my country have the 'Can Do' approach and the 'Will Do' spirit in them.'
>
> – Prime Minister Narendra Modi

Be it vedic mathematics, space science, drone technology, a revival of our rich literature, or a deep dive into our social milieu, *Mann Ki Baat*, has effectively and endearingly taken on the daunting task of engaging the younger generation to motivate them, and laying threadbare the transitory nature of the disproportionate stress they routinely encounter.

Imagine studying hard for an exam only to get stressed out at the nth hour, and turning to your granddad to be soothed by his calm demeanour and gently delivered pearls of wisdom. That's exactly how students and the student-in-everyone felt when Prime Minister Narendra Modi spoke about examination fear or education in general.

In Episode 88 of the show, he referred to a subject that many fear, as it is considered elite.

> 'My dear countrymen, you must have seen that a few days ago I held Pariksha Pe Charcha with students and my young

friends. During this discussion, some students said that they are afraid of their maths exam. Similar thoughts were also conveyed to me by many students in their messages. At that very moment, I decided that I would definitely discuss mathematics this time on *Mann Ki Baat*. Friends, mathematics is a subject which we Indians should be very comfortable with. After all, the people of India have contributed the most to the whole world in terms of research and the understanding of mathematics. You must have heard a lot about the zero, that is, the discovery of the zero and its importance. Often you will also hear that if the zero had not been discovered, then perhaps we would not have been able to see so much scientific progress in the world. From calculus to computers, all these scientific inventions are based on the zero. Mathematicians and scholars of India have even written that—यत किंचित वस्तु तत सर्वं, गणितेन बिना नहि!—which means that everything that is there in this entire universe, is based on mathematics.'

In December 2020, Prime Minister Modi reiterated his faith in students by saying that he was sure they could make studies quite interesting for themselves. He praised the fact that during the time of the COVID-19 pandemic, innovative methods were being adopted by the teachers all over the country, and course material was being creatively prepared by them, all of which was invaluable for online studies. He said,

'I request all the teachers to definitely upload these course materials on the Diksha Portal of the Education Ministry. This will greatly help the students who are staying in far-flung areas of the country.'

ENGAGING STUDENTS WITH ACADEMIC INCENTIVES

This was not the first time the PM discussed this matter in the broadcast history of *Mann Ki Baat*. As early as April 2018, the PM had spoken of exams, the fear experienced by students, and the subsequent relief.

> 'My young friends, by now you must have got off the treadmill of exams, exams and more exams. You must be wondering about spending your holidays. You must be contemplating how you will enjoy your vacations and the places you will travel to! I would like to talk to you today, to invite you to undertake a new task. I've seen a lot of young people these days, spending time learning new things. The significance of a summer internship has grown. It is an altogether new experience, which gives the opportunity to get to know life afresh, away from closeted walls, away from pen, paper and computers. Dear young friends, today I urge you to undertake a summer internship.'

He encouraged students to do something meaningful and to learn something significant for the sake of the society and the country. He encouraged college students, especially those who wanted to take part in transforming the country and wanted to do something for society with positive energy. To encourage them, Prime Minister Modi even added that the best interns who strived for excellence in schools and colleges would be rewarded with recognition at the national level. Not just that, those interns who accomplished their tasks well, would be awarded two credit points each by the UGC. By speaking of these academic incentives, he also hoped that, the youth would lend a hand in taking the cleanliness movement forward. In doing so, he actually achieved two-pronged success.

In January 2015, the PM took a new approach to effectively address many issues at once. He asked the boys amongst his young friends to do a simple thing which was to observe a sister or a friend's sister who was appearing for the Class X or XII exam. He said,

> 'You will see, whether it is Class X or XII, the girls will definitely help their mothers with household chores. Have you ever thought about how they manage to do household work and yet score well in exams? Nowadays, girls are far ahead of boys in examination results. Just observe this around you.'

Echoing the PM's view on Nari Shakti among young students, **Dr Kiran Bedi** says about the change in orientation that needs to occur in society: 'My message is not to the girls but to the parents, because it's the parents who are producing these girls. Earlier, it was the parents who were not supporting their daughters, but now parents and families are giving their daughters wings. Families are giving confidence to the girls, and the girls are finally finding recognition. That means, girls are the products of their families—if the family continues to play this positive role, no girl can be left behind. And boys can be made responsible too. So, I would say, make your sons responsible and your girls courageous. India will then reap remarkable demographic dividends.'

In August of that same year, the PM expressed how the months of July and August are very important for young people graduating from schools, since it is the peak season for college admissions. He mentioned a student, Satyam, who like hundreds and thousands of youths had left school to join college. He said,

'I firmly believe that my young friends must be enthusiastic and happy at the commencement of their college life. Leaving home for the first time, moving out of one's village, and coming out of the protective environment of home amounts to taking charge of the course of one's life. A multitude of young people leave their homes for the first time to chart a new direction for their lives.'

Offering his advice to the eagerly tuned-in youngsters, he iterated,

'Be calm, enjoy life and seek inner happiness. There is no alternative to books, one has to study, and yet one's bent of mind should be towards discovering new things. Old friends are invaluable. Childhood friends are precious but selecting, making and maintaining new friendships is a task that requires immense prudence. Keep learning something new, such as new skills and languages. Young people who leave their homes for the sake of studies should discover new places and get to know more about the people, language, culture and tourism aspects of such places.'

As he offered his best wishes to all the young people about to begin their new innings in college, he mentioned how one student in particular, Asharam Choudhury, who belonged to an extremely poor family in Madhya Pradesh—his father would earn his daily bread by waste-picking—had overcome life's many challenges to achieve success. In his maiden attempt, he had cracked the entrance exam for pursuing MBBS at AIIMS, Jodhpur. Prime Minister Modi said that there are many such instances of students from deprived families who, through sheer determination and perseverance, overcame all odds to stand out as beacons of inspiration to others. Enumerating other examples, the PM named students from all over the country—Prince Kumar of Delhi, whose father was a DTC bus driver, Abhay Gupta of Kolkata who had studied on footpaths and under street lights, Afreen Sheikh of Ahmedabad, whose father drove an auto rickshaw, Nagpur's daughter Khushi whose father was a school bus driver, Karthik of Haryana whose father was a watchman, Ramesh Sahu of Jharkhand whose father was a brick-kiln labourer—for their perseverance and diligence. He also mentioned Gurgaon's divyang angel Anushka Panda, who suffered from a hereditary disorder called spinal muscular atrophy. He said that with their combined resolve they had overcome each and every obstacle in their way.

> 'Our aspiration should be to reach from gurukul (seminary) to vishwakul (universal education).'

Any commendable incident from any part of the country infuses our Prime Minister's heart with energy and inspiration. In an early episode of the show, he referenced an incident that happened when he had been interacting with the Indian youth of San Jose, a city hailed as a technology hub. The PM had appealed to the young people there to think about how they could use their talents for India's benefit, and to do something in that direction whenever they found the time. The appeal was to change the Indian brain drain into brain gain. Two IT professionals from Rae Bareilly, Yogesh Sahu and Rajneesh Bajpayee, accepted his challenge and made a unique attempt. With their joint efforts, Yogesh and Rajneesh developed a SmartGaon app by utilising their professional skills. This app would not only connect the residents of villages with the whole world, but also allow them to obtain any information from the world on their own mobile phones. Residents of the Taudhakpur village in Rae Bareilly, the village chief, the District Magistrate, CDO and everyone joined in to create awareness amongst the masses. This incident of two young men living in America and following the American lifestyle and ideology, who had left India many years ago but remained emotionally attached to their village and worked towards finding solutions for the challenges faced by the people of their village, is hugely inspiring. *Mann Ki Baat* has made this connection possible.

Praising this exceptionally inspiring facet of *Mann Ki Baat*, **Sanjay Gupta**, chief editor and CEO, *Dainik Jagran* said, 'First of all, I would like to congratulate the Prime Minister for starting an inspirational programme like *Mann Ki Baat* in the country. Till now, the nation was devoid of any such programme conducted by top leaders of the country, but the citizens needed it. The way in which the Prime Minister enthusiastically talks about people's success stories in the show has not only encouraged people to come forward with their stories but has further inspired the citizens to follow their examples. The Prime Minister talks about multiple issues, all of which are apolitical. People residing in remote areas get the chance to connect with each other. The Prime Minister explains issues and concepts in simple language and talks about the achievements of people from all regions of India; this is very inspirational. We have started publishing similar success stories. We are glad that some of the success stories published by us have been selected and talked about by the Prime Minister in the show.'

In a seminal episode of the show, the PM addressed a crucial topic that has many students conflicted—having the courage to say 'No'. He asked students to have the courage to stand against detrimental conversations and say no to them. He went on to include parents in the ambit and said,

> 'I would like to share some views with the parents. These days none of us have time. All of us are running against time to earn our livelihoods. We are racing against time to improve the quality of our lives. But in this blind race, do we have the time to spare for our kids? Do we ever work for our kids' spiritual progress and discuss it with them, or do we only discuss material progress with them? How they are doing in their studies, what has been their progress in exams, what they should eat and not eat, where they should go and not go—majorly these are the topics that form the core of our interactions with our children. But do we share such a relationship that our children can bare their hearts to us? I request all of you to do this ... Your concern should extend to their inner depths, their thoughts, their logic, their books, their friends and their mobiles. I believe that no one else can do what a parent can for their kids.'

Over the years, the *Mann Ki Baat* episodes of February have naturally veered towards the subject of exams. In the show, the PM has an affable and empathetic approach towards his young listeners. In 2015, for instance, he spoke of the Cricket World Cup coinciding with the exam season. In another episode, he said he was sharing his inner feelings with students through initiatives such as Pariksha Pe Charcha. In his uniquely relatable manner, he had joked,

> 'I do not have the right to guide you on how to write a paper or how to pass exams well. I cannot guide you on the tricks to obtain better marks because I consider myself an average

student on such issues. I never scored well in any exams in my life. I was a very average student and on top of that, I had very bad handwriting. So, I think that most of the time I passed my exams only because the teachers could not comprehend my handwriting.'

His real intention had been to talk about precisely that, that the *intention* with which one approaches exams goes a long way in deciding its results. He had explained that a failure here or there, or failure in any one exam did not mean failure for life. Treating examinations, not as a burden but, as a festival is what he has tried to convey through many episodes. He has even encouraged parents to adopt a more understanding approach towards their children's performance in exams.

Actor **Anupam Kher** was all praise for the PM's innovative approach to exams. He tweeted: 'Today's #MannKiBaat by PM @narendramodi was simple, practical, innovative & so inspirational 4 students appearing 4 exams.:) #LifeLessons.'

By Episode 86, his young listeners knew that the terrifying exam season would be accompanied by a hugely motivating *Mann Ki Baat* episode from the PM. In the PM's own words,

'After my experience with millions of students of the country through the platform of Pariksha Pe Charcha, I can say with certainty that the youth of the country are brimming with self-confidence and can face every challenge.'

PEARLS OF WISDOM, PEPPERED WITH HUMOUR

Eminent screenwriter, filmmaker and historian, **Dr Chandra Prakash Dwivedi** praised Prime Minister Modi's singular approach to the youth in regard to exam fear. 'We have all appeared for examinations in our lives. But how one can handle the pressure of examinations, and how the family should deal with the pressure, are things that were never discussed with us during our school/college days. It is an immense pleasure to see the Prime Minister assuming the role of an elder person in the family. Sometimes he assumes the role of a father, sometimes of a grandfather and sometimes that of a friend. He teaches you that scoring good marks in examinations is not the most important thing. I remember one of his statements in which he said, "... it is not important that life should be successful, what matters is that life should be meaningful." That day, I understood the meaning of his words very well. I tell my friends that earlier I used to think differently about success and had different criteria for success, such as being materialistically prosperous and having a big house. However, this one sentence from the Prime Minister made me and millions of people think about what having a successful and meaningful life truly means,' he said.

Through the radio telecast, the PM has often said that it is one's desires that become resolutions, and resolutions can never be futile. Resolutions are accompanied by goals, and when goals and action come together, resolutions are achieved.

> 'That is why I say Desire + Stability = Resolution. Resolution + Action = Achievements.'

He has always encouraged students to dedicate themselves to their commitment and stay positive. He said,

> 'Don't be bothered about defeating others. Think of taking yourself further from where you already are. Test yourself every day against your own limits, so that however big a challenge comes in life, you will not have any problem. And

why should someone else take our exam? Make it a habit to take your exam yourself. Each day we will test ourselves. We will see if we have progressed from where we were yesterday. Have I reached further than yesterday, have I achieved more than what I achieved yesterday? Each day, every moment, keep testing yourself.'

He cited the example of a student, Arnav Mohta from Mumbai, Maharashtra who wrote to him saying some people make exams an issue of life and death. Similarly, Vinita Tiwari wrote to him from Varanasi that the news of children dying by suicides after the declaration of their exam results had saddened her. In response, the PM referred to R. Kamath who had sent in his thoughts on the subject. 'He has asked the students not to become worriers but warriors. Really, we should not sink in worries but should become like warriors on the battlefield. I believe that we should not drown in our worries; we should march ahead with the belief that victory will be ours,' the PM said.

This is exactly the credo that sees expression in Prime Minister Modi's immensely popular book, *Exam Warriors*.

Mann Ki Baat is almost like exam tips given to students before they enter their examination halls. Thousands of people have posted small messages on the NaMo app sharing their own tips. Shrey Gupta stressed the point that a healthy mind can only reside in a healthy body. Our daily schedule for all 365 days in a year should be in line with achieving our dreams and goals. Our very own chess grandmaster, **Vishwanathan Anand** has says that when he plays in international tournaments, he sits with a healthy composure. He is so focused, and that is a reflection of his inner tranquillity. Citing this example, the PM asked his young friends to laugh a lot, share jokes, and see how a calm atmosphere gets created on its own.

POLICY CHANGES TO EASE EDUCATION, EASE EXAMINATIONS

Expressing his view on the unconventional but much-needed change in the way education is perceived, education reformist and thinker **Mukul Kanitkar** says, 'We have been working for many years in the field of education. We did the work of organising Gurukuls which are a part of Indian tradition, and in the modern world of education, we have talked about the work of taking Indian knowledge and tradition forward. We have been working in this field, among the people, for quite a while. And the biggest need we have felt in this sector has been that of self-confidence and self-respect. The need to know that the work I am doing, running a Sanskrit school, running a Vedic Gurukul, running a Shastra Gurukul, is a great service to the tradition of this country. We used to try a lot to bring this feeling in the minds of our acharyas. The Prime Minister once made a small mention that a 16-year-old boy had cleared all 14 levels of the Tenali pariksha, and was the youngest ever to have completed the Mahapariksha. an encouraging message once, but we saw a huge rise in confidence in the atmosphere of our entire Gurukul after that.'

Unconventionally, in Episode 28, the Prime Minister reminded us of how we usually look at the arrangements made during the Kumbh Melas, which are celebrated for about 40–45 days, as the inherent strength of a festival. Hence, he reminded us that during examinations too, an atmosphere of festivity should be created within the whole family, amongst friends and around the neighbourhood. This in itself, he said, would convert pressure into pleasure!

Back in July 2015, he had raised the issue of 24-hour electricity supply to the villages of our country. He had said that this work was difficult but had to be done so that the students from villages did not get affected by the shortage of electricity during their exams. In reference to this, he spoke of the Deendayal Upadhyaya Gram Jyoti Programme. Through *Mann Ki Baat*, the PM has expressed these myriad thoughts. And not just his own thoughts; he has also lent a platform to the inspiring voices of others. In an episode that was relayed in early 2016, he thanked revered Morari Bapu for an encouraging message on managing stress. In Episode 75, he spoke of St. Teresa's College in Kochi, Kerala, where students were making reusable toys, that too in a very creative manner by converting old clothes, discarded wooden pieces, bags and boxes into toys.

He also spoke of teachers who are engaged in the inspirational work of teaching Sanskrit in foreign lands. One such person is Rutger Kortenhorst, a well-known Sanskrit scholar and teacher in Ireland who teaches Sanskrit to the children there. The PM said that Sanskrit played an important role in the strengthening of cultural relations between India and Ireland in the West and between India and Thailand here in the East. Dr Chirapat Prapandvidya and Dr Kusuma Rakshamani, continued to play a very important role in the promotion of Sanskrit in Thailand, the PM had let us know through the programme.

The Prime Minister said in Episode 94,

> 'My dear countrymen, when it comes to students, youth power, leadership power, so many outdated stereotypes have become ingrained in our minds. Many times, we see

that when student power is referred to, its scope is limited to the student union elections. But the scope of student power is very big, very vast. Student power is the basis for making India powerful. After all, it's the youth of today, who will take India forward into 2047. When India celebrates her centenary, this youth power, their hard work, their sweat, and their talent, will take India to new heights. The way our youth of today are working for the country and have joined in the nation-building process, fills me with confidence. The way our youth solve problems in hackathons, stay awake all night and work for long hours is very inspiring. A hackathon was held in recent years, with lakhs of the youth of the country who have together solved many challenges; they have given new solutions to the country.'

Addressing the concern over the National Education Policy, Prime Minister Modi happily shared that IIT Madras and IIT Kanpur have played a leading role in preparing India's indigenous 5G testbed. He said he hoped to see many more such efforts in the times to come and that taking inspiration from IITs, other institutions will also step up their R&D activities.

TAPPING INTO STUDENTS' ASPIRATIONS

Mann Ki Baat has been used by Prime Minister Modi to effectively give a podium to students who are unique in their aspirations. For instance, he shared the story of Riddhima Swargiyari from Guwahati, Assam, a student of class 7 who had written that she wanted to see India in the 100th year of independence as a zero-accident country and the cleanest country in the world, completely free of terrorism, included in the 100 per cent literate countries, and capable of food security with sustainable technology. The PM had also received a postcard from Navya Verma of Prayagraj, Uttar Pradesh, who had written that her dream for 2047 was of an India where everyone had a dignified life.

In Episode 93 of *Mann Ki Baat*, broadcast in September 2022, the PM had tapped into the aspirations of some talented students. Kritika Nandal was one of them who had got a very good result. The PM congratulated her and praised her for considering her mom to be her hero. Kritika shared with him that she wanted to become a doctor, to which he said that the life of a doctor is dedicated to the service of the people. Next, the PM spoke to a youngster from Kerala, Vinayak, who, aside from being a very good badminton player, was a great student. Prime Minister Modi asked Vinayak to share his mantra for success, to which the latter responded, 'Hard work and proper time utilisation.' Then, the PM spoke to Usman Saifi of Amroha in Uttar Pradesh whose favourite subject was mathematics. Saifi spoke about the teacher who had inspired him the most saying, 'Rajat sir. He inspired me, taught me very well. My mathematics was good from the beginning ... and it is a very interesting subject too.' Concluding the programme, the PM said, 'Friends, there are many other stories of such young friends whose courage and success in difficult conditions inspire us. I wanted to have a chance to talk to as many young people as possible but time has its own limitations. I appeal to all young friends that they share with us their stories in their own voice that can inspire the country.'

Indian educator, author, philanthropist and chairperson of the Infosys Foundation, **Sudha Murthy** says of the PM's leadership with respect to students, 'A country's head talks to people who did not receive benefits like us, who were born in different sectors of the society, who have had fewer opportunities, he encourages them to do well in life. Particularly so, because he chooses Episodes depending on current situations. Like during examination time, I heard the episode and it was such an encouragement for the students during a time when they require tremendous moral support. When our country's head, Prime Minister Modi is giving them that moral support, it's a great thing.

It can be said, that the Prime Minister has a unique relationship with the 'Amrit Kaal' generation, and through the programme, he has relayed every iota of his own mann ki baat to them. In his own words,

> 'Come make the exam festival into a celebration.'

3

Character Building for Nation Building

> 'I believe growth should be constant, sustained and inclusive. It's only meaningful if these three things are there. Otherwise they're just economic figures.'
>
> – Prime Minister Narendra Modi

Prime Minister Modi's appeal is unparalleled when it comes to leadership, accessibility, and his inspiring sense of ethics and values. When he urges us to evolve into better versions of ourselves, we do indeed feel like reaching deep within ourselves to find the best qualities in us and honing them further.

The Prime Minister has maintained that '*Mann Ki Baat*' is a platform for him to share inspiring stories of citizens and their noble deeds. In Episode 99, the PM introduced India to Sukhbir Singh Sandhu and Supreet Kaur from Amritsar, Punjab. After many years of prayers, the couple were blessed with a beautiful girl child they lovingly named Ababat Kaur. Her name stands for one who alleviates the sufferings of many and is devoted to serving others. As fate would have it, Ababat left this world when she was only 39 days old. And, instead of shrouding themselves in sadness, Sukhbir Singh and Supreet embraced everything

Ababat symbolised and took an incredibly inspiring decision—organ donation. In so doing, they inspired many to join in the cause.

Swapan Dasgupta, journalist, political commentator and former member of the Rajya Sabha describes this appeal thus: 'What is unique about *Mann Ki Baat* is that, in the programme relays, Prime Minister Modi has addressed subjects that are not political in character, but which, no responsible person holding public office has actually addressed. I'll give you some examples. The tension, the strain that students who undertake examinations go through, it's a real problem that almost all parents of children face. Prime Minister Modi thought it was important to address this question, to reassure people, to give tips about how they can actually escape this. He spoke about things like Indian toys. He spoke about how an entire tradition of Indian sports has been lost. Now, these are issues which have always been there, but to bring them to the top of the minds of people is a colossal achievement.'

Episode 48 reflected on precisely this trait of Prime Minister Modi when he said, 'I would like to say today that of all the feedback I receive for this programme, one of the points that touches my heart the most is when people tell me that, when we sit with all our family members to listen to *Mann Ki Baat*, we feel that the head of our family is sitting with us and sharing his ideas with us.'

This comment from us, the listeners of *Mann Ki Baat*, has moved our Prime Minister so much that he unhesitatingly expresses how satisfied he feels to know this,

> 'I am yours, I am one amongst you, I am with you, you have elevated me and, in this way, I will continue to

remain connected with you as a family member through *Mann Ki Baat.*'

The expansive subject of character development is an offshoot of this very concept—of a family elder encouraging us to be our best, so that we contribute organically to the growth and development of the nation. *Mann Ki Baat* frequently talks about people and institutions who make an extraordinary contribution to society. Their actions may seem small, but they actually have a very deep impact by changing our thinking and giving a new direction to society. Take the fervour and commitment displayed by villagers in Meghalaya towards water conservation that has turned out to be an exemplary model for all of India. The rural folk have donated their sweat, toiling collectively to change the course of a mountain spring. It was a purely indigenous, home-grown method. This has not only led to the prevention of soil erosion and crop damage but also facilitated the effective irrigation of fields. In July 2019, Prime Minister Modi congratulated the beautiful Northeastern state of Meghalaya for becoming the first state to have formulated its own water policy. Exactly a year later, he praised and congratulated the migrant workers of Barabanki—who had taken an initiative to return the Kalyani river to its pristine form—as an example of the small contributions that add to nation-building as a whole.

Spiritual leader **Sri Sri Ravi Shankar** says on the subject of character-building and diligent hard work contributing to national development, 'The Prime Minister is deeply steeped in spirituality and so he doesn't know what is tiredness. He keeps working 24x7 and inspires young and old alike. So, this *Mann Ki Baat* is such a boon to our country. Jai Hind!.'

DEVELOPMENT OF SOCIETY, ONE CITIZEN AT A TIME

In one of the early episodes, the Prime Minister referred to a farmer brother, Gurbachan Singh from Punjab, whose son was going to be married. Singh told the bride's parents that the marriage would be performed in a solemn manner and that there would be no need to spend much on the wedding reception. However, to their surprise, he did put forward one condition. Singh asked the bride's family to promise that they would not burn parali or stubble in their fields. The PM underlined the significance of this incident as it showed how a simple citizen's small gesture could make a huge difference that could benefit society as a whole.

Similarly, in Episode 91, he spoke of a little girl, Anvi. Prime Minister Modi said his meeting with Anvi had been so memorable that he had felt compelled to share her story as an example of great courage.

> 'Friends, Anvi is afflicted with Down's Syndrome since birth and she has also been battling a serious heart disease since childhood. She also underwent open-heart surgery when she was only three months old. Despite all these difficulties, neither Anvi nor her parents ever gave up. Anvi's parents gathered all the information about Down's syndrome, and then decided on a way to reduce Anvi's dependence on others. They started teaching Anvi how to lift a glass of water herself, how to tie shoelaces and button clothes on her own—small things such as those.'

By way of this example, the Prime Minister showed us how, at the appropriate place and time, and with a lot of patience, almost anything can be overcome. Encouraging the youth of the country has been a key tenet of the show. Entrepreneur and film producer **Ronnie Screwvala** praised this on his social handle: 'It's a great opportunity for young lads to clear their minds as PM@narendramodi addresses the nation today #MannKiBaat.'

In another episode, the PM spoke of Javed Ahmed, a brave survivor of a terrorist attack. Despite sustaining grave injuries, Ahmed's spirit has remained undeterred. The Prime Minister hailed his character, saying Ahmed harboured no grudge or anger against anyone. Instead, he had turned his crisis into compassion and dedicated his life to social work. Since the fateful episode 20 years ago, he has devoted himself to child education. By turning his focus to education, Ahmed has developed his own character and that of others. Ahmed also pursued a master's degree in social work, and is now leading a silent revolution as a messiah for the disabled, working as an informed citizen of the new India.

This same zeal for personal development that encompasses the development of others as well was seen in another example that the Prime Minister cited—that of the One Teacher, One Call effort being made in Bareilly for divyang children. This campaign was being led by the principal of a school in Daboragangapur, Deepmala Pandey. Due to this campaign, during the period when COVID-19 was prevalent, not only did the admission of a large number of children become possible, but more than 350 teachers joined the initiative with a spirit of service. These teachers would go from village to village seeking out divyang children, looking out for them and then ensuring that their admission took place in one school or the other. Lauding this campaign, the PM said,

> 'I deeply appreciate this noble effort of Deepmala and her fellow teachers for the sake of divyangjans. Every such effort

in the field of education is going to shape the future of our country.'

In Episode 74 of *Mann Ki Baat*, we were reminded of the endeavours of Babita Rajput of Agrotha village in Madhya Pradesh. Close to her village, there had once been a very large lake that had dried up. She mobilised other women in her village and built a canal to bring water to the lake. Through this canal, rainwater started flowing directly into the lake. Now, this lake remains filled with water.

Similarly, the work undertaken by Jagdish Kuniyal of Bageshwar, Uttarakhand, whose village and the adjoining areas were dependent on a natural source for their water requirements, was cited as a great example of innovative water harnessing. Many years ago, this water source had dried up, leading to the worsening of the water crisis in the entire area. Jagdish decided to solve this crisis through tree plantation. Along with fellow villagers, he planted thousands of trees in the entire area. Today, that dried-up water source is filled to the brim once again.

SHARING LIFE STORIES ABOUT PEOPLE'S LOVE FOR NATURE

Prime Minister Narendra Modi's love of nature and his sense of oneness with it is seen every now and then, such as in the photographs where he can be seen feeding peacocks and other animals. He even has a penchant for doing wildlife photography himself. In one episode, he spoke of Pawan Acharya from Alwar, Rajasthan, who, through the Prime Minister, wanted to request all Indians to use as many earthen lamps (diyas) as possible on Diwali to protect the environment, and to provide employment to many potter families.

In Episode 80, Prime Minister Modi said that one more thing should fill our hearts with joy and strengthen our belief in the greater good.

> ‘And what is that ... have you ever noticed? Generally, what had crept into our social fabric was acceptance of mediocrity—“It happens”, “It's okay—this will do!” But now I'm noticing my country's young minds focusing their minds on excellence. They want to do the best, using the best methods. This too will emerge as a major force for the nation.’

Singer **Kailash Kher** lauded the programme for its emphasis on unity with nature.

Through *Mann Ki Baat* the nation got acquainted with how the movement of Swachh Bharat has now advanced from cleanliness to beautification. We got to know about the story of Yogesh Saini—an engineer who left his job in America and returned to serve Mother India—and his team. He picked up the gauntlet to not just clean Delhi up but to beautify it. With his team, he began with the garbage bins of Lodi Garden. Through the medium of street art, he has decorated many localities of Delhi with aesthetically appealing paintings. From overbridges to school walls to hutments, he has given a free hand to his talent, garnering huge public support along the way, making it a truly effective campaign.

In Episode 13 of *Mann Ki Baat*, an example of love for nature was exemplified by girl students from Saint Mary Upper Primary School, Chittoor in Kerala. Prime Minister Modi said,

> ‘This letter is special in many ways. Firstly, these girls have created an image of Mother India with thumbprints on a huge piece of cloth. They have sent me an image of Mother India.

> Initially, I had wondered why they have created a map of India using thumbprints. But when I read their letter, I realised how beautifully they had conveyed a symbolic message. It is not as if these girls have tried to awaken the Prime Minister alone. They are trying to create awareness among the people in their region and their mission is the promotion of organ donation. They are organising a public awareness campaign for organ donation. They have organised plays to create an understanding of organ donation. Organ donation should become a habit as well as an instinct.'

Similarly, in Episode 22 of the programme, Prime Minister Modi spoke of an inspiring farmer from Pune who, at his granddaughter Sonal's wedding, had gifted all his relatives, guests, and friends a sapling of the Kesar variety of mango to plant. The Prime Minister also spoke of Nimit Singh of Gorakhpur, Uttar Pradesh who, after his B. Tech had decided to be self-employed and started honey production.

'EK ATMA CHINTAN': WHAT DOES IT MEAN?

In the very first episode of *Mann Ki Baat*, the Prime Minister spoke of the true spirit of celebrating Vijay Dashami, a festival that symbolises the triumph of good over evil. He mentioned Ganesh Venkatadari, a native of Mumbai, who had written to him saying that all of us must take a vow to eliminate ten bad habits from within ourselves on the occasion of Vijay Dashami and also pledge to eliminate dirt and filth on this occasion.

In Prime Minister Modi's words,

> 'Swami Vivekananda-ji used to say the same. My countrymen, 125 crore Indians have infinite strengths and

capabilities. We need to understand ourselves. We need to identify our inner strengths and, like Swamiji always used to say, we need to carry our self-respect, identify ourselves and move forward in life and be successful, in turn making our nation a winning and successful country. I believe, all our countrymen are efficient, strong and can stand against any odds with confidence.’

Mann Ki Baat has continued to highlight the steps taken by grassroots champions to make a difference in the nation’s holistic progress. In December 2019, he made us aware of Sankalp 95, an Alumni Meet organised by former students of the K.R. High School in Bettiah. Sankalp 95 means, the resolve undertaken by the 1995 batch of that high school, in which they resolved to do something for the society. They decided to shoulder responsibility in the area of Public Health Awareness. Under the aegis of Sankalp 95, the Government Medical College of Bettiah and many hospitals also joined the campaign. It was the beginning of an entire movement centred on public health.

Be it free medical tests, distribution of free medicines, or just spreading awareness, this effort has become a beacon of hope. The Prime Minister praised this effort stating,

‘We often say that when every citizen of the country takes a step ahead, our nation moves 130 crore steps forward!’

Only an avid learner can become an inspiring leader; endorsing this very concept, Prime Minister Modi saluted a 105-year-old student in an episode. If we wish to progress in life, develop ourselves and achieve something, he said that the first pre-condition is that the student within us must never die. Bhagirathi Amma from Kollam in Kerala, who is 105 years old, gives us this inspiration. She lost her mother when she was very young, and got married at a young age, but lost her husband soon after. However, Bhagirathi Amma did not let go of her courage and did not lose her spirit. She had quit school at the age of 10, but restarted her education again at the age of 105! Bhagirathi Amma wrote her level 4 exams and then eagerly awaited her results. She scored 75 per cent in her exams. Not just that, she scored 100 per cent marks in Mathematics. Amma now wants to continue her studies and to appear for higher exams.

Also, speaking of the edifying concept of Ek Atma Chintan, the Prime Minister said in the very first episode,

> ‘My countrymen, till the time we do not decide to walk, stand on our own, we will also not get guidance from others in our journey. We will not get people to hold our hand and help us in walking.’

Education reformist and thinker, **Mukul Kanitkar** describes the change that a programme like *Mann Ki Baat* has brought to the fore,

> ‘The first thing is that a programme like *Mann Ki Baat* by the Prime Minister, where he talks directly to society and the public, is a big deal for a participatory democracy. And it's not just a matter of him speaking what is on his mind. We have seen that in the last seven–eight years that the Prime Minister has shared stories and experiences that people have shared with him. The stories sent by his listeners, the success stories, he shares with all his listeners.
>
> Last year, we celebrated 75 years of independence ... the main thing in a democracy is that the ruler should also be a servant. This is the job of a public servant. The Prime Minister called himself the Pradhan Sevak. So, his biggest

task is that there should be dialogue. The Prime Minister has created a very big medium in *Mann Ki Baat* to bring about this system.'

WARDING OFF ADDICTION, CHOOSING HEALTH

As early as the third episode, Prime Minister Modi addressed the grave issue of addiction squarely and also presented to the nation a doable course of action.

> 'Some people feel that when a person is in despair, faces failures or is directionless, he easily falls prey to drugs. But I feel that people who lack ambition, do not have any set goals and targets, and have a deep vacuum in their lives are the ones with whom drugs will find easy access. If you want to avoid drugs and save your children from this menace then foster ambition in them, give them dreams to pursue, and make them individuals with a desire to achieve something in life. Then you will see that they will not be easily distracted.
>
> Their aim then will be to achieve something in life. Have you ever followed a sportsman's life? A sportsman is always motivated. In the bleak winters, everyone feels like sleeping in the warmth of a quilt, but a sportsman will still rise at four or five in the morning for his workouts. Why? Because his goal is set. Similarly, if your child is not aimless, there are less chances of him/her falling prey to the menace of drugs.
>
> Vivekananda had said, "Take a thought, make it your life. Ponder on it and dream about it. Make it an integral part of your dreams. Make it a part of your mind, brain, veins, and each and every part of your body, and forget everything else."'

Actor **Ajay Devgn** took to social media to express gratitude: 'It is through the medium of *Mann Ki Baat* that Prime Minister

Modi has been able to communicate to young India that addiction is neither cool nor a style statement. In reality, it is a precursor to destruction.'

In May 2020, he spoke of innumerable people who have willingly given their all in the service of others. One such gentleman is K.C. Mohan of Tamil Nadu who runs a salon in Madurai. Through sheer hard work, he saved Rs 5 lakh for his daughter's education. But he spent the entire amount in the service of the needy and the underprivileged in the difficult COVID-19 times. Similarly, Gautam Das of Agartala, whose only means of sustenance was plying a handcart, fed the needy by buying rice and pulses out of the savings from his daily earnings. Prime Minister Modi said,

> 'I have come to know of a similar example from Pathankot, Punjab. Divyang Raju, through a small investment raised with the help of others, got over 3,000 masks made and distributed. In these difficult times, brother Raju has arranged for the feeding of around a hundred families.'

Through the medium of *Mann Ki Baat*, the PM has also spoken of how important it is to not measure success in comparison to others, to not expend energy in useless competition. In the fifth episode of *Mann Ki Baat*, the Prime Minister said,

> 'Start competing with yourself, compete with yourself to do better, to do faster, to do more and to reach new heights. Concentrate on competing with yourself to make today better than the past. And you will find that this spirit of competition will give you such a lot of joy and satisfaction that you yourself can't imagine. We remember Sergey Bubka with admiration. This athlete broke his own record over

> 35 times. He would test against himself only. Every time he would set himself a new challenge and scale new heights. You also follow the same and then see that nothing can stop you from achieving success.'

Storytelling as a means of staying connected to one's roots, thus strengthening the idea of nation-building is another strain of the show. He took notice of people who had taken commendable initiatives in promoting the art form of qissagoi. He also spoke of the website *gaathastory.in*, run by Amar Vyas, along with other colleagues. He said that there were many endeavours that were popularising stories from rural India. People like Vaishali Vyavahare Deshpande are making this form popular in Marathi. Srividya Veeraraghavan of Chennai is also engaged in popularising and disseminating stories related to our culture, while two websites named, *Kathalaya* and *Indian Storytelling Network*, are also doing commendable work in this field. All of these found a mention in *Mann Ki Baat*.

DRAWING INSPIRATION FROM EXEMPLARY LEADERS

On 31 May 2015, Prime Minister Modi spoke of our nation's ex-President, A.P.J. Abdul Kalam.

> 'In his book *My Journey: Transforming Dreams into Action*, he mentioned an incident from his own life. He says that he had always aspired to become a pilot. However, when he had tried to become a pilot, he had failed and could not clear his exams. Now, you can see his failure gave him a great opportunity in life. He became a great scientist of our nation. He became the President of India and his contribution stands unparalleled in the field of nuclear energy in India.

Therefore, friends, please do not bend under the burden of failure. Failure is a kind of opportunity. Do not let the failure go without learning a lesson from it. Try to search for the hope and opportunity that lies hidden in your failure.'

Through the various episodes, the Prime Minister has managed to beautifully weave in the significance of nation-building and self-realisation in its many forms. In Episode 11, he said the old generation sometimes feels that the new generation does not understand anything. However, his own experience regarding youth has been different.

Sometimes when we talk to the youth, we learn so many things. He said,

'I have met so many youths who have taken the pledge Sunday on Cycle. Some say that I keep one day a week as Cycle Day as it is good for my health good for the environment and allows me to enjoy my youth too. Nowadays many cities in our country are witnessing cycle use and there are many people promoting its use. This is a good initiative both for improving health and saving the environment.'

Extolling the virtues of peace, social harmony and unity as cornerstones of self-realisation, the PM has called them essential elements of society. The Run for Unity programme organised in various parts of the country on 31 October 2019, also called Ekta ki Daud, is one such endeavour that has elicited his praise.

'In the true sense Ekta ki Daud is the real race for development.'

In Episode 25 of *Mann Ki Baat*, the Prime Minister touched upon the inspiration we can all draw in our lives from the sacrifice, devotion and zeal of the jawans of our security forces. He said that their well-being occupies his mind, heart and emotional universe all the time. His feeling and resolve that Diwali ought to be dedicated to our security forces saw a huge, positive response from the nation in the form of the Sandesh to Soldiers campaign. He said,

> ‘And today, in all humility, I wish to proclaim that there could not be a single soul in India who did not have unbounded love for our jawans, a sense of deep pride in the members of our security forces. The way these sentiments have been expressed is surely giving strength to all of our countrymen. Your messages to the jawans of our security forces have proved to be a great morale booster that cannot be easily imagined. Schools, colleges, students, villages, the underprivileged, traders, shopkeepers, political leaders, sportspersons and people from the cine world have all lit lamps for the country's jawans, and have joined in this campaign of sending a message of greeting and salutation to our jawans.’

DISCIPLINE: THE CORE QUALITY FOR NATION-BUILDING

Discipline is integral to self-realisation, and Prime Minister Narendra Modi has constantly underlined the role that both these qualities play in laying the foundations of success in our lives. In Episode 17, he mentioned how those who are disorganised and indisciplined do those things in the evening that they should have done in the morning, and then the work they had to do in the afternoon is done late at night. They might feel that their job is somehow done, but it results in so much wastage of energy and they are also saddled with unnecessary tension all the time. He reiterated,

> 'So we should not view anything as trivial or unimportant. Please see to it that you don't compromise on the time you have set for things. Don't get into this mess. Do things the way you have planned them.'

The idea of character-building leading to nation-building is sewn into every theme that Prime Minister Modi has touched upon. A strong foundation for a life well lived comes from this very quality of living for a larger cause, living for the nation, as is the case with the Prime Minister himself. It wouldn't be wrong to say that his own personal values have inspired many to become better versions of themselves over the course of *Mann Ki Baat*.

4

Jan Bhagidari to Combat the COVID-19 Pandemic

> India proved that at the time of crisis befalling our nation, at the time of crisis befalling humanity, how each and every Indian came together to put forth united efforts to deal with it.
>
> – Prime Minister Narendra Modi

In a special, televised public address, the Prime Minister called for the complete lockdown of the entire nation for the ensuing 21 days in order to contain the COVID-19 pandemic, saying that social distancing was the only way to mitigate its spread. He said,

> 'The most advanced countries of the world have been rendered absolutely helpless by this pandemic. Coronavirus is spreading at such a rapid pace that despite all the preparations and efforts, these countries are finding it hard to manage the crisis. The analysis of happenings in all these countries since the last two months, and the opinion of experts have proved that there is only one way to effectively deal with coronavirus—social distancing.'

Cautioning those who are careless, the Prime Minister said,

> '... carelessness and ill-conceived notions of a few can put you, your children, your parents, your family, your friends, the entire country in grave jeopardy. It will be impossible to estimate the price India will have to pay if this carelessness continues.'

Yes, he asked us to maintain social distance over the course of the challenging COVID-19 period, but in doing so, it won't be hyperbolic to say, he came closer to us than ever before, not just as our constitutionally elected Prime Minister, but as our universally beloved leader. It is true that whenever he addresses the nation, looking straight at us, we always pay attention. But, in March 2020, when he appeared before us, Prime Minister Narendra Modi towered over our combined fears, apprehensions, doubts and despondence with his compassionate yet commanding presence—he was ready to tackle a deadly pandemic, validated by a billion-plus hopes.

He also urged people to observe the lockdown imposed by the State with utmost sincerity. His decision was based on the experiences of health sector experts and the experiences of other countries, who had insisted that a twenty-one day lockdown was essential to break the chain of infection. This Janta Curfew, the PM said, was vital to protect the country and its citizens during the Corona pandemic.

A year later, he hailed our cumulative success. He said,

> 'My dear countrymen, last year it was in this very month of March that the country heard of the term Janta Curfew for the first time. Just have a look at the might of a great *praja*, the people of this great country ... Janta Curfew became

an object of bewilderment for the entire world. It was an unprecedented example of discipline; generations to come will certainly feel proud of that. Similar to that are the efforts we made to express honour and respect for our Corona Warriors, by banging thalis, applauding them and lighting lamps for them!'

His leadership during the COVID-19 crisis and its expression on the radio programme saw voluble resonance. **Dr Kiran Bedi** tweeted: 'One of his kind in billions is our @PMOIndia. Heard the #MannKiBaat. Thank God in this period of severe crisis he is leading us. Listen to the recording if anyone of u missed it. @ANI @PTI_News @airnewsalerts @DDNational @AkashvaniAIR'.

WHEN THE GOING GETS TOUGH, THE NATION GETS GOING.

India's Corona story is an unrivalled success story. The Prime Minister's timely resolve and his persistent communication through *Mann Ki Baat* and other platforms greatly reduced the impact of this disaster. He encouraged citizens to consistently keep strengthening their resolve, to exercise caution at every step, and to remember that *jaan hai toh jahaan hai.* He taught us patience, discipline and determination to keep our resolve, to keep our promise.

In the words of **Dr Devi Prasad Shetty**, Chairman & Executive Director of Narayana Health, a revered cardiac surgeon with around 34 years of experience and therefore the utmost authority on the subject, 'The best time to judge the leadership is when the leader and the country go through a crisis. The COVID-19 pandemic really differentiated the men from the boys and leaders from statesmen. It is very clear that the PM has risen much above other leaders and statesmen by the way he handled the country and took us through the entire journey of fighting against the coronavirus. See, with a country as big as ours in both population and size, and with literacy not among the best in the world, reaching out to people through storytelling on *Mann Ki Baat* is the only successful way to communicate. This is exactly what the Prime Minister did. He narrated various stories which were relevant and could be understood by the common man. You can't talk to them about technical aspects ... so narrating real-life stories, the implications of those stories and how some brave people went out of their way to make a difference, is hugely inspirational for the common man. That is the best way to reach out to them. And I hope he will continue to narrate stories in his typical way and style.'

When the Prime Minister said that the Central and State Governments countrywide were working swiftly to ensure that citizens did not face many inconveniences in their daily life, that provisions were being made to ensure the smooth supply of all essential items and that, along with the Central and State Governments, individuals from civil societies and institutions were constantly striving to reduce the problems of the poor during this period of crisis, we believed him.

Through *Mann Ki Baat*, Prime Minister Modi appealed to people to beware of false rumours or superstitions circulating at the time, while also endorsing Jan Bhagidari, people's participation. He also expressed confidence that every Indian would abide by the instructions of the government and local authorities during this crucial hour. The Prime Minister praised every Indian who came forward in the hour of crisis—manavta pe sankat. He said,

'India has shown that at a time of crisis befalling our nation, at a time of crisis befalling humanity. Indians can come together to put forth united efforts to deal with it.'

In June 2020, he communicated to us an inspiring story from Arunachal Pradesh. Mirem village of Siang district had attempted a unique feat that had become an inspiration for India, the PM said. Prior to the pandemic, most residents of this village had been staying away from the village, working elsewhere for their livelihood. During the pandemic, they started returning to the village. On noticing it, the resident villagers decided to make arrangements, in advance, to quarantine the returning villagers. They came together and erected 14 temporary huts, at a short distance from the village, to quarantine the returning villagers for a few days. The huts were equipped with toilets, water, electricity, and all essential items needed for daily use. It is not surprising that this awareness and collective effort on the part of the village folk of Mirem attracted widespread attention and accolades. Similarly, in Episode 67, the PM drew our attention to khadi masks that had become very popular during the COVID-19 pandemic. Self-help groups and other such institutions making khadi masks in the country, and people like Suman Devi in Barabanki of UP, were praised effusively by the Prime Minister in his monthly address.

THE DAUNTING BUT VICTORIOUS ODYSSEY

A remarkable achievement of *Mann Ki Baat* is that during the COVID-19 crisis, it became one of the most trusted sources of authentic information and encouragement, helmed as it was by a man the country trusted instinctively. In the 64th episode which was relayed in July 2020, the PM confirmed how beautifully the country was fighting against coronavirus unitedly, proving the apprehensions of many wrong. He spoke of the higher-than-average recovery rate in our country, the lower mortality rate and about how India had succeeded in saving the lives of millions of her people.

Never did he go easy on the need for precautions. Wearing a face mask, using a gamchcha or a light towel, practising six-feet distancing, frequently washing hands, not spitting anywhere and taking full care of one's hygiene and sanitation—he continued to reiterate that all these were weapons for protection from the coronavirus. He said,

> 'When a mask is required the most, we tend to remove it. At such times, I urge you that whenever you feel your mask is bothersome and you want to remove it, spare a thought for the doctors, nurses and other Corona warriors. You will find them wearing masks for hours together, diligently working to save our lives. They sometimes wear masks for a span of eight to ten hours. Doesn't that discomfort them? Just think about them ... you too will feel that as citizens, you should not be negligent at all nor allow others to be so.'

Highlighting the globally appreciated work of frontline healthcare workers, Prime Minister Modi exhorted them to continue working in the same selfless and dedicated manner. He also told us how during the coronavirus pandemic, our rural regions had come up as beacons of guidance for the entire country. One example he gave was of Balbir Kaur, the sarpanch of a village in Jammu, who had got a 30-bed quarantine centre constructed in her panchayat ward. She had also made arrangements for the availability of water on roads leading to the ward, ensuring that people did not face any problems in washing their hands. Not just that, along with volunteers, Balbir Kaur, with a spray pump slung on her shoulder embarked upon a mission of sanitisation of the entire neighbourhood. Similarly, a Kashmiri woman sarpanch—Zaitoona Begum of Chauntliwaar, Gaanderbal—fought the battle against the coronavirus and, along with that, created income opportunities for herself. She distributed free masks, and free rations in the vicinity; at the same time, she distributed crop seeds and apple saplings among people. The PM spoke to us about Mohd. Iqbal of Anantnag, who through his own efforts, designed and created a spray machine, that too at a cost of just 50,000 rupees.

In March of that year, the PM continued to drive the message of social distancing as the most effective way of fighting against the coronavirus. He said,

> ‘Friends, during the unlock period, we have to stay more vigilant compared to the lockdown period. Only your alertness can save you from the virus. Always remember, if you do not wear a mask, do not observe the six-feet social distancing norms, or do not take other precautions, you are putting others at risk besides yourselves, especially the elderly and children at home. Hence, I urge all countrymen ... and I repeatedly do so ... do not be negligent ... take care of yourselves and others too.’

To make the subject relatable, in April 2020, the Prime Minister elaborated his point with an analogy about fruits and diseases. He said,

> ‘When I talk about a mask, I remember an old thing. You also may remember that there was a time when a person

seen buying fruits would be questioned whether someone in the family was sick. It meant fruits could only be consumed during illness, such was the thinking that time.'

But with changing times, the way people thought about fruits had changed, Prime Minister Modi said.

'Similarly, the perception regarding the mask is also about to change. You will see that the mask will now become a symbol of civilised society.'

The Prime Minister also spoke about the harm of spitting in public and said people must shun this bad habit. In Episode 63, he added,

'It is now time to eradicate this bad habit forever. It is also said, better late than never. It may be later, but this habit of spitting should be given up. सावधानी हटी तो दुर्घटना घटी.'

He indicated that being vigilant was of utmost importance. He entreated people to even celebrate festivals by staying indoors. he said in Episode 63.

Not just conventional but age-old healthcare was also advocated on *Mann Ki Baat*. **Dr Nimesh Desai**, former director of the Institute of Human Behaviour and Allied Sciences says, 'I don't think there should be any controversy here. We have continued the use of western allopathy medicine for 75 years; they too should be made available to the people. A little conflict is there between the doctors, policy makers and the common people regarding whether a doctor of one particular system practices another medical system or not. A balanced view, as per me, is what we implemented ten years ago at the Evans Hospital where I worked for 23 years. If some patient came there, then allopathy medicine was not forced on them. Just like the cafeteria, we made all AYUSH systems available to them. People were free to take the treatment of whichever system they liked. So, a balanced view will be to promote Indian systems, and while our Indian/South Asian values must be promoted, the boundaries of science must also be maintained.'

In June 2020, as the COVID-19 pandemic raged, the PM reminded us to protect ourselves from it by using ayurvedic medicines, herbal decoctions and hot water. Precaution and protocol were both big themes for him.

Continuing the repetitive but significant theme of the importance of wearing a mask and maintaining Do Gaj Ki Doori, Mask Zaroori through the summer of 2020, he also praised the displaced labour force of our country, who became an embodiment of this mantra. He said,

> 'You can witness this for yourself—these days there are so many stories of our migrant workers who have become a source of inspiration for the entire country. In UP, migrant workers who returned to the village of Barabanki took an initiative to return the Kalyani river to its pristine, natural form. Upon witnessing this resolve to salvage the river, the farmers and other people from nearby areas also got enthused. After returning to their respective villages, whilst spending their mandatory time in isolation or quarantine centres, the manner in which our worker brethren have employed their skills to transform the conditions around them is amazing!'

He also lauded the filial bonding and strength of individual family units through his discourse.

SETTING CORRECTIVE MEASURES: VACCINATION DRIVE

In the first episode of the year 2021, Prime Minister Modi congratulated India on the completion of almost one year of our battle against COVID-19. Just as India's fight against the coronavirus became an example for the world, our vaccination programme too turned out to be exemplary. India undertook the world's biggest COVID-19 vaccine programme. Not just that—along with the biggest vaccine programme, we also vaccinated our citizens faster than anywhere else in the world. In just 15 days, India had vaccinated over 30 lakh COVID-19 warriors, whereas advanced countries such as the United States and the United Kingdom took 18 and 36 days, respectively, to get the same done! The PM said,

> 'The made in India vaccine is, of course, a symbol of India's self-reliance; it is also a symbol of her self-pride. On the NamoApp, Bhai Himanshu Yadav from UP wrote that the made in India vaccine has generated a new self-confidence for the people. Kirti-ji from Madurai wrote that many of her foreign friends messaged her to thank India. Kirti-ji's friends had written to her that the way India has helped the world in the fight against Corona has enhanced the respect for India in their hearts.'

Dr Pragya D Yadav, a research scientist from Indian Council of Medical Research (ICMR) validated this sentiment, 'When the COVID-19 crisis started, we were struggling with diagnosis. The first step then was the expansion of the laboratory network across the country. And once we got through with that, then the next challenge was to develop a vaccine because most of the developed countries were developing their own vaccine, and India had already started the process of isolating the virus. This was one of the most challenging journeys for us, from virus isolation to the delivery of a vaccine in record-breaking time of eight months, which included getting all kinds of approvals from the Government and a license from the WHO as well. I think it is one of the greatest success stories for the country and also indicates a new form of self-reliance. If I talk about the challenge, it was enormous; there was a country-wide lockdown and there was an international travel ban, so it was difficult to collaborate with the right agency to prepare this vaccine during the lockdown period. But in spite of all these restrictions, the government and pharmaceutical companies both worked together in such a way that we could deliver this vaccine to the common man of India. Not only that, we could also deliver vaccines to our neighbouring countries through Vaccine Maitri.'

Similarly, cardiac surgeon **Dr Devi Shetty** says, 'First of all, amongst all the countries in the world, India has done the best in facing the COVID-19 wave. The reason is that we are today the largest country in the world with 1.4 billion people. Many countries claim that they have done very well but you must realise what their population is: 20 million, 30 million, 50 million. Managing COVID-19 in a country of 1.4 billion people is unprecedented and compared to the population and number of possible complications, the number of deaths we have had are negligible. That was because of the foresight of the policymakers and the dedication and passion of all our doctors, nurses and technicians who continued treating COVID-19 patients, even though they didn't really know whether they would themselves survive or not. They came forward, moved very fast, took care of millions of people and virtually brought them out from the jaws of death. So, as a country, we should be very proud.'

In Episode 71 of *Mann Ki Baat*, in February 2021, Prime Minister Modi reiterated this very sense of pride in the made in India Corona vaccines reaching dozens of other countries. It was a big step for a self-reliant India. The vaccine production made us sit up and realise that for everything made in India—textiles, handicraft goods, electronic appliances, mobiles—we can feel pride in our self-reliance. The PM said,

> 'When we move forward with this thought, only then will we become self-reliant in the truest sense ... and friends, I am happy that this mantra of self-reliant India is reaching the villages of the country.'

He cited the example of Santosh from Garhmukteshwar, who turned adversity into opportunity. Santosh's ancestors used to make mats. When everything came to a halt at the time of COVID-19, he and his family began making mats with great energy and enthusiasm. Soon, they started getting orders for their mats not only from Uttar Pradesh but also from other states. With this, the hundreds of years old beautiful art of this region received renewed vigour.

FRONTLINE WARRIORS, DOCTORS, AND NURSES

Through *Mann Ki Baat*, Prime Minister Modi has effectively communicated to the country about its most invaluable assets: its citizens. Doctors, health workers and frontline workers who were waging a colossal battle against COVID-19 found a special place in the show. Dr Shashank Joshi, a prominent endocrinologist from Mumbai who resolutely held on for a whole year, without tiring, without halting, and senior pulmonologist Dr Naveed Shah who spoke about the importance of protective measures and India's own vaccines, Covaxin and Covishield, were both mentioned by the PM. He also spoke about the Boat Ambulance Service started at Dal Lake by Tariq Ahmad Patloo of Srinagar, a houseboat owner. He had fought the battle against COVID-19 himself, and this had inspired him to start the ambulance service. He continued to dispel misconceptions or myths amongst people by saying that no side effects had been found in vaccines that had already been administered.

Barely had the Prime Minister, and the nation, rested when COVID-19 raised its ugly head yet again. The Delta wave began testing the limits of all of us enduring misery. Many of our near and dear ones left us untimely. After successfully confronting the first wave of COVID-19, the country had been full of enthusiasm and confidence, but this storm shook it again. *Mann Ki Baat*, however, continued to focus on spreading a message of reassurance and positivity. Medical personnel, frontline workers working 24×7, ordinary citizens delivering medicines, vegetables, milk, fruits, etc. to families living in quarantine, those offering free ambulance services to patients, were all hailed by the PM.

Praising the superlative COVID-19 strategy adopted by the nation under the leadership of the Prime Minister, **Dr R S Sharma,** CEO, National Health Authority (NHA) says, 'During Covid time, the Honourable Prime Minister spoke in his *Mann Ki Baat* programme on a number of issues. He led from the front in this war against Covid. So basically, whether it was a question of educating the citizens about following Covid protocol, maintaining social distance, using masks, or a question of managing the vaccination platform or vaccination logistics, I think he has always shown the way. If you recall the Prime Minister set an example by himself going to AIIMS and getting the Covaxin vaccine, our own Indian vaccine to tackle people's initial misgivings about the vaccine. That gave people a lot of confidence. I think communicating well and the PM setting an example were actually very important interventions in the management of COVID-19 during those difficult times. I am told there were more than 50 meetings that he chaired with the chief ministers and with other professionals during those times so as to give them confidence. And he always told me don't be afraid, "jab tak dawa nahi tab tak dhilai nahi"—messaging like this was extremely important and I think his communication strategy at this time was par excellence.'

Even in such challenging times, in different corners of the country, voluntary organisations were coming forward and trying to do whatever they could to help others. A youth, Anandan Nair from Kerala, gave a new term to helping others—vaccine service. Similar messages by Shivani from Delhi, Himanshu from Himachal, and many other youths were appreciated by the PM. He said,

> 'On the one hand, the country is working day and night for hospitals, providing ventilators and medicines, and on the other hand, the countrymen are also fighting the challenge of Corona with a lot of heart. This resolve gives us so much strength and so much confidence. Whatever efforts are being made are of great service to society. They strengthen the power of society. Thousands of people are serving others by putting their own lives at stake.'

Mann Ki Baat also gave a stage to those recovering from COVID-19. Preeti Chaturvedi of Gurugram was one such person who shared her victory over the pandemic. Similarly, Pushpa Shukla from Bhubaneswar wrote to the PM sending him photographs of the vaccination programme, especially the ones for the elderly. By this time, Ram Dulaiya, a 109-year-old elderly mother from Jaunpur, UP, had taken the vaccination; similarly, 107-year-old Kewal Krishna from Delhi had also taken the dose of the vaccine. 100-year-old Jai Chaudhary from Hyderabad had also taken the vaccine and the PM's appeals to the people to get vaccinated only grew from there.

'DAWAI BHI, KADAI BHI'

Throughout the spring of 2021, the PM kept talking to lab technicians, cryogenic tanker drivers, the Oxygen Express loco drivers and armed forces personnel. Of the effort that went into that, **Dr Devi Shetty** says, 'It was perhaps one of the toughest periods that the medical community has gone through in our lifetime. Because when COVID-19 had just started all we had known was that there was a viral infection which was causing an epidemic, and nobody knew how the virus was going to behave. Nobody knew how patients were going to behave once infected with the virus. Everything was a mystery. With that kind of a backdrop, going near a patient with COVID-19 and taking care of them while being exposed to the virus could have been dangerous. Our nurses and doctors still came forward and offered their services knowing fully well that they could die in the process. And the worst thing was that when this happened there were no PPE kits, or N95 masks, or the vaccine, or any medicines against COVID-19. That meant that as a doctor if you got infected with COVID yourself, you had no mechanism to protect yourself against death. These are the real heroes who virtually risked their lives and moved forward and the country should be very very grateful to them.'

In Episode 74, Prime Minister Modi spoke to a lab technician, Mr Prakash.

> 'You have to encounter it from the front. It is a life-threatening affair in itself, and therefore it is very natural for the family to be worried. And because so many crores of people are being tested, the burden must have also increased. But for your own safety also, do you take precautions or not?'

Prakash, a technician at the ILBS lab, responded by saying that every protocol was being followed and that his family had remained untouched by the infection. The PM thanked him and thousands of other people like him who had been doing such arduous work, saving innumerable lives.

In the midst of this pandemic, the defence services—Navy, Air Force and the Army—and institutions like the DRDO, along with scientists, industry experts, and technicians were working on a war footing too. The PM spoke to Group Captain Patnaik from the Air Force asking him if like in warfare, running to save lives felt different.

The latter responded to the PM saying, 'Sir, we are fortunate to be able to help our countrymen at this moment of crisis. And these missions that have been assigned to us, we are fulfilling them very well. Our training and support services have been assisting us fully and the best thing, sir, is that job satisfaction derived is of a very high level. And this is why we are able to do continuous operations.'

Lauding the PM's many initiatives to keep the country's morale high, noted musician **Shankar Mahadevan** wrote.

In the midst of providing illustrious examples of selfless service, Prime Minister Modi also concurrently spoke to those people who were experiencing vaccine hesitancy; the people of village Dulariya, district Betul, Madhya Pradesh were among them. He spoke to Rajesh Hiraawe who was a member of the Gram Panchayat. The latter told him that there are 462 men and 332 women in the village but no one had taken the vaccine due to fearmongering on social media apps.

The PM dispelled this notion and assured him that by then, over 31 crore people had got themselves vaccinated, citing the example of his own mother. He entreated the village to come forward and take the vaccine. He also gave the example of Bandipora in Kashmir where Weyan village had achieved the target of 100 per cent vaccination. Similarly, three villages in Nagaland had also hit a 100 per cent vaccination rate. In appealing to Betul, the PM tore through the fear surrounding the vaccine. He asked them to believe in science, believe in scientists, adding that, '... at times when mothers-sisters tell a thing, people agree readily.'

The PM's appeal was that he didn't chide anyone, just tried to persuade them. Of the adoption of COVID-19 protocol in villages, he said someday it will be a subject of a case study for the world how, during this period, people residing in Indian villages, forest dwellers and tribal brothers-sisters, had displayed their capabilities and understanding. People in villages had set up quarantine centres, and had adapted the COVID-19 protocol as per local requirements. People of villages did not let anybody sleep hungry, and did not let work in the fields stop either.

The villages also ensured a daily supply of milk and vegetables to nearby cities, that is, they took care of themselves and of others too.

The decisive mantra for success in conquering COVID-19 was continuity, and the PM consistently conveyed exactly that. In Episode 75, Prime Minister Modi announced that as a nation, we will celebrate National Doctors day on the 1st of July. This day was dedicated to the birth anniversary of the great doctor and statesman of the country, Dr B.C. Roy. The day would mark our gratitude for the contribution of doctors in the COVID-19 period. Our doctors served us without caring about their lives. Therefore, National Doctors Day resonated with the listeners immediately.

The PM reminded everyone,

> ‘Hippocrates, one of the most respected persons in the world of medicine, had said: "Wherever the art of medicine is loved, there is also a love of humanity." Doctors are able to serve us with the power of this very love. Therefore, it is our duty to thank them with an equal measure of affection and to encourage them!’

Reminding his listeners to continue to expand the ambit of COVID services and service to the people, he also referenced Guru Nanak Dev who had started the tradition of langar. Prime Minister Modi reminded us of how the Sikh community all over the world had continued the tradition of feeding people and serving humanity during the period of COVID-19.

In October 2021, the Prime Minister started the show on an enthusiastic note. He said,

'The success of our vaccine programme displays the capability of India ... it manifests the might of our collective endeavour.'

Praising yet another frontline ASHA worker, Poonam of Uttarakhand, who had managed to achieve 100 per cent vaccination in her designated region, the PM said,

'It is on account of the hard work put in by lakhs of health workers like you that India could cross the hundred crore vaccine doses mark. Today, I am gratefully expressing thanks, not just to you but to every Bharatvasi, every Indian who raised the Sabko vaccine–Muft vaccine campaign to such lofty heights of success.'

As the world grappled with the pandemic, our Prime Minister, through *Mann Ki Baat,* cautioned us against complacency and advised us to maintain a strict vigil. He reiterated that COVID-19 had to be taken with the utmost gravity and directed officials to strengthen the ongoing surveillance measures, especially at international airports. He heaped immense praise upon those who deserved it the most, like teachers. He said,

'I am happy that not only have our teachers accepted this challenge but they have also turned it into an opportunity. Ways to incorporate more and more technology in studying, ways to imbibe newer tools, new ways to help students have been seamlessly embraced by our teachers ... they have passed it on to their students as well.'

Right from the early days, the Prime Minister stressed on the need to ensure that the entire COVID infrastructure at all levels is maintained at a high level of preparedness in terms of equipment, processes and human resources. He advised the States to audit their COVID specific facilities to ensure the operational readiness of hospital infrastructure, including the presence of oxygen cylinders, PSA plants, ventilators, and human resources.

He also directed officials to ramp up testing and genomic sequencing efforts. States were asked to share a larger number of samples with the designated INSACOG Genome Sequencing Laboratories (lGSLs) for genome sequencing on a daily basis. This supported the timely detection of newer variants, if any, circulating in the country and facilitated the undertaking of requisite public health measures.

On the occasion of our Independence Day in 2018, the Prime Minister had said,

> ‘The nation will never stop, never bow before anything, never get tired. We have to scale new heights. It is our aim to achieve enormous progress in the years to come.’

Our COVID-19 success prophetically proved just that!

SECTION II

Enabling Social Change

5

Enabling Nari Shakti

> 'In our society, women have been accorded the status of 'Shakti'. This power of women binds the society as a whole, the family as a whole, on the axis of unity and oneness.'
>
> – Prime Minister Narendra Modi

Women weave the fabric of the entire society into a single organic unit bursting with energy and vigour. A woman is the nucleus of her family, community, and humanity. The women of India have been revered since time immemorial, but at an elementary level, society has neither been fair nor kind to them. However, with time, we have seen a transformed consciousness and a perceptible change in the attitude of society and people. Albeit a bit slowly, the perception of women, of Nari Shakti is evolving to reflect the changing times. *Mann Ki Baat* has proven to be a fundamental catalyst in bringing about this change.

Dr Kiran Bedi, the first woman officer of the Indian Police Service (IPS) and the 24th Lieutenant Governor of Puducherry, had this to say about *Mann Ki Baat*, 'The most important requirement for a leader who wants to be successful is communication. He needs to convey his point, communicate from his heart and discuss his priorities. Our Prime Minister is doing the same. This is the first quality needed for leadership. A leader may be gifted with good character and long-term vision, but how will the next person know if he doesn't talk? So, when leaders talk, change comes in the country.'

Speaking about the improvement in the state of women, she says, 'Today women have gone all over, everywhere. Whether you take the sea, whether you take the sky, whether you take Siachen, whether you take the borders, women are everywhere. And now Agniveer has also come, girls are coming from Agniveer, what else do you want? I have been listening to the interviews of girls trying to join the armed forces, and how brave they have been. They are saying that we are doing the same training as everyone else. Everyone's hair is cut like mine ... I understand that as my recruitment became a message, similarly, their recruitment is also a message for future generations. The way they are giving interviews, showing bravery, courage, patriotism, with a futuristic and positive attitude, and having faith in the future of the country, I think they are also giving further messages.'

Truly, India is home to some of the most inspiring women in the world, and many of these women have achieved outstanding success in their respective fields despite the numerous hindrances in their path. Be it cricketer Mithali Raj, the first Indian woman cricketer to have made 10,000 runs—a feat that was lauded in *Mann Ki Baat* in March 2021—or our four talented women pilots who took command of a non-stop flight from San Francisco to Bengaluru in January 2021, examples of women power have been enumerated very warmly by Prime Minister Modi. In recent years, he has made Nari Shakti a top priority in his governance and has taken several steps to promote and empower women. His vision of Amrit Kaal envisions women partnering with India's growth story. Actor and politician Anupam Kher lent his voice to this aspiration, as did Mithali Raj.

It is, therefore, not surprising that the Prime Minister has used *Mann Ki Baat* to address many issues and achievements related to women. This process has not only sensitised people to women but also brought to the forefront the problems and hindrances women face. On the one hand, the programme has led to increased discussion and debate on women's issues. On the other, it has offered a little peek into their world by sharing endless stories of women across India, about their hard work and their accomplishments.

The fact that radio is still widely heard and that women in all corners of India understand the messages sent on it, were fully utilised to drive home important messages, be it the Beti Bachao, Beti Padhao campaign or the #SelfieWithDaughter movement. In Episode 69, Prime Minister Modi spoke of the vatsalya bhava (mother's love) of Rajmata Vijaya Raje Scindia. Relating his personal experience during an Ekta Yatra, Prime Minister Modi said,

> 'I was astounded to see Rajmata Sahab, that too on such a cold winter night. I offered my pranaam and said, "Mother, you at this midnight hour?" She said, "No son, here ... Modi-ji, you have this warm milk and sleep after that". She had brought turmeric milk for me. But, when I looked to the other side, I released it was not just me! The entire travelling establishment of the yatra, around 30-40 people including our drivers and other workers ... She visited each room and ensured that all of us had milk at 2 am in the night! I can

never forget this incident as it taught me about the love of a mother and motherly affection.'

TRANSFORMING MINDS, TRANSFORMING ATTITUDES

The women of India are not competing to be better than the men. They are fighting to be the best they can be. Women's empowerment will not happen overnight. It will take time, and it will require patience. It will happen only through a struggle. It will happen only when an equilibrium between new ideas and old learnings is found.

Eminent Indian corporate lawyer and businesswoman **Zia J Mody** addresses this paradigm shift, 'The law firm we belong to is very different. At the entry level there are more women than men. There are some challenges, but their remuneration is good. Our Prime Minister's speeches about girls' education being imperative, is helping. Our firm recruits/gets some brilliant girls, but the problem is that they get married; they become mothers. The idea of the first sacrifice always comes to a woman's mind. Still, we try a lot to retain women. Our success rate is 50 per cent. To manage the stress factor, we have to learn from the Prime Minister. He has indicated that employers must be responsible for retaining women. That is the challenge we will face in the coming years. But we will succeed.'

She continues to underline the subtle messaging from the Prime Minister himself, 'If you tell us your problem, we can find a solution. Because I am a woman and I have three daughters, it is easier for me to relate to them. The situation is different when it comes to women in courts, You have to get ready to argue every day, therefore, you have to work late-night and get up early in the morning. That is why we are still struggling to increase the women's bench strength. But I am convinced that women are the talent of the future. The Prime Minster has said that all along. And as far as the law is concerned, bring more women into the law and find ways to make them stay. I think, it will be the real success for us in the profession.'

As Mody says, the Prime Minister is indeed aware of the challenges women face in Indian society. But he is also aware of the readiness and dynamism of that same society to change, adapt and move with the times. In one episode, he said,

> 'Our society must recognise such daughters, honour them and feel proud of them. Programmes to felicitate them should be held throughout the country. We could do something more; we could highlight the achievements of these daughters by sharing their achievements on social media, using the hashtag #BharatKiLakshmi. The way we jointly ran a mega campaign Selfie with Daughter, which spread globally, similarly, this time, let us do a campaign encouraging the Laxmi of Bharat since it amounts to strengthening the paths of prosperity for the country and her citizens.'

Not just that, he used another episode of *Mann Ki Baat* to showcase the achievements of Sister Mariam Thresia, who, in her short lifespan of 50 years, worked for the good of the humanity. She became a noble example for the entire world. She rendered service in the fields of education and social upliftment, building many schools, hostels and orphanages. Throughout her life, she remained devoted to this cause. Prime Minister Modi paid a heartfelt tribute to Sister Mariam Thresia.

Equally, he has used the platform to speak against practices such as female foeticide, dowry and child marriage. There have been several reforms in these areas—from increasing the marriageable age of women to the abolition of triple talaq—all of which have contributed to elevating the position of women in the society. In Episode 40 of *Mann Ki Baat*, PM Modi quoted from the *Skanda Puran*,

'दशपुत्र-समाकन्या दशपुत्रान् वधघयन्। यत्फलं लभते मत्यघस्तल्लभ्यं कन्ययैकया.'

This means, a daughter is the equivalent of ten sons. The punya you earn through ten sons amounts to the same earned through just one daughter. This underscores the importance given to women in our society. Be it the erudition of the vidushis of the Vedic period, like Lopamudra, Gargi, Maitreyee, be it the learning and devotion of Akka Mahadevi or Meerabai, be it the governance of Ahilyabai Holkar or the valour of Rani Lakshmibai, woman power has always inspired us. They have always brought glory to the nation.

Prime Minister Modi has always believed that giving women a level playing field to see them thrive is important. In one of the later episodes, he also gave the example of the women of Deurgaon Village in Chhattisgarh who run a self-help group to clean the village roads, squares and temples, in one of the later episodes.

IDEAS THAT SHAPED THE NARRATIVE

Mann Ki Baat has now witnessed the birth of many campaigns that have had a far-reaching impact on the psyche of the country. The platform is effectively being used to hammer home the importance of educating a girl child. The campaign Beti Bachao, Beti Padhao finds several mentions through the 100 episodes of

Mann Ki Baat as it became a fertile ground for ideas to germinate, resulting in the spread of knowledge and change in society. The impact of such dialogue has been far-reaching. The PM spoke about it in Episode 29, where he said,

> 'I have heard that in the Cuddalore district of Tamil Nadu, child marriage has been banned under a special campaign. About 175 child marriages have been prevented so far. The district administration has opened bank accounts for over 55,000 to 60,000 daughters under the Sukanya Samridhi Yojana. In the Kathua district of Jammu & Kashmir, all departments have been connected with the Beti Bachao, Beti Padhao Yojana under the convergence model. In addition to the convening of gram sabhas, efforts are being made by the district administrations to ensure the adoption of orphan baby girls and their future education. In Madhya Pradesh, the Har Ghar Dastak campaign focuses on visits to every village and every house to encourage the daughters' educations. In Rajasthan, Apna Bachcha, Apna Vidyalaya campaign aims to re-admit those girls who dropped out of school. It encourage and motivate them to start studying again. I mean to say that the Beti Bachao, Beti Padhao movement has also developed in many shapes and forms. This entire movement has become a people's movement. New imagination and new concepts have been linked and connected with it. This movement has been moulded as per local requirements.'

Another such example of amplification was the idea of the Selfie with Daughter campaign. On his June 2015 *Maan ki Baat*, Prime Minister Modi appreciated sarpanch Sunil Jaglan, who had launched the Selfie with Daughter campaign. He said,

> 'A few days back the sarpanch of a small remote village of Haryana, Sunil Jaglan-ji launched the Selfie with Daughter campaign. It resulted in such an environment that every father wished to click a selfie with his daughter and post it on social media. I liked this idea, and that too, for a special reason. In Haryana, the number of girls compared to boys is dismally low. Around another 100 districts in the country have a similar situation of skewed sex ratios. But it is the worst in Haryana. If a sarpanch of a small indistinct village in Haryana gives this meaning to the Beti Bachao, Beti Padhao programme, I am certainly overwhelmed.'

An unprecedented tsunami followed on social media. There were several posts from people in India and around the world posting selfies with their daughters. The campaign aimed to evoke pride in parents for having a girl child, and it was beautifully received by the public at large. The emotions portrayed through the campaign were beautiful. It tried to create an understanding, it aimed to bring about change, and it resulted in a revolution in people's thought processes. Soon after the PM's speech, people began responding by posting photos of themselves with their daughters. Maharashtra's Chief Minister Devendra Fadnavis, Union Minister Nirmala Sithraman, MP Pratap Simha, Gujarat minister Shankarbhai Chaudhary, former IPS officer Kiran Bedi, film personality Shekhar Kapur, USA's Assistant Secretary of State Nisha Biswal, journalists Kanchan Gupta, Chitra Subramaniam, Umesh Upadhyay and Richa Anirudh are among those who shared their #SelfieWithDaughter moments.

A travel writer from Canada @JimByersTravel tweeted 'Love India PM's concept of #SelfieWithDaughter. Very proud of my daughter, Kathleen.' The support for the campaign was unprecedented. In Episode 57, the PM urged listeners to celebrate India's Nari Shakti, the power and achievement of women, thereby felicitating the Lakshmi of India. It received an overwhelming response, which the PM acknowledged in the next episode, Episode 58. The PM quoted 17th-century poetess Sanchi Honnamma's poem in Kannada,

Penninda permegondanu himavantanu.
Penninda broohu perchidanu
Penninda janakaraayanu jasuvalendanu.

It means, Himwant, the mountain god, attained fame on account of his daughter Parvati, Rishi Brighu on account of his daughter Lakshmi and King Janak on account of his daughter Sita.

Prime Minister Modi said,

> 'Our daughters are our pride ... Their prodigious virtuosity cradles our social fabric, ensuring its bright future.'

Prime Minister Modi has given countless examples of ordinary women achieving extraordinary feats; he has spoken of numerous women whose tales would otherwise have been lost. He has urged his listeners to read more about them to get inspired and encouraged. He even lauded minor but meaningful achievements of women. He spoke of Bhagyashree Sahu of Rourkela, Odisha, a student of engineering, who started learning and mastered the art of Pattchitra. She began painting on soft stones. On her way to college, Bhagyashree often found these soft stones. She collected, cleaned and started painting these stones in the Pattachitra style for two hours daily. She also gifted these painted stones to her friends. During the lockdown, she started painting on bottles too. And now, she even conducts workshops on this art form.

The noted dancer and a muse to many, classical Indian dancer **Sonal Mansingh** reiterates this stance of *Mann Ki Baat* saying, 'Brilliant, dignified and successful, we can use many adjectives for him, but those would fall short as Shri Narendra Damodardas Modi is the pride of today's India. I call him Vishwa Bandhu because Vishwa Guru is India. He has spoken about all aspects of life, answered all questions of the country and the society, especially all the questions of students, and those related to youth, environment, dried rivers, well, ponds, diversified culture, etc. So, there is no issue that he has not touched upon ... He has spoken about women, Nari Shakti, and the defence services where women are now given employment. The contribution of women is being hailed as Nari Shakti. We were left speechless when we saw Nari Shakti in the Cobra commandos, Airforce, Navy, and Army in the parade on 26 January.

All these words (in *Mann Ki Baat*) come from his heart, sometimes expressing his grief as he is very emotional. It's quite astonishing for him to address his people, bring forward their words, and speak about their stories, speaking to us so that we know what is happening in other parts of society. In every *Mann Ki Baat*, he has spoken about his inner feelings. He has a sharp vision for every issue. He thinks about them, finds solutions for problems and asks for feedback and comments. Our Prime Minister's heart is like an ocean. It may seem quite uncertain from the outside. But deep inside, it is very calm, patriotic and loves society and the people of India. And his feelings of gratitude are like waves of an ocean. So I feel gratitude for such a kind Prime Minister.'

STEPPING BEYOND THE ORDINARY REALM

Over the episodes of *Mann Ki Baat*, the Prime Minister gives countless examples of women who have stepped beyond their traditional roles in the household and have contributed to society and the nation.

Take the example of the women of Phulpur. They joined a self-help group in Kadipur and learned the art of making slippers. With the help of the Gramin Aajeevika Mission, a slipper manufacturing unit was set up, where modern machines now produce slippers. The women inspired the entire region with their resolve and hard work and are an example for the nation. Prime Minister Modi, in Episode 60 of *Mann Ki Baat*, expressed his appreciation for them by saying,

> ‘They not only managed to pluck out the thorn of helplessness from their feet but by becoming self-reliant, they also gained the support of their families. Today, due to the resolve of these women, not only has the financial condition of their families been fortified, but their standard of living has also improved.’

The fact that the awakening of one woman, can lead to the mobilisation of other women, leading to a positive change in the entire society is a unique facet that *Mann Ki Baat* reports. Just a small trigger was sufficient to bring about a huge change. Today, whether women are in politics, defence, social work, entrepreneurship, or sports, the list is long, and their contributions are endless.

The Prime Minister occasionally refers to the varied contributions. In Episode 44, he mentioned Navika Sagar

Parikrama, where six Indian women circumnavigated the globe for 254 days aboard the INSV Tarini. He said,

> 'I congratulate these daughters and their spirit of adventure for bringing laurels to the country, for raising the glory of the Navy and for, so significantly, conveying to the world that India's daughters are no less.'

This was seconded by actress **Preity Zinta**. She tweeted, 'Great to see our PM support the INSV Tarini team #women empowerment #Mannkibaat.'

The enunciation of such events, where women have stepped out of their traditional roles, has been celebrated in the programme. It paves the way for many others to follow. The PM's mention of this episode was widely celebrated by people from all backgrounds.

An empowered woman is a harbinger of change in society. *Mann ki Baat* uncovers stories where women have, on several occasions, led from the front to bring significant changes in the development of the place where they live. Like the case of Babita Rani from Bundelkhand, who built a canal with the help of other women to bring water to a dried lake. Or the case of Usha Dubey, a teacher from Singrauli in Madhya Pradesh, who has turned a scooty into a mobile library. Every day she goes to some village or the other with her mobile library and teaches children there. Children lovingly call her *kitabon waali didi* (the elder sister with books). Or the instance of a self-help library in Rayo village in Nirjuli of Arunachal Pradesh, funded by Meena Gurung and Dewang Hosayi. This is how women have taken the lead in bringing about a transformation in their lives.

In Episode 53 of *Mann Ki Baat,* Prime Minister Modi spoke about Jamuna Tudu of Jharkhand, famously nicknamed Lady Tarzan, who most valiantly took on the timber mafia and the Naxalites. She saved 50 hectares of the forest and also inspired 10,000 women to unite and protect the trees and wildlife. On the birth of every child, the villagers plant 18 trees. Also, 10 trees are planted to celebrate the marriage of a girl in the village. In the same episode, the PM mentioned the story of Rajkumari Devi of Muzaffarpur in Bihar, fondly called Kisan Chachi (farmer aunty). Her story is awe-inspiring. She has established a precedent in the area of female empowerment and farming, by adding 300 women from her area to a self-help group, motivating them to become financially independent. She has not only trained the village women on how to pursue other gainful means of employment but, most importantly, she has integrated technology with agriculture. All these instances establish that women have converted probabilities into possibilities and plans into realities.

In Episode 74 of *Mann Ki Baat,* the PM spoke to Shirisha Gajni, a loco pilot of Oxygen Express, who shared her experience during the coronavirus pandemic. Gajni and all her female team members, delivered oxygen at various places through the oxygen express. Prime Minister Modi said that it is through their strength and dedication that the nation was able to fight coronavirus. The PM's impetus to Nari Shakti has seen tremendous resonance with social media. These tales of exceptional service and commitment to the cause of self-help are remarkable. All these episodes bear witness to the fact that Indian women are not afraid of effecting changes systemically. The women of New India are exploring every possibility, from start-ups to stand-ups, from Sainik schools to defence colleges, from judiciary to legislative offices, from offices to homes, every role is awe-inspiring and venerable.

THE WAY FORWARD

During these radio addresses, Prime Minister Modi has highlighted the achievements of Indian women. In addition to the measures mentioned above, the Prime Minister has also taken a personal interest in the welfare of women in India. He often visits different parts of the country to meet with women and discuss their problems and aspirations. During these visits, he encourages women to work towards achieving their dreams and assures them support for their efforts. This personal touch has been widely appreciated by the people of India and has encouraged more and more women to step forward and take charge of their lives.

It can be said conclusively that Prime Minister Narendra Modi's initiatives and heartfelt conversations have positively impacted the status of women in India. Women are now more empowered and have access to better education, healthcare and job opportunities. The Prime Minister's focus on *Nari Shakti* has also helped to reduce the gender gap in India and has provided women with the confidence to pursue their dreams and aspirations. Sportswoman **Babita Phogat** has expressed her thoughts via Twitter. She tweeted, 'माननीय प्रधानमंत्री श्री

@narendramodi

जी ने आज #MannKiBaat कार्यक्रम के माध्यम से जल संरक्षण का संदेश दयिा। जल हमारे जीवन के लिए बहुत उपयोगी है। जल है तो हमारा कल सुरक्षति है, इसलिए हम सब को मलिकर अपने कल को बचाना है ताकि हमारी आने वाली पीढ़ी जल से वंचति न रहे।

Women have expressed their views on the vision of Nari Shakti held by the Prime Minister. As an employer, women are sensitised to the fact that it is their responsibility to give flexibility to women and offer solutions to retain them in the workforce. This resonates with the Prime Minister's vision too. **Zia Mody** agrees there will be a definite impact.

> 'Women are the talent of the future, and the Prime Minister has said this all along, and I could not agree more.'

The laboratory of *Mann Ki Baat* now bears testimony to the fact that one voice, one emotion, and one call are enough to create a revolution and transform our thinking.

There have been significant changes in how the woman of today is perceived. But there is still a long way to go before equality is reached. Through his *Mann Ki Baat* addresses, the Prime Minister has been able to reach out to millions across the country and inspire them to become part of the Nari Shakti movement. For women to grow and prosper, to break the glass ceiling, to rise and fly, society has to step up, a family has to be supportive, and a neighbourhood needs to come forward. If a small step in this long journey is taken through collective consciousness and efforts, a step can become a leap and a leap can become a lap, in the long run to the finishing line.

6

Mainstreaming Every Part of India

> 'From the farthest of latitudes and longitudes of India-east or west, north or south, ocean beds or Himalayan peaks, I have left no stone unturned to reach the corners and fulfil Mahatma Gandhi's vision of inclusion. I have committed myself to his vision of empowering and uplifting the person sitting at the last mile.'
>
> – Prime Minister Narendra Modi

Among other things, *Mann Ki Baat* has become a very effective vehicle for carrying, seeding and germinating the thought of one India, unbroken, in nature. Ek Bharat, Shreshtha Bharat isn't just a bugle call for those of us who are motivated by patriotism. It is a theme that reverberates through the very spirit of India and unites us at junctures in history that need us to come together without exception; such as the COVID-19 pandemic, aggression at our borders, or even jubilation at our Oscar wins in March 2023 (for *RRR* and *The Elephant Whisperers*). Unfortunately, for the longest time, this very spirit remained stunted when it came to being one with the states in the northeast, the non-mainland regions, and our tribal communities.

In Episode 72 of *Mann Ki Baat,* Prime Minister Narendra Modi congratulated Naveen, a citizen who had reached out to him saying that he would be exploring ten places to celebrate India's 'Amrit Kaal', starting with a visit to the land of the illustrious unsung hero, Birsa Munda. Prime Minister Modi said,

> 'Naveen from Jharkhand has sent me a message on NamoApp, along with some pictures. He has written that he watched programmes on Amrit Mahotsav and decided that he would visit at least ten places connected with the freedom struggle. The first name on his list is the birthplace of Bhagwan Birsa Munda. Naveen has written that he will disseminate stories of the tribal freedom fighters of Jharkhand to other parts of the country. Bhai Naveen, I congratulate you on your thought.'

He revisited the inspiring story of the legend in Episode 82:

> 'If we have to learn to love nature and the environment, then for that too, Dharati Aaba Bhagwan Birsa Munda is one of our greatest inspirations. He strongly opposed every such policy of foreign rule which was detrimental to the environment. Bhagwan Birsa Munda was always at the forefront while helping the poor and the distressed. He also made society aware of eliminating social evils. Who can forget his leadership during the Ulgulan movement? This movement shook up the British and, as an aftermath, the British had put a large price on Bhagwan Birsa Munda's head ... The more you know about the unique contribution of our tribal populace in the freedom struggle of India, the more you will feel proud.'

Engaging each and every citizen of India and encouraging them to embrace this unit of the nation is something that is central to the Prime Minister's vision. As veteran journalist and thinker **Swapan Dasgupta** said,

> 'Each time he mentions some achievement by some person in some corner of India, whether it's in Uttarakhand, whether it's in Pondicherry, whether it's in West Bengal, wherever, people who were not known, who don't make it to the television, who don't make it to the newspapers, that gives such an enormous boost to their self-confidence. It makes people realise that they are being acknowledged somewhere and that some people are taking note of what they are doing quite silently. So, I think this is a unique institution that he has set up for direct communication. He uses radio because it enables. In my view, the Prime Minister has actually shown that there is a large world outside the realm of politics and that the task of the true leader is to engage with all facets of life.'

INTEGRATING THE DISPERSED SELF INTO THE LARGER, NATIONAL SELF

Bhagwan Birsa Munda's life remains an inspirational force for our people. Even today, folk songs and stories about his courage and valour are very popular in the central region of India. But heroes come in all forms, and *Mann Ki Baat* celebrates as many of them as possible. Take the example of Bijay Shanti of Manipur, whom the Prime Minister referenced in September 2020. Her contribution towards conceptualising modern alternatives for traditional agriculture has led to tremendous progress, with newer experiments and techniques. Bijay Shanti launched a start-up to develop thread from the lotus stem; her efforts and innovations have opened up new avenues in lotus farming and textile. Her story captivated the interest of the audience instantly.

India's and the Prime Minister's focus on integrating different peoples, traditions and cultures within the country is a core theme of the show. He said in a later episode,

> 'You surely know of bamboo, which grows abundantly in the Northeast. Now, using the same bamboo, artisans of Tripura, Manipur and Assam have started crafting high-quality water bottles and tiffin-boxes. If you glance at the craftsmanship of these bottles, you will not believe that bamboo can be used to create such fine products. Moreover, these bottles are eco-friendly. Before actually making them, the bamboo is first boiled, adding neem and other medicinal shrubs. Thus, these bottles also acquire medicinal value.'

He spoke in another episode of the shining example from Bishunpur, Jharkhand, where more than thirty groups are collectively cultivating lemongrass. It takes four months for lemongrass to mature and its oil fetches a decent price in the market. Thematically connecting India, he said,

> 'I also wish to refer to two regions of the country—both are hundreds of kilometres apart, yet are contributing to making India self-reliant in their own unique, novel ways. One is Ladakh, the other is Kutch. The mere mention of Leh–Ladakh creates images of picturesque valleys, mountain peaks and whiffs of fresh air. On the other hand, any reference to Kutch evokes images of an unending desert with no vegetation in sight. In Ladakh, a distinct fruit called *chooli* or apricot, also known as khubani, is grown. This product has the capacity to transform the economy of the area.'

Similarly, in July 2021, the Prime Minister praised farmers in Ukhrul, Manipur who were engaged in apple farming.

There was a time when even the idea of relaying a common message to 'one' India was not thought of. But today, through *Mann Ki Baat,* it is possible to get a national, even universal, message out to everyone. Noted social activist and philanthropist **Nabam Atum** said,

> '*Mann Ki Baat* is a very effective programme. Since India became independent, no other Prime Minister has done such a programme. Prime Minister Modi's programme started in 2014, and throughout these eight-nine years, he has kept his soul among the people and he lives among the people in their hearts. Prime Minister Modi is there in every village and is a subject of discussion in every house. He has worked for the development of poor people, for backward people like us. He has enabled good schemes and wonderful programmes so that the poor who suffer from sorrow and pain are benefited. If you speak of education, health, family welfare, agriculture, horticulture, in every aspect, our community is getting benefits. For this I am deeply thankful to the Modi government.'

Speaking of his own, personal impression of the PM's work, he went on to elucidate,

> 'As a social worker, I met Modi-ji in Mumbai in 2012, when the One India Award was conferred on me by Prime Minister Modi. I have never seen a Prime Minister like Modi-ji. His *Mann Ki Baat* is transmitted to villages, and people gather around the radio in their homes and listen to him. They pay attention to what is said about welfare schemes. The earlier government used to hide schemes from the people. Earlier,

when governments used to send money from Delhi, it used to go to ministers and it didn't come to the people, but now Modi-ji tells us about how much money is being spent, about the outlay of the schemes, which section of society is able to receive it, who is going to get the benefit of the scheme, he gives information about all these things. People are blessed to have Modi-ji as their leader. In my village, roads are being constructed, there is connectivity where there were no roads or railways, we are getting electricity, drinking water. In the border areas, in sensitive areas like Arunachal Pradesh, we feel secure. We feel more secure when Modi-ji goes to the border to celebrate Diwali with the people there and distributes sweets ... We feel good seeing these things. We feel more secure as, at every place, there is the army and the air force who guard the border area. With *Mann Ki Baat*, we feel that Modi-ji is among us, he is sitting in front of us and talking to us like a family member. This is a very good programme.'

THE TOURISTIC APPEAL OF OUR VERDANT STATES

In Episode 70 of *Mann Ki Baat*, while wishing the country a very happy Bihu, Pongal and Makar Sankranti, Prime Minister Modi spoke of the importance of tourism in the integration of the country. Through the powerful medium of *Mann Ki Baat*, he let the country know that the regional office of the Ministry of Tourism had started an 'Incredible India Weekend Getaway' in the villages of Bengal. Artisans from West Midnapore, Bankura, Birbhum, Purulia and East Bardhaman organised workshops for visitors and the sale of handicrafts during these getaways was encouraging. He also mentioned that, all over the country, people are making our art forms popular by employing novel methods with creative fervour.

In Episode 57 of the show, the Prime Minister referred to World Tourism Day. He said,

> 'My dear countrymen, you will be happy to know that certain reputed tourism agencies of the world which benchmark standards of travel and tourism have observed that India has shown a lot of improvement in the Travel & Tourism Competitive Index.'

When a leader like Prime Minister Modi puts emphasis on the contribution of every single individual in the functioning of the country and the need to live by the motto, 'By the people, of the people, and for the people', everyone prospers. Take the instance of Sudeep from Assam, who has transformed his bamboo products into a global brand, or that of Meena Gurung and Dewang Hosayi, who funded a self-help library that is open 24x7 for everyone in the Rayo village of Arunachal Pradesh.

It is through the messaging in *Mann Ki Baat* that the nation came to know about the achievement of the Kaziranga National Park & Tiger Reserve Authority, which has been carrying out an annual waterfowl census for some time. The census records the population of water birds and also the state of their habitat. By February 2021, the number of water birds had increased by about 175 per cent compared to the previous year. A total of 112 species of birds were sighted in Kaziranga National Park during this census. Of these, 58 species happened to be winter migrants from different parts of the world, including Europe, Central Asia and East Asia. The most important reason, the PM said, is that here, there is better water conservation along with very little human interference.

He then drew his listeners' attention good-humouredly to the aspect of positive human interference in the cause of a greater good.

> 'Just take the example of Shri Jadav Payeng of Assam, with whom some of you must certainly be familiar. He has received a Padma Award for his work. Shri Jadav Payeng is the person who actively contributed to raising about 300 hectares of plantations on Majuli Island in Assam. He has been constantly working for forest conservation and is also involved in motivating people for plantation and conservation of biodiversity.'

RETHINKING UNITY: COOPERATIVE FEDERALISM AND EMPOWERMENT

In a bid to ensure equal treatment for all citizens and the integration of every part of the country, the Indian government has come up with several provisions since Independence. Undoing the injustice done by British rule presented its own challenges. Throughout the colonial period, the Northeastern region was treated separately and differently from other regions of British India. Geographically remote and with limited representation, the Northeast and even the islands of India remained isolated for the longest time. As a result, a sense of incompatibility gave way to a feeling of resentment at the time of Independence and integration, and an anti-India sentiment emerged amongst the region's people, especially when the Indian government cold-shouldered local aspirations. Given the historical background of the region, it was not surprising that this provoked antagonism.

But *Mann Ki Baat* became a catalyst for driving a deep sense of unity, despite the challenges. In Episode 61, the Prime Minister spoke of one such instance of redressal: the ethnic tension that forced the Bru–Reang tribe to leave Mizoram and take refuge in Tripura in 1997. The community lived in temporary camps in Kanchanpur in northern Tripura and spent a significant part of their lives as refugees. They had no home, no land, no access to medical treatment for their families, and no education for their kids.

> ‘Just imagine, how difficult it must have been for them to live for 23 long years in trying circumstances in camps. How painful it would have been to spend every moment, every day of their lives, hurtling towards an uncertain future. Governments came and went, but there was no cure for their pain. Despite that, their unwavering belief in the Indian Constitution and culture continued. It’s as a result of that belief that their lives are on the threshold of a new dawn today. As per the agreement, the path to a dignified life has been opened for them. Finally, the new decade of 2020 has brought a new ray of hope to the life of the Bru–Reang community. Around 34,000 Bru refugees will be rehabilitated in Tripura. Not just that, the government will provide assistance of close to Rs 600 crore for their rehabilitation and all-round development. Each displaced family will be provided a plot of land. They will be assisted in the construction of a house. In addition, rations will be provided to them. They will now be able to benefit from the public welfare schemes of the state and central governments. This agreement is special for many reasons. It symbolises the spirit of cooperative federalism.’

Prime Minister Modi said. Lauding the chief ministers of both Mizoram and Tripura, the PM openly expressed his gratitude to them and the people of both states. The new agreement also epitomised the inherent compassion and sensitivity of Indian culture.

Even in the case of Jammu and Kashmir, the conflict in and around that region had its roots in British imperialism. Different religious groups and communities began to perceive themselves as persecuted minorities due to British policies in the region. The region's autonomy, coupled with its isolation and various political vendettas, made it seem incompatible with the rest of the country. In his characteristic fashion, Prime Minister Modi started threading together stories from all our states to underline the idea of one Bharat. In Episode 64 of *Mann Ki Baat*, he mentioned a Kashmiri woman sarpanch—Zaitoona Begum of Chauntliwaar, Ganderbal—who had decided that her panchayat would fight the battle against the Corona virus while also creating opportunities for earning an income. She distributed free masks and rations to those who needed them. At the same time, she distributed crop seeds and apple saplings, so that farmers and horticulturists would not suffer losses. The PM concluded,

> 'Friends, there is another inspiring example from Kashmir. Shriman Mohd Iqbal is the Municipal President of Anantnag. He required a sprayer for sanitisation of his area. He was informed that the machine would have to be brought from another town, that too at a cost of six lakh rupees. On this, Shriman Iqbal-ji, through his own efforts, designed and made a sprayer machine, at a cost of only 50,000 rupees. There are many similar examples.'

In October 2020, in Episode 67, the Prime Minister congratulated the people of the Pulwama region, who have been playing an important role in educating the entire country. He informed us that today, when children anywhere in India do their homework or prepare notes, somewhere behind this lies the hard work of the people of Pulwama. The Kashmir Valley meets almost 90 per cent of the country's demand for pencil slats and timber casings, and of that, a very large share comes from Pulwama. We would never have known about this, had it not been for *Mann Ki Baat*.

RE-CONTEXTUALISING THE SPIRIT OF NAYA BHARAT

Even while serving as a karyakarta at the grassroots level in the 1970s and 1980s, Prime Minister Modi was clear about his vision for his country. He wanted a united India, with every section of the population having a role to play in its growth and development. On the radio show, this idea of a united India, where all its people know about each other and interact without any inhibitions—an India free of biases—is beautifully articulated. As Mahatma Gandhi rightly observed, the decades following Independence were a testing time for our civilisation, especially when it came to mainstreaming marginal regions and celebrating diversity, and we are still far from our goal of mutual coexistence of diverse cultures and traditions within such a large geographical area.

Through *Mann Ki Baat*, the Prime Minister focused on strengthening communication with those who had been marginalised for many years. In almost every episode of the programme, the focus has been on speaking to listeners about different things happening across the country, irrespective of region, culture or tradition. The radio platform seeks to translate the vision of the PM for uniting the country and inspiring implementable action. For instance, while addressing a gathering of 40–50 pradhans of different villages in the Kashmir valley, several issues came to the fore and extensive discussions took place, some on the heavier side and others on the lighter side. When a mention was made of schools in Kashmir that had been set on fire, the pradhans too felt that it was not just the schools, it was the future of the children who studied there that had been set ablaze.

Likewise, in one of the episodes, while addressing queries concerning Board examinations, this is what the PM said:

> ‘I am feeling happy that when the Board examinations were held, 95 per cent of the sons and daughters of Kashmir, the young students, appeared in the examinations. The sheer volume of students who appeared in the Board examinations shows our children from Jammu and Kashmir are committed to attaining newer heights of progress, to build a bright future through the medium of education.’

It is wonderful to see how Prime Minister Modi has fully embraced the notion that it is time India's rich culture gets its due credit. Whether domestically or internationally, he has reinforced this point. In one of the episodes of *Mann Ki Baat*, while speaking about Indian culture, he said,

> ‘... tribal communities have been an integral part of our land, our heritage. Their contribution to the development of the country and society is very important.’

In Episode 97, he spoke about how tribal societies have always tried to preserve their traditions. The government is also making efforts to preserve and research aspects related to the life of tribal communities. The PM named many great personalities who had worked on tribal languages like Toto, Ho, Kui, Kuvi and Manda and received Padma Awards for their achievements. Those working with the Siddhi, Jarawa and Onge tribes have also been honoured. Some of the names mentioned by the PM were Hirabai Lobi, Ratan Chandra Kar and Ishwar Chandra Verma. Not just that, in 2023, the echoes of the Padma Awards were heard elsewhere. For instance, those who showed the right path to misguided youth in Naxal-affected areas were honoured. Ajay Kumar Mandavi, a wood carver in Kanker, and Parshuram Koma Khune, who is associated with the famous Jharipatti Rangbhoomi of Gadchiroli, also received an award. Similarly, Ramkuiwangbe Niume, Bikram Bahadur Jamatia and Karma Wangchu, who are involved in the preservation of their respective cultures in the Northeast, were honoured.

In another interesting episode of *Mann Ki Baat*, Prime Minister Modi spoke about the richness of India's languages and how every community is trying to preserve their language, tradition and customs in their own way. He shared the story of Sikari Tissau of Assam:

> 'Tissau-ji of Karbi Anglong district has been documenting the Karbi language for the last 20 years. Karbi, the language of our Karbi tribal brothers and sisters ... is now disappearing from the mainstream. Shriman Sikari Tissau decided that he would protect their identity ... and today his efforts have resulted in the documentation of much information about the Karbi language. He has also received accolades and has been felicitated with awards at many places for his efforts. I take this opportunity to congratulate Shriman Sikari Tissau-ji

> through *Mann Ki Baat*, but in many corners of the country, there will be many people who are working in this direction through different initiatives, and I also congratulate them all.'

In another episode, the PM read out a letter from the former Governor of Meghalaya, V. Shanmuganthan. It was about how a tiny village in Meghalaya—Mavalyannong—had set out on a mission for cleanliness and more or less every generation was completely dedicated to the cause. He also mentioned that a few years ago, it had won the award for the 'cleanest village' in Asia.

The sharing of a letter from a Northeastern region may be a very small gesture, but the impact it has had is immense. For the Prime Minister's efforts towards disseminating such relevant information have inspired a similar drive in the rest of the country.

Once, while having a light-hearted conversation with his listeners on *Mann Ki Baat*, Prime Minister Modi proudly spoke about how the cricket team from Kashmir had defeated Mumbai on their home ground. He said,

> 'I do not view it as a matter of someone's victory and another's loss. I view it differently. All the stadiums in Kashmir have been inundated after the floods. Kashmir is passing through a tough phase. The circumstances have been extremely grim, with these boys not standing a chance to practice. But the team spirit shown by these boys, their conviction, and their determination are awe-inspiring. These boys have shown us that one can overcome the most trying circumstances if one remains focused on one's goals. This news gave me immense pleasure, and I take this opportunity to congratulate all these players on their victory.'

Prime Minister Modi is one of the very few individuals who knows what is required to fully realise the immense potential of the Indian democratic system. He has stated that, while it is important to unite the people, it may also be time to normalise the idea of dividing India into different administrative zones—North, South, East, West, Central and Northeast—for more efficient yet integrated functioning.

Prime Minister Modi began his journey early, and has worked tirelessly towards uniting the country at different levels and through different platforms. One such medium to unite the country and gain deeper insights into India's rich and diverse culture is *Mann Ki Baat*. In one of the episodes, while promoting India as the favoured destination for both domestic and international tourists, he spoke about his own favourite destination, which is not Dubai or Singapore, but the Northeast. Describing the divine beauty of this region, he said,

> 'Last week I had the chance to travel to the Northeast. I was there for three days. Many times, the youth express their desire to see the Taj, Singapore or Dubai. But I would urge all nature lovers, all who want to experience the divinity in nature, to take a tour of the Northeast. I had gone earlier too. This time, when I went as the Prime Minister, I tried to explore its potential. Our Northeast has tremendous potential and possibilities. It's a land of beautiful people and beautiful surroundings. The love and respect accorded by the people there is something that will stay with me forever. The kinship and affinity shown by the people of the Northeast touched me deeply.'

Who would have imagined that news like this would circulate throughout India and become a medium to mainstream these regions? It still feels like a pleasant dream that is yet to take a formal shape. But, going back to the analogy at the outset of this chapter, it wouldn't be hyperbolic to say, let's *Natu Natu* to the one beat that throbs in the heart of a united India.

In the Prime Minister's words,

> 'Considering everyone as its own and living with the spirit of togetherness is embedded in the ethos of this holy land.'

7

Farmers' Welfare for India's Welfare

> 'Our farmers are the "annadatas". When our farmers prosper, India will prosper.'
>
> – Prime Minister Narendra Modi

Prime Minister Narendra Modi has been consistent in ascribing utmost respect and recognition to our farmers. In Episode 65 of *Mann Ki Baat*, he hailed the spirit of the Indian farmer, saying: *Annanam pataye namah, kshetranam pataye namah* (Bow to the food provider, salute to the farmer).

Even during COVID-19, our farmers proved their mettle. The Prime Minister directed the nation's attention to the astonishing fact that during the pandemic, the sowing of kharif crops had increased by 7 per cent compared to the previous year; the sowing of paddy had increased by approximately 10 per cent; pulses close to 5 per cent; coarse cereals almost 3 per cent; oilseeds around 13 per cent and cotton nearly 3 per cent. He extended felicitations to the farmers and hailed their perseverance, saying that our farmers and our villagers are the bedrock, adhaar, of Atmanirbhar Bharat.

At a farmers' rally in Bareilly, UP in February 2016, he urged farmers to plant more trees and focus on animal husbandry along with traditional practices of agriculture, and stated that for the welfare of the farmers, industries, as well as the services sector, were important, as they offered several opportunities for collaboration. Water management, he said, was also vital for the agriculture sector to flourish and it was important to accord priority to it.

Highlighting several aspects of farmer welfare that aimed to strengthen agricultural infrastructure, Prime Minister Modi said that 'jal' and 'jameen', both are key elements of agriculture and must be taken care of. Similarly, in his enriching conversations on *Mann Ki Baat,* he focused on the soil health card and the government's desire to make the benefits of various schemes reach every farmer. His references to individual efforts also garnered much praise from listeners.

Congratulating the Prime Minister on *Mann Ki Baat* and its impact on the rural sector, author **Sudha Murthy** said, 'I salute our leader Shri Modi-ji and his *Mann Ki Baat.* I work with poor people and uneducated people in the rural areas of India—I know their difficulties and I have realised, in the last ten years particularly, that there has been a great change in the social sector. This is only because the leader of the country has understood the difficulties of the social sector and implemented new projects which have enabled people to talk about their problems while simultaneously enjoying the benefits and being atmanirbhar. There are so many different schemes and initiatives, and women in rural areas have also received a lot of benefits.'

HIGHLIGHTING INDIVIDUAL CONTRIBUTIONS FOR OVERALL SUCCESS

Referencing the many experiments for creating wealth from agricultural waste that are being run successfully across the country, Prime Minister Modi cited the instance of a banana farmer from Tamil Nadu in Episode 21 of *Mann Ki Baat*,

> 'Murugesan-ji from Madurai made a machine to make ropes from the waste of bananas. This innovation of Murugesan-ji will solve the issues of environment and agricultural waste too, and will also pave the way for additional income for the farmers.'

In the same episode, he spoke of another farmer–entrepreneur who had made a huge difference to many. He said,

> 'Virendra Yadav-ji is one such farmer–entrepreneur who has impacted the lives of thousands through his awareness. Virendra Yadav-ji used to live in Australia. Two years ago, he came to India and now lives in Kaithal, Haryana. Just like others, the stubble in the fields was a big concern for him too. Work is being done on a massive scale to find a solution to this issue. However, today in *Mann Ki Baat*, I am especially mentioning Virendra-ji because his efforts are different and show a new way forward.'

Virendra Yadav bought a straw baler machine to make bundles of straw. For this, he received financial assistance from the agricultural department. With this machine, he began to make bundles of stubble and sold them to energy plants and paper mills. As a result, in just two years, he traded in stubble in excess of Rs 2.5 crore and earned a profit of approximately Rs 50 lakh. The benefit of this also accrued to the farmers who owned the fields from which Virendra sourced the stubble. Through the example of this initiative Prime Minister Modi invoked the mantra of 'waste to wealth'.

To the youth, especially the lakhs of students studying agriculture, Prime Minister Modi made a request. He wanted them to visit villages in their vicinity, talk to the farmers and make them aware of innovations in farming, as also the recent agricultural reforms.

The celebrated agricultural economist **Dr Ashok Gulati** has been a witness to the salient reforms discussed on *Mann Ki Baat*. He said, 'The Modi government, which is completing almost nine years very soon, started off with a dream, and after two successive droughts of 2014–2015 and 2015–2016, agriculture still survived. But in 2016, Modi-ji announced that he had a dream of doubling farmers' income by 2022–23. And then he set up a committee. We thought it was a political statement and he may be talking in nominal terms, but the committee said that no, we are not talking in terms of nominal income but real income, i.e., at constant prices, and to do that, major steps were taken. After the droughts, they shortlisted about 99 irrigation projects. Rs 40,000 crore were allocated to them, and the committee said these have to be completed in the next five years, so that resources will not be a constraint. If you have irrigated agriculture, then you can fight droughts, you can fight climate change, and many other things.

Many states are moving steadily on that front and on better price discovery through eNam, which was very innovative, and now they are talking about digital infrastructure for agriculture. These are going to be big moves that can give better pricing to the farmer because the farmer has two basic concerns: one is how to increase productivity and the other is, how to get a better price for his produce.'

In September 2020, speaking of another key achievement—the right to sell fruits and vegetables anywhere and to anyone—Prime Minister Modi cited the example of Shri Kanwar Chauhan of Sonipat, who used to face great difficulties in marketing his fruits and vegetables outside the mandi. In 2014, when fruits and vegetables were excluded from the APMC Act, he and his fellow farmers were greatly benefited. He went on to form a Farmer Producer Organisation. Today, their produce is being supplied directly to Azadpur Mandi in Delhi, and also to big retail chains and five-star hotels. Not only this, more than 60 farmers in his village, through the construction of net houses and poly houses, are producing various varieties of tomato, cucumber and capsicum and earning between 10 and 12 lakh rupees per acre every year.

Farmers across the country have been similarly empowered to market fruits and vegetables and whatever else they are cultivating in their fields—paddy, wheat, mustard, sugarcane. They now have the freedom to sell where they wish to, and get a higher price for their produce.

An example of the benefits of excluding fruits and vegetables from the purview of APMC comes to us from Maharashtra, from the Sri Swami Samarth Farm Producer Company Limited, which is another Farmer Producer Organisation. Farmers in Pune and Mumbai have been running weekly markets in which the produce of about four and a half thousand farmers, from nearly 70 villages, is sold directly, without the involvement of any middleman. During the pandemic, the Lucknow-based

Irada Farmers Producer Company Limited procured fruits and vegetables directly from the cultivators' fields and sold them directly in the markets of Lucknow, independent of middlemen.

When rural youth are directly involved in the process of farming and selling to the market, farmers of the village are gainfully employed. Thus, the Prime Minister, through the effective medium of his radio programme, was able to take a genuine farming issue and pave the way for a long-term solution that could be emulated by crores of farmers.

FARMERS AT THE INTERSECTION OF TECHNOLOGY AND SCIENTIFIC INNOVATION

Typically, when we talk of science, we restrict the discussion to physics and chemistry or to labs, but the reach of science extends well beyond that. Prime Minister Modi has been instrumental in ensuring that scientific prowess is demystified to the point that it becomes useful to the common citizen of India. This has contributed tremendously to the Atmanirbhar Bharat campaign.

Addressing the nation in Episode 71 of *Mann Ki Baat*, the Prime Minister suggested an alternative approach to farming through which farmers would become stakeholders in major reforms that are underway in the country while using the benefits of scientific research. Here are some examples the PM cited as indicative of this approach. Ismail Bhai, a farmer from Gujarat, wanted to do farming, but his family was not supportive because his father had often incurred losses as a farmer. Ismail Bhai resolved that he would dispel the notion of farming being a loss-making activity. He started farming with the use of new methods and innovative techniques. Using drip irrigation, he cultivated potatoes, and today his potatoes have become the hallmark of sound farming practices. Ismail Bhai is also helping hundreds of farmers in his region.

The PM's thrust to move science forward with the mantra of 'Lab to Land' is exemplified in Chintala Venkat Reddy from Hyderabad, whom he mentioned in one of the episodes of *Mann Ki Baat*. A doctor friend of Reddy's once told him about the diseases caused by the deficiency of Vitamin D and the dangers thereof. Reddy, a farmer, thought about what he could do to solve this problem. He began to develop special varieties of wheat and rice that contained Vitamin D. Eventually, he received a patent from the World Intellectual Property Organization, Geneva. Venkat Reddy was also honoured with the Padma Shri by the Government of India.

A self-help group (SHG) of women in Jharkhand have accomplished a similar feat. They created an app, 'Ajivika Farm Fresh', through which vegetables and fruits could be ordered for delivery to homes directly from the fields of farmers. Produce worth more than Rs 50 lakh was delivered during the lockdown. Likewise, Atul Patidar of Barwani, Madhya Pradesh has connected four thousand farmers in his area through the digital medium. Through Patidhar's e-platform farm card, farmers are able to get the essentials of agriculture—such as fertiliser, seeds, pesticide and fungicide—home delivered. Agricultural equipment is also available for hire on this digital platform.

The PM went on to praise another farmer who embodied the spirit of scientific innovation.

> 'Similarly, Urugen Futsog of Ladakh is working very innovatively. At those daunting heights, Urugen is growing about 20 crops organically, that too in a cyclic way, that is, he utilises the waste of one crop as manure for the other crop.

Isn't it amazing? In the same way, Kamraj Bhai Choudhary from Patan district in Gujarat has developed good seeds of drumstick at home itself. Some people call drumsticks sargava or moringa. Drumsticks that are grown with the help of good seeds are of good quality too. Now, by sending his produce to Tamil Nadu and West Bengal, he is raising his income also.'

ORDINARY FARMERS MAKING EXTRAORDINARY CONTRIBUTIONS

In an early episode of *Mann Ki Baat*, Prime Minister Modi lauded persons and institutions who made extraordinary contributions to society. He said the efforts of everyday citizens may seem small but have a very deep impact on changing our thinking and giving a new direction to society. He spoke of a village, Kallar Majra, which is near Nabha in Punjab. Kallar Majra came into the limelight because the farmers there mix stubble with sand by ploughing their fields rather than burning the stubble. Prime Minister Modi congratulated the people of the village effusively and extended his appreciation to everyone who was working to keep the environment clean and pollution free.

The PM mentioned the contribution of Abdul Majeed Wani, a resident of the Shar area of Tral in Pulwama, towards the larger, unifying themes of Atmanirbhar Bharat. Wani was selling his GI-tagged saffron with the help of the National Saffron Mission at the Trading Centre in Pampore through e-trading. Prime Minister Modi said,

> 'Many people like him are involved in this activity in Kashmir. Next time you decide to buy saffron, think of buying saffron

> from Kashmir. Only the warmth of Kashmiri people is such that it imparts a unique, distinct flavour to the saffron.'

Even during the COVID-19 phase, Prime Minister Modi praised the strides made by the agricultural sector, which had protected itself from the pandemic to a great extent. In Episode 77, he said,

> 'Not only did it keep itself safe, but the sector also progressed, moving forward. Do you know that even in this pandemic, our farmers have achieved record produce? The farmers produced record output and this time the country went on to procure a record number of crops. This time, in many places, farmers have got more than the minimum support price (MSP) for mustard. Due to the record food grain production, our country has been able to provide support to every countryman. Today, 800 million underprivileged denizens are being provided free rations in this hour of crisis. So, no such day ever occurs in a needy home when the stove is not lit!'

WELFARE OF CITIZENS IS PARAMOUNT

In Episode 6 of *Mann Ki Baat*, the PM stated that it is our duty to ensure that as the nation progresses, so do our farmers, by increasing yield. He spoke of the introduction of the 'Soil Health Card':

> 'If a person falls sick, a laboratory test is undertaken for them. Similarly, a lab test can be undertaken for our motherland. So, we are working not only to protect your land but also to make it healthy.'

In Episode 74, broadcast in May 2021, he said,

> 'You must definitely have heard about the mangoes of Vizianagaram in South India. Now who wouldn't like to eat the mangoes from there? Therefore, now Kisan Rail is ferrying hundreds of tonnes of Vizianagaram mangoes to Delhi. The people of Delhi and North India will get to eat Vizianagaram mangoes, and the farmers of Vizianagaram will earn well. Kisan Rail has so far transported nearly 2 lakh tonnes of produce. Now the farmers are able to send fruits, vegetables, grains to other remote parts of the country at a very low cost.'

Speaking of other novel approaches towards agriculture and farmer welfare, **Dr Ashok Gulati** says,

> 'Normally, when we speak about agriculture, we only think about rice and wheat because it has been fed into our minds from the early 1960s-70s. That is also why there was a shortage of wheat. Currently, half of the agricultural sector comprises livestock and horticulture. The former includes milk, curd, chicken, poultry and fishery, while the latter includes fruits and vegetables. So, if there is diversification, it must be done in a good way. If we move forward in this way, it will be good for our nation. The country will attain improved food and nutrition security. Also, it will increase the income of farmers. They have to come out of the wheat and rice cycle, we need to come out of that.'

Time and again, Prime Minister Modi has spoken of the need for modernisation. Adopting new alternatives and innovations is as important as continuing with traditional farming methods, especially for creating new employment opportunities in the agricultural sector and increasing the income of farmers. In one of the episodes, he spoke of how bee farming is emerging as a credible alternative. It is becoming the foundation of a honey revolution or sweet revolution in the country, he said. He referred to a village called Gurdum in Darjeeling, West Bengal, which has steep mountains and geographical difficulties, and yet, people here started the work of honey bee farming, and today, there is a sizeable demand for this honey, resulting in increased income for farmers. The natural organic honey from the Sunderbans in West Bengal is in great demand in our country and the world, he pointed out.

Narendra Modi spoke of a personal experience he had in Gujarat.

> 'An event was organised in the year 2016 in Banaskantha, Gujarat. In that programme, I had told the people that there were so many possibilities here ... why don't Banaskantha and the farmers here write a new chapter of the sweet revolution? You will be happy to know that in such a short time, Banaskantha has become a major centre for honey production. Today, farmers of Banaskantha are earning lakhs of rupees annually through honey.'

The idea of honey bee farming resonated tremendously with Prime Minister Modi's listeners, as it allows for income not only from honey but also bee wax, for which there is demand from pharmaceutical, food, textile and cosmetic industries. And the initiative would contribute not only to farmer welfare but also to the Atmanirbhar Bharat campaign. He said in Episode 75 of *Mann Ki Baat*,

'Today the whole world is looking at Ayurveda and natural health products. In such a situation, the demand for honey is increasing even more rapidly. I wish more and more farmers in our country would join bee farming.'

In the same vein, the Prime Minister noted in Episode 77 that farmers in our country are continuing to do wonders in many areas; he mentioned the farmers of Agartala, who produce very good jackfruit. Anticipating the high demand for jackfruit in the country and abroad, these farmers brought their produce to Guwahati by rail, so it could be sent onwards to London. He also mentioned how, in 2018, the government gave the GI tag to 'Shahi Litchi' so that its identity would be reinforced and the farmers would get more benefits.

BENEFITS FOR ALL WITHOUT EXCEPTION

In Episode 19 of the programme, Narendra Modi spoke about to the Gorwa Gram Panchayat, which had taken up the task of creating farm ponds, achieving an increase in the groundwater level. This meant that whenever water was required for crops, farmers had access to it. Due to this, their agricultural production increased by 20 per cent. Similarly, in the next episode, Prime Minister Modi spoke highly of farmers in Telangana, who had, through Mission Bhagirathi, made a commendable effort to optimally use the waters of the Godavari and Krishna rivers. In Andhra Pradesh, 'Neeru Pragati Mission' had been using technology for groundwater recharging.

The Prime Minister referred to Jal Yukt Shivir, a people's movement that promises to be of great help in saving Maharashtra from a water crisis in the future. He said,

> 'Chhattisgarh has started the Lok–Suraj, Jal–Suraj campaign. Madhya Pradesh has started the Balram Talaab Yojana and dug nearly 22,000 ponds, which is no small figure. Work is also being carried out on their Kapil Dhara Koop Yojana. In Uttar Pradesh, there is the Mukhya Mantri Jal Bachao Abhiyaan. In Karnataka, water conservation efforts are in the form of Kalyani Yojana, under which they are trying to revive wells once again. In Rajasthan and Gujarat, there are many ancient baolis, deep tanks or masonry wells with steps going down to the water. These states are making a very big effort to revive these as "water temples".'

Water conservation as a unique facet of farmer welfare is something that Prime Minister Modi has stressed on through the enumeration of other examples. He spoke of Santosh Negi from Pauri Garhwal in Uttarakhand, who, before the onset of the monsoon, dug 250 small trenches which were four feet deep, along the side of the playground in his school, so that rainwater would collect there. This way, the playground remained unspoiled, there was no danger of children drowning in the water bodies, and they managed to save crores of litres of rainwater.

In October 2022, among various initiatives for farmer welfare, the PM launched the Pradhan Mantri Bhartiya Jan Urvarak Pariyojana (One Nation One Fertiliser scheme). Under the scheme, the Prime Minister launched Bharat Urea Bags, which helps companies market fertilisers under the single brand name, 'Bharat'. In Episode 9 of *Mann Ki Baat*, he cited a deeply personal experience to inspire farmers to move towards natural farming. He asserted,

> 'This monsoon season, there should be mass plant sowing campaigns conducted by youth and social organisations.

And I can take a leaf from my personal experience and offer you a suggestion which has been very successful. This is an intensely rural technology. Whenever you sow a plant, place an earthen pot near it. You just need to fill it once or twice a month. You will see how fast the plant grows into a lush green tree. I have even been telling the farmers to plant trees on the boundaries of their fields instead of putting up barricades. These will become your biggest asset in the long run.'

While recording these episodes, the PM struck a chord as an elder offering wise counsel to his audience. His evocative conviction in the idea that '*hamare kisan, hamare gaon Atmanirbhar Bharat ka aadhar hain*' resonates unmistakably for everyone who listens to his words.

8

Harnessing Jal Shakti

> 'Water is also an offering from the God. Even if a drop of water is wasted, we should feel remorse and pain. Water storage, water conservation and proper water irrigation are all of equal importance'.
>
> – Prime Minister Narendra Modi

How can we save every drop of water during the coming rains? How do we begin an exercise to ensure that every drop of water in a village stays within the village? How do we move towards making water conservation a matter of everyday habit but also of unique prioritisation? These are the questions posed by our PM in his ongoing dialogue with the nation through *Mann Ki Baat*.

The importance of water conservation is something that he has dwelled upon almost at the start of every new annual water cycle i.e., the crucial months of April-July in India. All along, the Prime Minister has told us, that as a people, we must show up for and own the responsibility of water harvesting and water conservation.

An example of this could be seen in March 2023, when India announced that it will showcase its traditional water management techniques and the ability to implement mega water projects in the G20 Environment and Climate Sustainability working group. Concurrently, we also asked member nations to share their best practices in the area of water management in order to enable knowledge exchange and cross-learning. Union Jal Shakti Ministry Special Secretary Debashree Mukherjee said that the technical sessions during the three-day meeting will focus on five areas—climate resilient infrastructure, groundwater management, water sanitation and hygiene, climate change mitigation and resource efficiency and circular economy. This is not a solitary event; it is one of the many initiatives focusing on water management that *Mann Ki Baat* has engendered.

As early as March 2016, Prime Minister Modi had announced the government's decision to construct five lakh ponds and farm water reservoirs. Under MNREGA too, the emphasis is laid on creating assets for water conservation. Every village, he insisted, should save water. He encouraged citizens to plan ahead, and get connected with government schemes so that a people's movement could be ignited. Only then, he felt, would the importance of water be fully understood and realised. He reiterated the idea that everyone must join in the campaign for water conservation; that there are many such villages in the country, many progressive farmers and many conscientious citizens who have already done this kind of work. But much more was still needed to done in this area.

> 'I hope we will do, with complete focus, whatever is necessary for water conservation. We have a couple of months to go before the onset of monsoon. Do remember,

the more we save water, the more our farmers will benefit and more lives will be saved.'

In one of the episodes, the PM said that some states, especially Gujarat and Andhra Pradesh, had made full use of technology for water conservation. He expressed the desire that in the future the exceptionally successful efforts of these states be applied to other states also through the Niti Aayog. He said that people's participation was a strong base for solving such problems.

Mann Ki Baat became the confluence of perfect planning, use of appropriate technology, and time-bound action, in order to achieve optimum results in drought management, water conservation, and for saving every single drop of water.

Prime Minister Modi said in one of the episodes,

'The bond with our roots must be strengthened as much as possible.'

In another episode he said,

'My faith is that water is a gift from God. When we go to a temple, we are given an offering of prasad and even if a small bit of that spills, we feel bad in our hearts. We not only pick it up but also pray five times for God's forgiveness. Water is also an offering from God. Even if a drop of water is wasted, we should feel remorse and pain. And so, water storage, water conservation and proper water irrigation are all of equal importance.'

Through the radio programme, he encouraged processes like implementing the maxim 'Per Drop More Crop' through micro-irrigation and cultivating crops that require minimal water intake. The fact that, in many states, even sugarcane farmers are using micro-irrigation, some are using drip irrigation and some are using sprinklers was also lauded by him. As is the case with issues of common national import, the Prime Minister's connection with people and, through them, with other relevant themes is unsurpassed. He said,

'When I discussed with the eleven states, I noticed that even for cultivating paddy for production of rice, some of them had employed drip irrigation successfully and got higher yields, thereby also reducing the requirement for water as well as for labour.'

Journalist, anchor and presenter Richa Anirudh is an admirer of the radio show. She tweeted: 'Connecting very beautifully with the citizens ... @PMOIndia #MannKBaat'.

The PM also mentioned that there were many states which set themselves on very ambitious targets, especially Maharashtra, Andhra Pradesh and Gujarat—these three states had done massive work in the field of drip irrigation. And they were also striving to bring two to three lakh hectares of additional land under micro-irrigation every year. He said,

> 'If this campaign gets underway in all the states, then not only will it benefit cultivation, but more water will also be conserved. Our farmer brothers in Telangana, through Mission Bhagirathi have made a commendable effort to optimally use the waters of the Godavari and Krishna rivers. In Andhra Pradesh, Neeru Pragati Mission has been using technology for ground water recharging.'

Prime Minister Modi also mentioned several others states contributing financially to the mass movement: Jal Yukt Shivir is one such people's movement, which is helping save Maharashtra from a water crisis in the future; Chhattisgarh has the Lok-Suraj, Jal-Suraj campaign; Madhya Pradesh is running the Kapil Dhara Koop Yojana and the Balram Talaab Yojana, under which nearly 22,000 ponds have been dug. In Uttar Pradesh, there is the Mukhya Mantri Jal Bachao Abhiyaan; in Karnataka, the Kalyani Yojana, under which an attempt to revive wells is being made. In Rajasthan and Gujarat, there are many ancient baodis—deep tanks or masonry wells with steps going down to the water—and for their revival, the states are making big efforts. Rajasthan has started the Mukhyamantri Jal Swavlamban Yojana, the Water Self-sufficiency Campaign. Jharkhand, although being a predominantly forest area, still has some parts which face a water problem. They launched a very big campaign for building check dams and started an exercise to check and stop the flow of water. Some states also started a campaign for building a number of small dams at distances of 10 to 20 kilometres in the rivers themselves to check the flow of water. A lot of these efforts became inflection points for jan bhagidari because the PM mentioned them in his monthly address.

MASS MOVEMENT FOR WATER CONSERVATION

In Episode 88, the PM gave us the concept of amrit sarovars or 75 water bodies that are emblematic of the amrit kaal. Everyone talks about our responsibility towards conservation of water, but to make it a priority, water conservation must be come a collective, social responsibility. The idea that each citizen must focus on conserving each drop of rain water is something that we understand innately; it is neither a part of the academic curriculum nor a part of our languages, but it has been a way of life for centuries for our forefathers. The PM said,

> 'Those of you who have had a chance to visit Tamil Nadu might have noticed that in some temples in the state, there are carvings on stone depicting irrigation systems, water conservation methods and drought management methods. There are vast stone inscriptions in these temples and devotees get a chance to read these educative messages. Be it Mannarkovil, Chiran Mahadevi, Kovilpatti or Pudukottai—you will get to see detailed stone inscriptions to this effect. Several baolis (stepwells) are famous as tourist spots, but please do not forget that these are the living symbols of the water conservation campaigns which our forefathers had accomplished.'

Commending the work done by ordinary citizens such as Pawan Gaurai of Belagavi, Sitanshu Mohan Parida of Bhubaneswar, Yash Sharma, Shahab Altaf and many others, through *Mann Ki Baat,* the PM reiterated that water is of great importance to our culture. The PM quoted Rigveda's *Apah Suktam* about water:

> 'आपो हिष्ठा मयो भुवः, स्था न ऊर्जे दधातन, महे रणाय चक्षसे,
> यो वः शिवतमो रसः, तस्य भाजयतेह नः, उषतीरिव मातरः |'

This means that it is water which is the life force and also the source of energy. Please bless us like a mother and may your blessings continue to be showered upon us.

THE SOLUTION IS INHERENT IN THE PROBLEM

Water scarcity affects many parts of the country every year. Yet, only 8 per cent of the water received from rains in the entire year is harvested in our country. This is where Prime Minister Modi's unique approach comes into play.

> 'I believe, like the other problems on hand, we can also solve this predicament by the participation of the people, *jan* bhagidari and their power, jan shakti. We are bound to find a solution through the strength, cooperation and resolution of one hundred and thirty crore citizens. Therefore, keeping the importance of water in mind, a new Jal Shakti ministry has been created in the country. This will allow for faster decision-making on all subjects related to water. A few days ago, I tried to do something different. I wrote a letter to the sarpanchs and gram pradhans across the country, saying that in order to save water, to collect water, to save every drop of rainwater, they should convene a meeting of the gram sabha and sit and discuss the resolution to this problem with the villagers. I am happy that they have shown exemplary enthusiasm on this front and on the 22nd of this month, crores of people contributed free labour (shram daan) across thousands of panchayats. People in village after village resolved to accumulate every single drop of rainwater.'

Referring to Birsa Munda's land, where cohabiting in harmony with nature is a part of the culture, the PM told the nation how people there were ready to play an active role in water conservation. Similarly, through the show, he praised the denizens of those villages that had over time become involved in raising awareness about the water temples in their respective villages. His constant refrain that collective effort begets massive positive results and that there isn't any single formula for dealing with water crisis across the country, has seen huge adoption in theory and in practice by citizens.

In Punjab, for instance, drainage lines are being fixed to get rid of the problem of water logging. The construction of the water-tank in Telangana's Thimmaipalle is changing the lives of the people living in the village. There has been a major change in Rajasthan through the construction of small ponds in the fields at Kabirdham. The PM said in an episode,

> 'I was reading about the collective endeavour in Vellore of Tamil Nadu where 20,000 women came together to revive the Nag river ... I have also read about the women of Garhwal, who are working together on the good work of implementing rainwater harvesting. I believe that many such attempts are being made and we can turn the impossible into possible when we are together and strive with collective resolve. When people will join hands, water will be conserved.'

In June 2019, through the *Mann Ki Baat* programme, he put forth three recommendations. The first was that just like the cleanliness drive had been given the shape of a mass movement by our countrymen, we should start a mass movement for water conservation as well. We should together resolve to save every drop of water since it is God's prasad to us. He said water is like the philosopher's stone—a mere touch of the philosopher's stone could transmute iron into gold—because water too spreads prosperity wherever it goes. He also urged luminaries belonging to different walks of life—films, sports, media, and people belonging to social, cultural and devotional organisations—to lead the promotion of water conservation through innovative campaigns, He entreated his listeners to awaken the society, and unite and join the society in this endeavour.

His second recommendation to us, his own extended family, was to share the many traditional methods that have been in use over the centuries in our country for the conservation of water. He cited a brilliant example:

> 'I urge all of you to share these traditional methods of water conservation. If any of you gets an opportunity to go to Porbandar, the place of birth of revered Bapu, then there is a house behind the house of revered Bapu, where a 200-year-old water tank still exists. It is still capable of storing water and has a mechanism to harvest rain water!'

His third recommendation was for us all to honour those that were making a significant difference to the cause, to share information concerning the people, NGOs and anyone else who was making a big contribution towards water conservation, in order to create an extensive database of individuals and organizations dedicated to water preservation. He encouraged us to share our experiences using the #JanShakti4JalShakti hashtag.

THE EXPOSITION OF JAN BHAGIDAARI

The concept of people's participation in a cause comes to life only when it is lauded. The Prime Minister has been generous in educating us about the living examples of water conservation. In Episode 61, he spoke of the Jal Shakti campaign in Jalore (Rajasthan), Barabanki (UP) and Suniyakot village along the Almora-Haldwani highway in Uttarakhand. In doing so, he hailed the ethos of public participation. Even his listeners got to know about the extensive and innovative efforts that were underway, in every corner of the country, for the sake of conserving water. The PM said,

> 'It gives me joy to let you know that the Jal Shakti campaign that commenced last monsoon is making rapid, successful strides with the aid of public participation. A large number of lakes and ponds have been built. And the best part is that in this campaign, people from all strata of society contributed wholeheartedly. Take for instance Jalore district in Rajasthan. There, two historical stepwells had turned into storehouses of garbage and dirty water. But one fine day, hundreds of people from Bhadrajun and Thanwala panchayats made a resolve to rejuvenate them under the Jal Shakti campaign. Much before the rains, people immersed themselves in the task of cleaning out the filthy water, garbage and morass. For this campaign, some donated money; others their labour and sweat. As a result, these stepwells have turned into their lifelines now. A similar story is from Barabanki in Uttar Pradesh.'

The Prime Minister also spoke of the efforts that went into the rejuvenation of Sarahi Lake, spread across 43 hectares, which was on the verge of breathing its last. It was the sheer force and conviction of the villagers, who, through the power of their collective resolve, pumped life into it. They did not let any deterrent come in the way of this mammoth mission. Together, they built a one-metre-high embankment along all the four sides of the lake. He exulted,

> 'The lake now is brimming with water; the surroundings wake up to the melody of the chirping of birds.'

Suniyakot village, along the Almora-Haldwani highway in Uttarakhand, also emerged as a similar example of Jan Bhagidaari. To tide over an acute water crisis, villagers took it upon themselves to ensure that water reached their village. Their resolve was so firm that they raised money among themselves to lay a pipe almost a kilometre away and set up a pumping station. Just like that, a two-decade-old agonising problem came to an end. Through the medium of the radio programme, we got to know that the country is replete with innumerable such stories that lend strength to the resolve of the new India. People came together to share their stories, photos and videos of water conservation and water harvesting on social media using the #Jalshakti4India hastag.

In the summer of that very year, in June 2020, we tuned in to hear about the rain water harvesting underway in one thousand schools of Vadodara, which is a sign of the efficacy of the campaign. As a consequence, it was estimated that on an average, about 100 million litres of water was being conserved annually in Vadodara.

THE EXPANSION OF JAN BHAGIDAARI

Exactly six months later, in Episode 73, Prime Minister Modi informed us about a similar amazing feat achieved by the Battor village panchayat of Panchkula in Haryana, which had hitherto faced the problem of water drainage because of which dirty water would spill over into the surrounding areas, and spread disease. But the people of Battor decided that they would create wealth even from this waste water. The village panchayat started filtering the dirty water coming from the village after collecting it at a place, and then used the filtered water for irrigation of the fields in the village, thereby, liberating their village from pollution, filth and diseases while irrigating the farmers' fields too. The Prime Minister once said,

> 'Friends, I touched upon the subject of water conservation in *Mann Ki Baat* and today I feel that it was an issue close to your heart even before I referred to it, a matter of universal human interest. I have experienced the fact that this topic has stirred the nation's heart strings collectively. Many an informed, effective endeavour is afoot across the country. People have shared information on traditional methods. The media has embarked upon quite a few innovative campaigns. Be it the government or the NGOs, something or the other is being carried out on a war footing. Witnessing the might of the collective is in itself heart-warming and satisfying,'

Pontificating on the water conservation journey that the nation had successfully undertaken, he spoke of village Aara-Keram, not very far from Ranchi in Jharkhand. The fervour displayed by villagers there towards water conservation is exemplary, the PM told us. The rural folk donated sweat, toiling collectively to change the course of a mountain spring. It was a purely indigenous, home-grown method of the kind that the PM had wanted the countrymen to adopt in the preceding year. Aara-Keram's effort not only put a stop to soil erosion and prevented crop damage, but also facilitated the effective irrigation of the fields. Similarly, he praised the beautiful Northeastern state of Meghalaya, which had become the first state to formulate its own water policy.

> 'In Haryana, crops that require meagre water are being encouraged. Farmers are thus saved from suffering losses.

I specially congratulate the Haryana Government for establishing a connect with the farmers to wean them away from conventional modes of farming and leading them towards crops that do not require much water,' he concluded on the subject.'

Similarly, in the summer of 2021, via Episodes 78 and 79. Prime Minister Modi continued to spread the message of water conservation and asked us to spread awareness of the same through forums such as exhibitions and street plays, thus using the festive fervour to convey the message of water conservation with ease.

He spoke of the people of Adhawan village in Banda district of UP, who have also made an innovative effort for conserving water by following the principle *'Khet ka pani khet mein, gaon ka pani gaon mein'*. Under this campaign, high bunds were raised around several hundred bighas of fields of the village. As a result, rain water started collecting in the field, and then percolating into the ground. Subsequently, the farmers also planted trees on the bunds of the fields, generating an extra source of income for themselves.

He also heaped praise on Sachidanand Bharti of Pauri Garhwal, Uttarakhand, because of whose hard work, the huge water crisis in the Ufrainkhal area of Pauri Garhwal has come to an end. Where people used to pine for water, today there is a continuous supply of water throughout the year.

'Friends, in the hills there exists a traditional method of water conservation, which is called Chalkhal. It involves digging a big pit to collect water. Bharti-ji added some new methods to this tradition. He regularly got small and big ponds dug. Due to this, not only did the hills of Ufrainkhal turn green, but the problem of drinking water of the people was also solved. You will be surprised to know that Bharti-ji has got more than 30,000 such water tanks constructed. 30,000! This monumental work of his continues even today and is inspiring many people.'

MOMENTS THAT TURNED INTO A MOVEMENT

In Episode 87, Narendra Modi spoke of his pride and joy that many people in the country had made water conservation a life mission. He spoke about Arun Krishnamurthy from Chennai who is running a campaign to clean the ponds and lakes in his area. He took up the responsibility of cleaning more than 150 ponds and lakes and successfully completed it. Similarly, he spoke about Rohan Kale, an HR professional from Maharashtra, who was running a campaign to preserve hundreds of stepwells in Maharashtra. Many of these wells were centuries old and a part of our heritage.

Bansilalpet kuan in Secunderabad is another such stepwell. Due to years of neglect, this stepwell had got filled with mud and garbage. But a campaign to revive it was started with public participation.

In April 2022, the PM reminded us that water conservation is one of the resolves with which the country is moving forward. He recited the above shloka, which means that in the world, water is the basis of the life of every living being, it is the biggest resource, which is why our ancestors have laid so much emphasis on water conservation. From the Vedas to Puranas, to save water everywhere, to build ponds, lakes etc., has been termed as the social and spiritual duty of a person. In Valmiki's Ramayana, special emphasis has been laid on water conservation, on connecting water sources. Similarly, students of history know, how engineering developed in India around water even during the time of Indus-Saraswati and Harappan civilisations. In ancient times, there was an interconnected system of water sources in many cities. This was a time, when the population was not that great, there was no shortage of natural resources, and there was an abundance of water, and yet, awareness among the people about water conservation was very high. The PM urged the citizens to become aware of old ponds, wells and lakes in our areas as part of the Amrit Sarovar Abhiyan. With this, local touristic places could also be developed in cities, and in localities, the people will get a place to walk around.

> 'Friends, every effort related to water is related to our tomorrow. It is the responsibility of the whole society. For this, different societies have made various efforts continuously for centuries. For example, the Maldhari, a tribe from the Rann of Kutch use a method called Vridas for water conservation. Under this, small wells are built, and trees and plants are planted nearby to protect it. Similarly, the Bhil tribe of Madhya Pradesh uses their historical tradition Halma for water conservation. Under this tradition, the people of this tribe gather at one place to find a solution to the problems related to water. Thanks to the suggestions received from the Halma tradition, the water crisis in this area has reduced and the ground water level is also increasing.'

In Episode 90, again during the monsoon months, he reminded us to make special efforts towards water conservation, since in our country, for centuries, this responsibility had been taken by the society together. Revisiting an older episode of the show, he spoke yet again of baolis and cited the example of Udaipur, Rajasthan, where there is one such stepwell which was hundreds of years old: Sultan Ki Baoli. It was built by Rao Sultan Singh, but due to neglect, gradually this place had become deserted and turned into a dumping ground for garbage. But the resolve of well-motivated youths of that area changed the very picture and destiny of Sultan Ki Baoli. They named this mission of theirs—Sultan se Sur-Tan. 'You must be wondering, what is this Sur Tan! In fact, with their efforts, these youths have not only rejuvenated the stepwell, but have also linked it to the notes and melody of music. After cleaning the Sultan's stepwell, after decorating it, a programme of harmony and music took place there. There is so much talk of this change that many people from abroad have started coming to see it.' He ended the segment saying how can we all create a similar sense of awareness about our water bodies by connecting them with music and other social programmes. Water conservation is actually life conservation, and so he reminded us of many river festivals that are being held to celebrate water.

WATER CONSERVATION VIA AMRIT SAROVARS!

The concept of creating amrit sarovars during the Amrit Kaal has perhaps been the most crucial pivot for *Mann Ki Baat*'s messaging on these issues. It has echoed through the length and breadth of the nation over the course of several episodes.

> 'I have come to know of a brilliant effort from Warangal in Telangana. A new gram panchayat has been formed here, named Mangtya Valya Thanda. This village is close to a forest area. There was a place near the village where a lot of water

used to accumulate during the monsoon. On the initiative of the villagers, this place is now being developed under the Amrit Sarovar campaign. This time, due to the rains during the monsoon, this lake is filled to the brim with water.'

In another episode, the Prime Minister spoke gushed about the Amrit Sarovar built in the Mocha gram panchayat area in Mandla, Madhya Pradesh. This Amrit Sarovar has been built near the Kanha National Park and has further enhanced the beauty of this area. The newly constructed Shaheed Bhagat Singh Amrit Sarovar in Lalitpur, Uttar Pradesh also draws a lot of people. This lake built in the Niwari gram panchayat area is spread over 4 acres. The tree plantation on the shoreline of the lake is enhancing its beauty. People are also coming from far and wide to see the 35 feet high tricolour near the lake. The Amrit Sarovar campaign was a success in Karnataka's Bilkerur village of Bagalkot district also, where people have built a very beautiful amrit sarovar.

Along with being a primary agent for water conservation, the Amrit Sarovar Abhiyan is a gift for today and a boon for our future. Under this campaign, that was mentioned several times on *Mann Ki Baat*, old water bodies are being rejuvenated at many places. Amrit sarovars are being used for quenching the thirst of animals as well as for farming. Due to these ponds, the ground water table of the surrounding areas has risen. At the same time, the greenery around them is also increasing. Not just this, people at many places are also engaged in preparations for fish farming in the amrit sarovars.

In *Mann Ki Baat*, the PM has said,

> 'My dear countrymen, our Upanishads mention a life mantra—*Charaiveti-Charaiveti-Charaiveti*—you must have heard of this mantra too. It means keep going, keep going.'

The PM reiterated this mantra for our benefit once more in the historic Episode 100 of the show. Nothing could be truer of his resolve, and through him, the people's resolve to restore, conserve and preserve water.

9

Aatmanirbhar Bharat for Developed India

> 'Come, we will buy only local, products, emphasise on local products, carrying the fragrance of the sweat of our countrymen. "Vocal for Local" should be our guiding philosophy.'
>
> – Prime Minister Narendra Modi

Becoming fully self-reliant is akin to becoming fully cognisant of our full potential. For a country like ours, Prime Minister Modi's vision of a one-on-one conversation through radio to talk about landmark initiatives in the arenas of social change—such as nurturing the idea of a self-reliant India—is crucial. Take the example of Episode 84, where he alluded to our national song *Vande Mataram*: 'I am sure you must have enjoyed listening to that with a feeling of pride. The spirit that is embodied in *Vande Mataram* fills us with pride and enthusiasm.'

In the spirit of self-reliance, PM Modi had called out 'Jai Anusandhan', or hail innovation, from the Red Fort. He had also talked about making this decade the Techade of India. IITs coming together on one platform to showcase their innovations and research projects, and students and researchers from the fields of healthcare, agriculture, robotics, semiconductors and 5G communications displaying more than 75 projects made on these themes have drawn his attention and praise. For example, on *Mann Ki Baat,* he felicitated a team from IIT Bhubaneswar that had developed a portable ventilator for newborn babies which could run on battery and be used easily in remote areas. Sucha device could prove very helpful in saving the lives of babies born prematurely.

In a recent episode, he spoke of how Gandhi-ji had inspired not just him but all of us to move in the direction of atmanirbharta. 'A hundred years ago when the non-cooperation movement started, Gandhi-ji had written, "Non-cooperation movement is an effort to make the countrymen realise their self-respect and their power."' *Mann Ki Baat* has become the perfect vehicle for showcasing the idea of atmanirbharta.

MAKING A HISTORIC PROMISE A CONTEMPORARY PREMISE

In January 2018, Prime Minister Modi spoke of how empowerment for all is another form of self-reliance. Today our Nari Shakti is assuming all kinds of leadership roles, becoming self-reliant in the process, he said. He cited the extraordinary example of the tribal women of Chhattisgarh. When we refer to Adivasi women, often a stereotypical image comes to our minds, i.e., women carrying firewood on their heads navigating jungles and their pathways. But the women of Chhattisgarh present a different picture. Dantewada in Chhattisgarh is a Maoist-activity affected region, rife with violence, with an atmosphere of terror hanging over the area. In this dangerous atmosphere, Adivasi women have become self-reliant by starting to drive e-rickshaws. In a short span of time, a number of women have become part of this movement. Prime Minister Modi said,

> 'This has three benefits—on the one hand, self-employment has empowered them; on the other, the Maoist-infested region is witnessing a transformation. And simultaneously, it is also strengthening efforts towards the protection of the environment. I laud the efforts of the District Administration which has played a significant role in the successful endeavour of these women by ensuring availability of grants and by imparting training to them.'

Echoing this sentiment of self-reliance as a motivation for innovation, **Deepali Upadhyaya**, programme director, NITI Aayog, says,

> 'Atal Tinkering Labs programme is an initiative of the Government of India wherein 10,000 tinkering labs have been set up across the country. Students from these tinkering labs have been innovating to find solutions to various community problems. When the Honourable Prime Minister of our country mentions them on *Mann Ki Baat*, which is a national platform that connects the entire country with him on a one-to-one basis, it really encourages not just students, parents and teachers but also the community at large to think about innovation as an important aspect of learning, as an important mindset that needs to be inculcated in children to make them ready for the future. Another thing that it does is that it motivates all students and not just the ones who are in the Tinkering labs. These students from other schools then express a desire to visit the

Atal Tinkering Labs, and feel encouraged to find innovative solutions for community problems.'

The very next month, Prime Minister Modi talked about India's self-reliance in science. He reminded us that right from Sir Jagadish Chandra Bose and Hargobind Khorana to Satyendranath Bose, our scientists have brought laurels to India. The subatomic particle, boson, as we all know, has been named after Satyendranath Bose. The Prime Minister said that, at the inauguration of the Wadhwani Institute for Artificial Intelligence, he had got to know of interesting, miraculous accomplishments in the field of science. Artificial Intelligence (AI), through self-learning, can enhance robotic capabilities and allow machines to operate at much smarter levels as compared to earlier. This technology can be harnessed to better the lives of the underprivileged, the marginalised and the needy. For instance, can we make better predictions about natural disasters? Can we use AI to assist farmers with information on crop yield? Can AI be used as a tool to simplify the outreach of health services and modernise medical treatment? Taking this a step further, using self-reliance to become a driver for mass social change, the PM urged the scientific community to deliberate on how AI can help us make life easier for our divyang brothers and sisters. These were all questions posed by him, and through him by his listeners, in the interest of achieving atmanirbharta.

As early as October 2014, Prime Minister Modi equated self-reliance with khadi as a glorious example of our cultural as well as social legacy. 'Whenever, we think of Mahatma Gandhi, naturally we are reminded of khadi. You may be wearing a variety of clothes with different fabrics and company brands in your family. But is it not possible to include khadi too? I am not telling you to use only khadi products. I am just insisting that you use at least one khadi product, like a handkerchief, a bath towel, a bedsheet, a pillow cover, a curtain or anything of that kind. If you have an inclination for all kinds of fabrics and clothes in your family, you can also buy khadi products on a regular basis. I am saying this because, when you buy khadi products, it helps poor people to light lamps on Diwali. Also, you can avail a special discount on khadi products from 2 October onwards for a month. It is a very small thing, but it has a very big impact which binds you with the poor.'

Praising *Mann Ki Baat* for raising important issues, **Vijay Shekhar Sharma,** CEO, Paytm, wrote on social media, 'What a great concept of delivery-in and delivery-out for this Diwali as mentioned by our honourable @PMOIndia in today's #MannKiBaat!'

Much later, in another episode, the Prime Minister spoke of how the imprint of self-reliance had shown in India's start-up culture. To promote start-ups in the field of medicinal plants, an incubator by the name of Medi-Hub TBI is operational in Anand, Gujarat. In a very short time, this incubator, associated with medicinal and aromatic plants, has supported the business ideas of at least 15 entrepreneurs. Sudha Chebrolu is one such citizen who launched her start-up with assistance from Medi-Hub TBI. Another such entrepreneur is Subhashree, whose company is working to manufacture herbal room and car fresheners. She has also created an herbal terrace garden which has more than 400 medicinal plants.

This is how, through the show, the Prime Minister has let us know that the nation's betterment is the responsibility of the government as well as of individuals. If we intend to progress, then we need to identify our own potential, understand our strengths as Indians, and move ahead with confidence. Prime Minister Modi has encouraged the listeners of *Mann Ki Baat* to be guided by the sayings of Swami Vivekananda.

> ‘Vivekananda-ji used to tell a story about a lioness who was carrying her two cubs and, on the way, saw a flock of sheep at a distance. She had a desire to prey on them and started running towards the flock. Seeing her running, one of the cubs joined her too. The other cub was left behind when the lioness moved on, after preying upon the flock. The cub who was left behind was brought up by a mother sheep. He grew up among the sheep, started speaking their language and adapted to their ways of life. He would sit, laugh and enjoy with them. The cub who went with the lioness also grew up. Once, he happened to meet his brother who behaved like the sheep and was shocked to see him. He thought in his mind, "He is a lion and is playing with sheep, talking like sheep. What is wrong with him?" His ego was hurt, and so he went to talk to his brother. He said, "What are you doing, brother? You are a lion." His brother replied, "No, I am a sheep. I grew up with them. They have brought me up. Listen to my voice and the way I talk." The brother who grew up as a lion said, "Come, I will show you, who you really are." He took his brother to a well and told him to look at his reflection in the water, and asked him if both of them had similar faces. "I am a lion, you, too, are a lion." At this, his brother's self-esteem got awakened; he attained self-realisation and even a lion brought up among sheep started roaring like a lion because his inner entity was awakened.’

Similarly, Modi, too, has himself inspired and reminded us Indians of our strengths and capabilities.

> 'We need to understand ourselves. We need to identify our inner strengths and like Swami-ji always used to say, we need to carry our self-respect, identify ourselves and move forward in life and be successful, which in turn, will make our nation a winning and successful country. I believe, all our countrymen with a population of 125 crores are efficient, strong and can stand against any odds with confidence.'

INDIA AT THE JUNCTURE OF FESTIVE SELF-RELIANCE

In 2019, in Episode 60 of *Mann Ki Baat,* the Prime Minister spoke of the Himayat Programme of Jammu, Kashmir and Ladakh, which is associated with skill development and employment of teenagers and youth from 15 to 35 years of age. The programme is meant for those who were forced to leave school and college midstream. Under the aegis of this programme, in just two years, 18,000 youths have been trained in 77 different trades. Out of these, around 5,000 people are productively employed, and many have moved towards self-employment. The success stories of lives which have changed under the aegis of the Himayat Programme, are truly moving, and it has become a wonderful example of how important it is for all of us, the citizens of our country, to become self-reliant and live our lives with dignity.

Picking on the theme of festival tourism, Modi spoke of the limitless possibilities in the field. Notably, Diwali is not limited to Indian communities or even India geographically; governments, citizens and social organisations wholeheartedly celebrate Diwali with gaiety and fervour. In a way, they nurture a microcosm of

India in their respective places. Using the platform of *Mann Ki Baat*, the Prime Minister spoke of how it is customary in every family to buy something new from the market on the occasion of a festival. He urged us to buy local products by saying that there was no need to go to the tehsil if our need could be met in our village, or if an item could be found in the tehsil, then there is no need to go to the district. He said that, as Indians celebrating such an auspicious festival, it was our duty to buy handloom products made by our weavers, our khadi artisans. He concluded the show extending his best wishes to everyone on Deepawali, and urging us to come forward and become a patron of local things to witness for ourselves, how we can all play an important role in making Mahatma Gandhi's dream of self-reliance come alive.

In the same episode, he recalled how he had urged from the ramparts of the Red Fort on 15 August that, as a nation, we ought to make it a priority to buy local products. He urged us to continue promoting locally made products and continue prioritising them while shopping. Linking local products with our status and pride, he said, can become a viable medium to bring prosperity to our fellow countrymen.

> ‘Friends, Mahatma Gandhi viewed this spirit of swadeshi as a lamp illuminating the lives of millions as well as bringing prosperity in the lives of the poorest of the poor. A hundred years ago, Gandhiji started a huge public movement to promote Indian products as one of its objectives. This was the path shown by Gandhi-ji towards self-reliance.’

He also entreated us to pledge that, until 2022, when India would complete 75 years of independence, we remain steadfast—at least, for about two-three years—in buying local products,

products made in India, made by the hands of our citizens. He appealed to not just our emotions but also reason by saying,

> 'I do not advocate this for a long time, just till 2022, till the completion of 75 years of independence. And this work should not be carried out by the government, instead young people should step forward at various places, form small organisations, motivate people and decide that, "Come, we will buy only local products, emphasise the use of local products, carrying the fragrance of the sweat of our countrymen." That will be an exultant moment for my free India; let these be the dreams with which we proceed!'

In Episode 67 of the show, while again advocating for Vocal for Local, he cited the example of khadi that has not only remained a symbol of simplicity over a long period of time, but has also been making waves as an eco-friendly, body friendly, all-weather fabric that works as an excellent fashion statement. 'Not only is the popularity of khadi rising it is also being produced in many places of the world. There is a place in Mexico called Oaxaca. There are many villages in this area where the local villagers weave khadi. Today, the khadi from this place has gained popularity by the name Oaxaca khadi. How khadi reached Oaxaca is no less interesting. A young person of Oaxaca, Mark Brown once watched a movie on Mahatma Gandhi. Brown got so inspired by watching this movie on Bapu that he visited Bapu's ashram in India, understood his work and learnt about him in depth. It was then, that Brown realised that khadi was not just a cloth; it was a complete way of life.'

Prime Minister Modi also celebrated the fact that, on Gandhi Jayanti, the khadi store in Connaught Place in Delhi had witnessed purchases of over Rs 1 crore in just a day. Khadi masks also become very popular during COVID-19. Self-help groups and other such institutions were making khadi masks in many places of the country. Suman Devi of Barabanki in Uttar Pradesh, along with her friends, formed a self-help group and started making khadi masks. Gradually, more and more women started joining her, and now, they are producing thousands of khadi masks. The beauty of our local products is that often a complete philosophy is enshrined in them; *Mann Ki Baat* served as a perfect reminder for this maxim.

ATMANIRBHAR BHARAT AS A TRIBUTE TO OUR VEER YODHAS

In June 2020, Prime Minister Modi reminded us that our pursuits and endeavours should be in the direction of enhancing the country's capabilities and capacities to safeguard our borders. Appealing to the noblest part of our nature, he said that a self-reliant India would be a tribute to our martyrs in the truest, deepest sense. Citing an instance of a listener from Assam, Rajni, he said that, after watching what had happened in eastern Ladakh, she had taken a vow of buying only local ... and for the sake of local, she was also ready to be vocal. Not just her, *Mann Ki Baat* has received messages along these lines from every corner of the country.

Another listener, Mohan Ramamurthy from Madurai, wrote in to say that he wishes India to become self-reliant in the defence sector. It's true that, prior to independence, in the realm of the defence sector, our country was ahead of many countries in the world. Take the multitude of ordnance factories for instance. However, many countries that lagged behind us then are ahead of us now. While a lot could have happened in the interim, it didn't. But today, in the fields of defence and technology, India is relentlessly endeavouring to advance; India is making huge strides towards self-reliance. Naturally, no mission can be successfully achieved without people's participation. And that is why, on the path towards a self-reliant India, as a citizen, our collective resolve, commitment and support is necessary. So, when the Prime Minister urges us to buy local, and become Vocal for Local, we know that we play a crucial role in strengthening the country. We know that, in its own way, this is our civic duty, our way of giving our service to the country. To paraphrase Modi's words, we should also remember that the stronger our country is, the greater the possibilities of peace in the world.

'*Vidya vivadaya dhanam madaay, shaktih pareshaan paripeednayakhalasya sadhoh vipareetam etat, gyaanaydaanaych rakshanay*,' which means, a person who is wicked by nature, uses education to foster conflict, wealth for conceit and strength to trouble others, but a gentleman uses education for knowledge, wealth for helping and strength for protecting. This sentiment is reflected in the way India has always used her might. India's solemn resolve is to safeguard her honour and sovereignty, Modi said.

> 'India's aim is a self-reliant India. India's tradition is trust and friendship. India's spirit is brotherhood. We shall keep moving ahead abiding by these principles.'

Commending the show on its significant boost to self-reliance, author **Sudha Murthy** says, 'Our great visionaries have always felt that promotion of science and technology should be given top priority for the economic development of the country. If we look at the country's major space missions, like *Chandrayaan*, *Mangalyaan*, cryogenic engine developments and related launch vehicles PSLV and GSLV, we have established a whole technology indigenously. DRDO is dedicatedly working at enhancing self-reliance in defence systems and is undertaking design and development, which is leading to the production of world-class weapons systems and equipment. We have established capability in Light Combat Aircraft, Airborne Early Warning and Control Systems, Unmanned Aerial Vehicles, Missile systems both tactical and strategic, Radar and Electronic Warfare systems. Numerous developments have been made in the field of robotics, artificial intelligence, internet of things, 3-D printing, additive manufacturing, biotechnology and quantum computing—the scientific world is challenged by innovations of creative engineering outcomes. With the government giving policy directions and support for indigenous development of systems and equipment within the country, it is the responsibility of all engineers and young generations to come forward and take up start-up projects and contribute wholeheartedly to make India's defence atmanirbhar and self-reliant in the true sense.'

SOLDIERING ON, SANGHE SHAKTI, KALAU YUGE

The journey towards self-reliance was and is ongoing. What *Mann Ki Baat* did was offer a platform that propelled it forward definitively. In Episode 64, we were made aware of a unique initiative that used bamboo, something that grows abundantly in the Northeast. Using bamboo, the artisans of Tripura, Manipur and Assam have started crafting high-quality water bottles and tiffin boxes. Not only are these products eco-friendly but also medicinal, since they are treated with neem prior to finishing.

Yet another example from Jharkhand showed us how small local products can be hugely successful. In Bishunpura, Jharkhand, more than thirty groups are collectively cultivating lemongrass. It takes four months for lemongrass to mature and its oil fetches a decent price in the market. Due to increased health awareness, this product is much in demand.

Some youths from Bihar who decided to move away from their routine jobs exemplify the ambition to think of doing something new and to think innovatively. One day, they decided to start cultivating pearls. In their area, people did not know much about this line of work, but this group of people gathered all the requisite information, went to Jaipur and Bhubaneswar for the requisite training and started cultivating pearls in their village. As a result, they have started earning really well from it and have also started training migrant labourers from Muzaffarpur, Begusarai and Patna, who were returning home from other states. What a wonderful example this is that opened the avenue of self-reliance for so many.

In September 2020, Prime Minister Modi referred to the agricultural sector of the country, to our farmers, our villages as the very basis of a self-reliant India. In their strength, he said, lies the foundation of atmanirbhar bharat. He lauded how, in the recent past, the agriculture sector had liberated itself from many restrictions and tried to break free of many myths. He said that farmers would often write to him about the many dimensions being added to the farming sector and the changes it was undergoing. Self-reliance, in the present times, mandates modern alternatives: i.e., the more we offer to agriculture, the more it will progress with newer innovations and techniques.

Bijay Shanti of Manipur who launched a start-up to develop thread from the lotus stem was cited as an example of new avenues in the fields of lotus farming and textiles.

Correlating the idea of self-reliance to the festival of Raksha Bandhan, the PM said,

> 'Friends, a few days from now, the auspicious festival of Raksha Bandhan will be celebrated. These days, I am noticing that many people and institutions are campaigning to celebrate Raksha Bandhan this time in a different manner. And many people are linking the festival with Vocal for Local. This is true that, in society, if the business of a person near our home increases on account of our festivals, and thus, in turn, his festival becomes merrier, then the joy of the festival increases manifold.'

The Prime Minister concluded the programme by reminding us to celebrate National Handloom Day on the 7 August. He told of this day's remarkable historic background, as it was on this very day in 1905 that the Swadeshi Andolan had begun. Handlooms of India and our handicrafts encompass a glorious history of hundreds of years and are yet another expression of our self-reliance. It should, therefore, be an endeavour on the part of all of us to use Indian handlooms and handicrafts as much as possible, and to also spread the message to as many people in our network as possible. The more the world knows about the richness and diversity of Indian handloom and handicrafts, the greater our local artisans and weavers will benefit. This was the pulse that the PM tapped into exactly a year later in July 2021 when he elaborated on the enormous benefit that the handloom industry creates towards the cause of self-reliance.

> 'Just the way champion proponents of freedom had joined hands for a cause, we have to come together for the development of the country. We have to live for the country, work for the country ... and in that, even the smallest of efforts can produce big results. We can contribute to nation building even while performing our routine chores ... such as by supporting Vocal for Local. Supporting local entrepreneurs, artists, craftsmen, weavers should come naturally to us. The National Handloom Day on the 7 August is an occasion when we can strive to do that.'

Narendra Modi reminded us that in the rural and tribal regions of our country, handloom is a major source of income. It's a sector that comprises lakhs of women, weavers and craftsmen. Therefore, the smallest efforts on our part can give rise to a new hope among weavers. By purchasing something and sharing the experience with our peers, we can celebrate 75 years of Independence, responsibly, he said. He also made it a point to appreciate the small but significant efforts of ordinary citizens.

> 'You must have noticed that, 2014 onwards, we have often touched upon khadi in *Mann ki Baat*. It is only on account of your efforts that today the sale of Khadi has risen manifold. Could anyone even think that, in any Khadi store, the sales figure would cross one crore rupees ... But you have made that possible too. Whenever, wherever you purchase a khadi product, it does benefit our poor weaver brothers and sisters. That is why, in a way, buying khadi is a service to our people, a service to the country. I urge you my dear brothers and sisters, to make it a point to definitely buy handloom products being made in rural areas and share it by using the hashtag #MyHandloomMyPride.'

THE INDIAN TOY STORY

The August 2020 episode of the programme laid stress on an initiative that was started under the aegis of the Ministry of Women and Child Development, the Ministry of Education and the Ministry of Micro, Small and Medium Enterprises (MSMEs). The Prime Minister shared his experience of working together with the University of Gandhinagar students on a unique experiment under the programme Toy Production in India. They discussed how to make new toys available to the children of India, and how India could become a big hub of toy production.

Prime Minister Modi reminded us of what Gurudev Rabindranath Tagore had said about toys—the best toy is that which is incomplete; it is a toy that children complete together with friends while playing. Gurudev Tagore had said that, during his childhood, he used to make his own toys and games with his friends with materials available at home, using his own imagination. But one day, the elders started interfering with those fun-filled moments of childhood. Their interference made the toy—and not the game—the centre of attraction. The child, who hitherto used to mingle with everyone during play and remain immersed in the game, started acting aloof. In a way, the feeling of being distinct from the rest of the children, took over his mind. In that expensive toy, there was nothing to create, nor was there anything to learn. That is, an appealing toy had subdued, veiled and withered a brilliant child. This toy exuded pomposity, it exhibited wealth and a little nobility, but it curtailed the growth and grooming of the child's creative spirit. The toy remained, but the game was over and the blossoming of the child stopped too. Therefore, Gurudev used to say that toys should be such that they bring out the childhood of a child and also his or her creativity.

In the National Education Policy, it is not surprising that a lot of attention has been given to the impact of toys on different aspects of children's lives. Given that there has been a rich tradition of local toys in our country and the fact that we have many talented and skilled artisans who possess expertise in making good toys, the manufacture of Indian toys can be an excellent expression of India's spirit of self-reliance.

Through *Mann Ki Baat,* we were made aware of many parts of India that are developing as toy clusters—Channapatana in Ramanagaram, Karnataka; Kondapalli in Krishna, Andhra Pradesh; Thanjavur, Tamil Nadu, Dhubri, Assam; Varanasi, Uttar Pradesh. The global toy industry is worth more than Rs 7 lakh crore, but India's share in this is small. The Prime Minister asked us to assess why, for a nation which has so much heritage, tradition, variety and young population, India's share in the toy market so little. He said that be it cottage industries, small industries, MSMEs, big industries or private entrepreneurs—all of them should look towards creating and promoting our toys. The Prime Minister cited the example of C.V. Raju in Vishakhapatnam, Andhra Pradesh. At one time, the Etikoppaka toys of his village were very popular. The speciality of these toys was that they were made of wood and had no angles or corners. Since these toys were round from all sides, there was no scope for injury to children. Raju has now started a sort of new movement for Etikoppaka toys along with the artisans of his village. By making excellent quality Etikoppaka toys, C.V. Raju has brought back the lost glory of these local toys.

Through *Mann Ki Baat*, Prime Minister Modi encouraged us to think of ideas based on which we could make games. He actively called upon the young talent of the country to make games in India and make games based on India too. He said,

> 'It is also said, Let the game begin! So, let us start the game. Friends, be it virtual games, be it the sector of toys in the self-reliant India campaign, they all have a very important role to play, and therein lies an opportunity too.'

Episode 72 also spoke of how the country was blessed with newer capabilities. Abhinav Banerjee from Delhi had written to the PM saying that, when he had gone to Jhandewalan to buy some toys and gifts for the children in his family, he had noticed that many shopkeepers were selling Indian toys to customers, emphasising their quality, saying that they were better toys since they were made in India. Similarly, customers too have been demanding India-made toys. He stated,

> 'Indeed, this is it—a big transformation in the mindset ... this is living proof of the same. A huge change has begun in the minds of our countrymen ... that too within a year. It is not easy to gauge this change. Even economists would not be able to assess it on their parameters.'

SWADESHI, AT OUR CORE

Today, when we as individuals, are trying to make the country self-reliant, it is precisely these kinds of examples that work as seeds for the banyan tree of self-reliant India to grow.

Technology falls within this ambit too. Everyone acknowledges the capability of Indians to offer innovation and solutions. So, when there is dedication and sensitivity, this power becomes limitless. The Prime Minister spoke of the AatmaNirbhar Bharat App innovation challenge to encourage participation. He praised our youth who participated enthusiastically in the challenge. Around 7,000 entries were received; of these, nearly two-thirds were from the youth of tier two and tier three cities. This, in and of itself, was an auspicious indication of a self-reliant India as well as for the future of the country.

Echoing India's growing pride in self-reliance, actress Sherlyn Chopra had this to say, 'Achieving the $400 billion exports target is a reflection of India's capacities and a manifestation of rising global demand for Made in India goods. #MannKiBaat #VocalForLocal #LocalForGlobal.'

In Episode 68, Prime Minister Modi spoke of Sri Aurobindo. The more we read **Sri Aurobindo**, the greater insight we get. He said that, as we move forward with the campaign Vocal for Local, Sri Aurobindo's philosophy of swadeshi shows us the path. Sri Aurobindo used to say that swadeshi means that we give priority to the things made by our Indian workers and artisans. He cited a very profound poem in Bangla.

Sui chhuto poy-monto ashe tunga hote.
Diya-shalai kathi, tau aasepote ||
Pro-deepti jalite khete, shutee, jethe.
Kichhute lok noya shadhiaan ||

That is, even the sewing needle and matchstick come here on a foreign ship! The people are not free even in eating, drinking, sleeping!

The gist of what Sri Aurobindo said echoed in the example of Venkat Murli Prasad from Vishakhapatnam who had made the effort to create ABC, that is the AatmaNirbhar Bharat Chart. The PM said,

> 'This is very interesting. Venkat-ji has prepared a list of all those items that he uses on a daily basis. It comprises electronics, stationery, self-care items, besides many other things. Venkat-ji has said that knowingly or unknowingly, we are using those foreign products whose substitutes are easily available in India. He has now vowed that he would use only that product that bears the mark of our countrymen's toil and sweat.'

It was also an opportune moment for him to promote the ethos of zero effect, zero defect. He reiterated,

> 'I urge manufacturers and industry leaders of the country ... people of the country have taken a firm step ... moving a bold step forward ... Vocal for Local is reverberating in each and every household ... in such a scenario, it is time to ensure that our products meet global standards. Whatever is global best; we should make it in India and prove it. For that, our entrepreneur friends have to come forward. Start ups too have to come forth. Once again, I congratulate Venkat-ji on his stellar effort.'

MADE IN INDIA TAG A STATEMENT OF QUALITY

In January 2021, while celebrating Episode 70, the Prime Minister lauded yet another swadeshi endeavour—the Made in India vaccine. It is, of course, a symbol of India's self-reliance and a symbol of her self-pride.

'These days I, too, receive similar messages for India from Presidents and Prime Ministers of different countries of the world. You must also have seen recently how the President of Brazil in a tweet thanked India. Every Indian felt gladdened by that.'

In the episode that aired the following month, Modi mentioned a resident of Bettiah, Pramod, who worked as a technician in an LED bulb manufacturing factory in Delhi. During his work in the factory, he had learnt the intricacies of the entire process of manufacturing of LED bulbs in great detail. During the COVID-19 crisis, Pramod had to return home. What he did next is a shining example of self-reliance; he started a small unit to manufacture LED bulbs in his hometown. He recruited some youngsters from his area and completed the journey from being a factory worker to becoming a factory owner in a few months; that too while living in his own house.

In Episode 74, Prime Minister Modi said that his purpose in talking about so many people to the listeners of *Mann Ki Baat* was so that we could be motivated by them. He referenced Ranjan from Kolkata who had questioned what self-reliant India meant. It's true that self-reliance is not just a government policy, but rather a national spirit. Ranjan believes that being self-reliant means deciding one's own fate, that is controlling one's own destiny. The PM said that Ranjan was 100 per cent correct.

'Further to what he has said, I too would say that the first condition for self-reliance is to have pride in the things of one's own country; to take pride in the things made by people of one's own country. When every countryman takes pride, every countryman connects; self-reliant India doesn't remain just an economic campaign but becomes a national spirit. When we see the fighter plane *Tejas*, made in our own country, doing acrobatics in the sky, when we see made-in-India tanks and made-in-India missiles our pride increases. When we see made-in-India coaches in metro trains in wealthy, advanced nations, when we see made-in-India corona vaccines reaching dozens of countries, then our heads rise higher.'

Modi has stressed that it is not the only bigger things that will make India self-reliant. This is why, be it textiles made in India, handicraft goods made by talented artisans of India, electronic appliances of India, mobiles of India, *Mann Ki Baat* has raised our awareness and led to a feeling of national pride. Modi has motivated his listeners by saying that, when all countrymen put their minds and their might into it, achieving self-reliance, atmanirbharta, will be seamlessly transformed from dream to reality.

10

Promoting Science and Technology

> 'We have two things in abundance in today's 21st century India. First, data and second, technology. Both of them have the power to take India's science to new heights.'
>
> – Prime Minister Narendra Modi

THE X FACTOR: *JAI VIGYAN, JAI ANUSANDHAN!*

Prime Minister Narendra Modi has been instrumental in demystifying science and technology and removing notions around their exclusivity. Science benefits one and all. And thanks to Prime Minister Modi talking about science simplifying everyday lives through the medium of *Mann Ki Baat,* its social acceptability and resonance have increased manifold. Since scientific innovation has multiple touchpoints, the many references to it over the course of the show may have seemed repetitive but it has remained interesting for the listeners.

The Sukhet model to reduce pollution in the villages was one such initiative that the PM cited. Under this model, dung and other household waste is collected from farmers in villages and in return, they are given money for cooking gas cylinders. The work of making vermicompost from garbage collected from the village is also ongoing. Therefore, there are four benefits of the Sukhet model that are directly visible. One, the village is freed from pollution, second, the village is freed from filth, third, money to buy LPG cylinders goes to the villagers and fourth, the farmers of the village get bio-fertiliser—all made possible because of innovative, scientific thinking.

Talking about a widespread concern regarding the inclusion of scientific processes, **Dr Nimesh Desai**, former director of the Institute of Human Behaviour and Allied Sciences, says, 'Aatma nirbharta ... is a good thing: we must respect the past and move forward. After 75 years, we must have the confidence that we can adapt our healthcare sector to the Indian context. Especially from my experience as a psychiatrist, I can say that implementing Western science directly in India or other South Asian societies will be wrong. Mindsets are different, there are cultural differences, and philosophical issues are different. The most important thing is the inner resilience that Indians have which is found very rarely anywhere else. That had been visible in the earlier crisis and the recent pandemic as well. So, we must encourage our cultural and spiritual values and develop such medicines and counselling which can be used not only in India but in other Asian and African countries, similar to how the vaccines were used.'

Technology too, as a related area of focus, has seen an ongoing commitment from Prime Minister Modi because he finds innovation crucial for driving social change and empowering the common citizen. He has naturally veered towards the subject time and again. In his Budget session address in Rajya Sabha, in February 2023, he said,

'We are using technology for empowering common citizens.'

UNLEASHING THE POWER OF SCIENCE AND TECHNOLOGY

In the very early episodes of *Mann Ki Baat,* Prime Minister Modi emphasised that science and technology is like the DNA of development. At the time, he had said that the launch of five heavyweight satellites was a huge achievement which deserved to be widely reported, but that it had merely been touched upon briefly here and there by a few newspapers. Similarly, he had said that it is sad but true that nowadays, out of 100 children, only one or two students say they want to become scientists when they are questioned about their aspirations. This is certainly a cause for concern. Our future generations should, in fact, be taking an active interest in science and technology, be keen on research and be encouraged to become a part of the scientific community. He cited the establishment of the National Discovery Mission as one such step in the right direction. Our former president, Dr APJ Abdul Kalam, had inaugurated it and leading academic institutions such as the IITs and IIMs are being encouraged to take students under their wings.

His words are echoed by **Dr VR Lalithambika**, director, Directorate of Human Space Programme, ISRO: 'In the hugely popular *Mann Ki Baat,* the Hon'ble Prime Minister of India has been touching upon developments in diverse areas which cover all aspects of Indian life and culture. He has placed a special emphasis on the youth of India and on them realising their true potential and with that, the potential of the country. Each month, *Mann Ki Baat* inspires and makes each of us proud and aware of our glorious heritage. It also makes us aware of the diverse and specialised capabilities of our country. This is enthusing the whole generation to excel and will enable us to lead the world in diverse domains. *Mann Ki Baat* has often dwelt upon the challenges and opportunities in science and technology, including in my domain of space technology. This would, no doubt, steer many talented youths to this area. Nari Shakti has been a small but strong current in Indian science and technology. It's heartening to see many opportunities being available for technical leadership, and the capable women who are helming important government departments on scientific research, premier academic institutions as industry leaders and start-ups which are yielding cutting edge technologies.'

Touching upon Nari Shakti as part of our growing scientific prowess, Prime Minister Modi cited the example of Kunni Deori of Orissa who successfully harnessed solar energy to run a silk yarn factory with other women of the village. In doing so, she has set a brilliant example on the use of renewable energy, and has also given a fillip to the local industry and to Nari Shakti!

FROM HIS ADDRESS TO THE SCIENCE CONGRESS

Over the years, the Prime Minister's commitment to science and technology has remained consistent. At an event in January 2023, the PM stated that India had two things in abundance: data and technology. Both of them had the power to take India's science to new heights. He also said that India was among the top three countries in the world in terms of PhDs and the start-up ecosystem.

He reiterated how we're scaling new heights in the space sector as well. Private companies and start-ups are taking advantage of opportunities. Start-ups can find a way forward by associating with R&D labs and academic institutions. Similarly, India is making its mark in the world as a quantum frontier, moving fast in the direction of quantum computers, quantum chemistry, quantum communication, quantum sensors, quantum cryptography and new materials. At this event, the PM appealed to young researchers and scientists to gain expertise in the field of quantum and to take a lead.

SPACE EXPLORATIONS AND PUSHING CHILDREN TO REACH FOR THE STARS

In the *Mann Ki Baat* Episode 29, the PM spoke of Shobha Jalan who had written to him on the NaMoApp that many in the public were not aware of the achievements of ISRO, and that she would like him to provide some more information on the recent launch of 104 satellites and the interceptor missile.

The Prime Minister remarked,

> ‘Shobha-ji, thank you very much for paying attention to this shining example of India’s pride. Whether it is eradicating poverty, preventing diseases, connecting with the world, or disseminating knowledge and information, technology and science have made a mark. 15 February 2017 is a day of immense pride for India. Our scientists have brought laurels to the nation, witnessed by the whole world. And we know that over the last few years, ISRO has accomplished various unprecedented missions with flying colours. After the successful mission of sending Mangalyaan to planet Mars, recently, ISRO scripted a world record in the arena of space. In a mega mission, ISRO has successfully launched 104 satellites simultaneously into space. These satellites belonged

to various countries such as America, Israel, Kazakhstan, Netherlands, Switzerland, UAE and, of course, India.'

Prime Minister Modi highlighted how India had created history by becoming the first country to launch successfully 104 satellites into space simultaneously. Highlighting the achievements of *Cartosat-2D*, he said,

'Brothers and sisters, one out of these 104 satellites is extremely important. It is the *Cartosat-2D*, which is India's satellite and the pictures clicked through it will be of great help in mapping resources and infrastructure, evaluating development and planning for urban development. Particularly for my farmer brothers and sisters, our new satellite, *Cartosat-2D*, will be immensely helpful on a whole lot of subjects such as knowing how much water is there in our existing water sources, how this should be best put to use and what things to keep in mind in this regard. Almost immediately after its launch, our satellite sent back some pictures. It has commenced functioning. It is also a matter of exultation for us that this entire campaign was led and steered by our young scientists, our women scientists.'

In *Mann Ki Baat*, the Prime Minister has continuously emphasised on the role of women and youth in the shining progress of the country. He said that the tremendous participation of youth and women is a major part of ISRO's success. Thanks to his encouragement, scientists are adhering consistently to the objective of bringing space science to the common man and in the service of the nation, they are breaking one record after another.

Sharing the aspirational impetus of the Prime Minister, **Dr Tessy Thomas**, director general (Aeronautical Systems), DRDO says,

'It goes without saying that a nation's development and prosperity is judged by the status of science and technology in the nation. India is one of the top-ranking countries in the field of basic research. Indian science is regarded as one of the most powerful instruments of growth and development, especially in the emerging scenario and competitive economy. Our great visionaries have always felt that the promotion of science and technology should always be given the top most priority for the economic development of the country.

The sustained efforts of scientists and technologists have made the country an emerging power in many areas and have propelled us to the elite club of nations with a presence in space, defence, and nuclear technologies. If we look at the country's major space missions like *Chandrayaan*, *Mangalyaan*, Cryogenic engine development, and related launch vehicles PSLV and GSLV, we have established a whole area of technology indigenously. DRDO works towards enhancing India's self-reliance in defence systems and undertakes design and development leading to the production of world-class weapon systems and equipment. We have established capability in Light Combat Aircraft, Airborne Early Warning and Control Systems and Unmanned Aerial Vehicles, missile systems, both tactical and strategic, and radar and electronic warfare systems.

With numerous developments in the field of robotics, artificial intelligence, the internet of things, 3-D printing additive manufacturing, biotechnology and quantum

> computing, the scientific world is now experiencing the innovations of creative engineering outcomes.'

FROM STARS IN THE SKY TO GUARDIANS OF OUR DEFENCE

The PM also addressed the crucial issue of India's security and defence having acquired great capability. He reiterated how, in the field of defence, India has successfully test-fired the Ballistic Interceptor missile. During its trial, this missile, based on interceptor technology, destroyed an enemy missile at an altitude of about 100 km above the surface of the earth. This is significant, cutting-edge competency in the arena of security. The PM said in an episode:

> 'And you will be happy to know that hardly four or five countries in the world possess this capability. India's scientists have demonstrated this prowess. Its core strength lies in the fact that if, even from a distance of 2,000 km, a missile is launched to attack India, our missile can pre-emptively destroy it in the space itself.'

Deepali Upadhyaya, the programme director for the Atal Innovation Mission, expresses great enthusiasm for the impetus to science and technology that *Mann Ki Baat* has given, 'Atal Tinkering Labs programme is the initiative by the Government of India wherein 10,000 tinkering labs have been set up across the country. Students from these tinkering labs have been making innovations with respect to various community problems. When the Honourable Prime Minister of our country mentions them on *Maan Ki Baa*t, which is a national platform that connects the entire country with him on a one-to-one dialogue basis, it really encourages not just the students but the community at large towards innovative thinking. It also motivates parents and teachers towards thinking about innovation as an important aspect of learning, and as an important mindset that needs to be inculcated in children for them to become ready for the future. Another thing that it does is that it inspires students, not just the ones who are in the tinkering labs, but also other students from other schools who express an interest in visiting the Atal Tinkering Labs, who want to experiment and solve a community problem through innovative solutions.'

When asked about the fillip that the scientific community has received as a result of the show, India's pride, and the first citizen to have travelled to space, **Wing Cdr (Retd.) Rakesh Sharma** said, 'Everybody says space is the last frontier, and we are there amongst the top leading nations. We have been extremely successful. But I won't say space exploration is coming to end, even though the original dreams have already been realised by ISRO. And at the moment we have begun to explore our celestial neighbourhood. So, I would say even the sky is not the limit; there is a lot more to happen in this field in the coming years.'

SCIENTIFIC SOLUTIONS FOR THE BENEFIT OF THE COMMON MAN #INNOVATEINDIA

When referring to the sheer perseverance of scientists, Prime Minister Modi has said several times that the attraction to science for our young generation should increase. When science is harnessed keeping in mind the needs of common folk, when those principles to meet people's requirements and when appropriate mediums and technologies are deliberated upon, it paves the way for science to make the most valuable contribution to general humanity.

During the 14th Pravasi Bharatiya Diwas, Niti Aayog and India's Ministry of External Affairs organised a unique competition. Ideas for socially useful innovations were invited. These innovations were identified and showcased, people were informed about them and how they could be harnessed for use by the common people and their mass production and commercial utilisation were also discussed.

There are times when a problem presents an opportunity for science to find a solution. Our society is also increasingly turning out to be a technology-driven one. In a way, technology is becoming an inseparable part of our lives. In recent days, one can see a lot of emphasis being laid on Digidhan. Gradually, people are moving towards digital currency. Digital transactions in India are witnessing a very rapid surge. All these tenets have been touched upon by Prime Minister Modi via *Mann ki Baat*.

In Episode 41, in response to a phone call from Komal Tripathi, the PM addressed the significance of science yet again. He said,

> 'My young friends have asked me many questions related to science. They keep writing on quite a few points. All of us have seen that the sea appears blue, but we know from routine life experiences that water has no colour at all. Have we ever thought about why water acquires colour in rivers and seas? The same thought occurred to a young man in the 1920s. The same question gave rise to a great scientist of modern India.'

SCIENTISTS AS THE PRIDE OF INDIA, TECHNOLOGY AS A CATALYST FOR CHANGE #TRANSFORMINGINDIA

This land has given birth to many great scientists. On the one hand, there has been a tradition of great mathematicians like

Bodhayana, Bhāskara I, Brahmagupta and Aryabhata. On the other, in the field of medicine, Sushruta and Charaka have bestowed upon us a place of pride. Right from Sir Jagdish Chandra Bose and Har Gobind Khorana to Satyendra Nath Bose, Indian scientists have brought laurels to India. The famous particle BOSON was named after Satyendra Nath Bose.

At the inauguration of the Wadhwani Institute for Artificial Intelligence in Mumbai in February 2018, the PM noted that it was interesting to find out about the ongoing miraculous accomplishments in the field of science. Artificial intelligence aids in the making of robots, bots, and other machines meant for specific tasks. Through self-learning, machines today can be enhanced.

Prime Minister Modi's address in Episode 21 of *Mann Ki Baat* on National Science Day focused on Yogeshwaran from Kerala who had written on the NamoApp that the discovery of the Raman Effect had changed the direction of science in its entirety. Snehil from Nasik also sent him a very good message related to this, saying that there are many scientists from our country without whose contributions science would not have progressed as much. He added that the way we know of other scientists of the world is the same way we should also know about the scientists of India. When we talk of science then many times people restrict it to physics-chemistry or labs, but the spread of science is much more than that. And there is a lot of contribution of the power of science to the Aatmanirbhar Bharat campaign. Through *Mann Ki Baat*, the PM was able to put weight to the words that science should move forward with the mantra of 'lab to land'.

SCIENTIFIC PROWESS AS LAB TO LAND

Narendra Modi spoke of other shining expositions of the scientific spirit in a later episode.

> 'Chintala Venkat Reddy-ji from Hyderabad is an example. A doctor friend of Reddy-ji once told him about the diseases caused by the deficiency of vitamin D and the dangers thereof. Reddy-ji is a farmer, and he thought about what he could do about solving this problem. After this he worked a lot and developed breeds of wheat and rice that specially contained vitamin D. For his effort, he even received a patent from World Intellectual Property Organization, Geneva. Our government is fortunate that Venkat Reddy was also honoured with the Padma Shri last year.'

Similarly, the PM mentioned Urugen Futsog of Ladakh who is working very innovatively. Urugen is growing about 20 crops organically, that too in a cyclical way. He also mentioned Kamraj Bhai Choudhary from Patan district in Gujarat who has developed good seeds of drumsticks at home itself. So, in these cases, one can see that what began as scientific innovation is also an economic innovation.

CHANDRAYAAN-II: SCIENCE TEACHES FAITH & FEARLESSNESS

The PM's second address in the 2nd episode of *Mann Ki Baat 2.0* referenced *Chandrayaan-II*.

> 'My dear countrymen, I firmly believe that you must have felt immensely proud of India's achievement beyond the skies ... in outer space ... *Chandrayaan-II*. Through the A-Sat,

we have acquired the capability of destroying a satellite three hundred kilometres away in a mere three minutes. India has become the fourth country in the world to possess this capacity.'

On 22 July 2019, the nation watched with pride as *Chandrayaan-II* launched into space from Sriharikota. Visuals of *Chandrayaan-II* lifting off filled the countrymen's hearts with glory, zest and joy and echoed the message of the Prime Minister. *Chandrayaan-II* is a mission that is special on many counts. When speaking of it, Prime Minister Modi firmly stated that faith and fearlessness should guide all scientific endeavours.

'We should trust our talents and capacities, we should have faith in them. You will be glad to know that *Chandrayaan-II* is Indian to the core. It is thoroughly Indian in heart and spirit. It is a completely swadeshi, homegrown mission. This mission has proved beyond doubt, once again, that when it comes to attempting an endeavour new-age areas with innovative zeal, our scientists are second to none. They are the best ... they are world-class,'

The important lesson of never losing hope in the face of stumbling blocks or obstacles is also a consistent theme. The PM said,

'The world watched the tapasya, the awesome perseverance of our scientists. We should also feel proud of the fact that despite hindrances, there is no change in the arrival time [of *Chandrayaan-II*] ... many are amazed at that. We have to face temporary setbacks in life ... but always remember—the capacity to overcome them resides within us. I fervently hope that the *Chandrayaan-II* mission will inspire our youth towards science and innovation. After all, science is the path to progress. We are now expectantly waiting for the month of September when the Lander Vikram and Rover Pragyan will land on the lunar surface.'

Through the medium of *Mann Ki Baat*, it is heart-warming to see Prime Minister Modi discuss books published on subjects such as science, technology, innovation, history, culture, business, biographies and so on.

VIKRAM-S – SKY IS NOT THE LIMIT

Prime Minister Modi's address in Episode 95 of *Mann Ki Baat* was a special occasion. Beaming with pride, he announced,

> 'My dear countrymen, on 18 November, the whole country witnessed new history being made in the space sector. On this day, India sent its first rocket into space, which was designed and prepared by the private sector of India. The name of this rocket is *Vikram-S*. As soon as this first rocket of an indigenous space start-up made a historic flight from Sriharikota, the heart of every Indian swelled with pride.'

The *Vikram-S* rocket is equipped with many features and is lighter than other rockets, along with being cheaper. The cost of its development is much less than the cost incurred by other countries involved in space missions. Indian space technology exemplifies world-class standards at a low cost and has now become a hallmark for India. Interestingly, some crucial parts of this rocket have been made through 3-D printing.

As such, the name *Prarambh* given to the launch mission of *Vikram-S* suits it perfectly. The launch signals the dawn of a new era for the private space sector in India. This is the beginning of a new age full of self-confidence for the country. The PM referred to children who once made paper airplanes and used to fly them with their hands:

> 'You can imagine those children who once used to draw shapes in the sky, looking at the moon and stars, are now getting a chance to make rockets in India itself. After space was opened to the private sector, these dreams of the youth are also coming true. As if these youth making rockets are saying, the sky is not the limit.'

Through the radio show, he discussed how India is sharing its success in the space sector with its neighbouring countries as well. He lauded India for launching a satellite, jointly developed by India and Bhutan, which was a reflection of the strong Indo-Bhutan relations. In his words:

> 'Friends, you must have noticed that in the last few episodes of *Mann Ki Baat*, we discussed a lot on space, tech and innovation. There are two special reasons for this. One is that our youth are doing wonderful work in this field. They are thinking big and achieving big. Now they are not going to be satisfied with small achievements. Secondly, in this exciting journey of innovation and value creation, they are also encouraging their other young colleagues and start-ups.'

DRONE TECHNOLOGY: FUTURE FORWARD

In Prime Minister Modi's address in Episode 82 of *Mann Ki Baat*, he spoke of how, in the preceding few years, the pace at which the use of modern technology has increased in our country was echoing with the listeners.

In the episode, he pointedly said that he wanted to discuss a topic that had caught the imagination of our country. 'This topic is drones and drone technology. Up until a few years ago, when the word 'drone' used to come up, what used to be the first feeling in the minds of the people? Of the army, of weapons, of war. But today, if we have any wedding procession or function, we see a drone shooting photos and videos. The spectrum of a drone's usage and its capabilities has widespread uses.'

Drones played a significant role in the COVID-19 vaccine campaign. In Episode 56, the PM spoke of a young student who, with the help of his drone, saved the lives of fishermen.

> 'Friends, earlier there were so many rules, laws and restrictions in this sector that it was not possible to unlock the real capabilities of a drone. The technology that should have been seen as an opportunity was seen as a crisis ... We decided that this mindset has to be changed and new trends have to be adopted,'

Due to the PM's address, after the introduction of the new drone policy, foreign and domestic investors started investing in many drone start-ups. Many companies are also setting up manufacturing units. The army, navy and air force have also placed orders worth more than Rs 500 crores with Indian drone companies.

IN-SPACE : BEYOND FRONTIERS

Narendra Modi's address in Episode 90 of *Mann Ki Baat* is a significant turning point in the push to promote science and technology.

> 'My dear countrymen, there is hardly anyone who has not had fantasies pertaining to the sky. During one's childhood, stories of the moon and stars in the sky attract everyone. For the youth, touching the sky is synonymous with making dreams come true. Today, when our India is touching the sky of success in so many fields, how can the skies, or space, remain untouched by it!'

In the past few years, many big feats related to the space sector have been accomplished in our country. To add to these, the PM announced:

> 'One of these achievements of the country has been the creation of an agency named IN-SPACe ... an agency that is promoting new opportunities in the space sector for the private sector of India. This beginning has especially attracted the youth of our country. I have received messages related to this from many young people.'

The PM spoke also of Dhruva Space, a start-up in Hyderabad that is working on high-technology solar panels for satellite deployers. He conveyed to the country how he had met Tanveer Ahmed of Digantara, another space start-up trying to map waste in space, and how he challenged Tanveer to develop technology to solve the problem of waste in space.

THINKING BIG, ACHIEVING BIGGER

In his classic friendly avatar, the PM spoke of his meeting with Tanvi Patel of Mehsana in one of the later episodes.

> 'Friends, in the programme of IN-SPACe, I also met beti Tanvi Patel, a school student of Mehsana. She is working on

In a historic collaboration, Prime Minister Narendra Modi and then US President Barack Obama came together to address the first-ever joint radio address by the two heads of state, on 27 January 2015.

Prime Minister Narendra Modi interacted with *Mann Ki Baat* contributors during the MyGov town hall in New Delhi, on 6 August 2016.

President Pranab Mukherjee unveiled the first book based on the initial 26 episodes of *Mann Ki Baat* at the Rashtrapati Bhavan, on 30 May 2017. Vice President Mohammad Hamid Ansari, Lok Sabha Speaker Sumitra Mahajan, Finance Minister Arun Jaitley, and other distinguished dignitaries also attended the event.

Prime Minister Narendra Modi presented *Mann Ki Baat: A Social Revolution on Radio* to the Japanese Prime Minister, Shinzo Abe, on 14 September 2017. Incidentally, the Japanese premier also penned the foreword for this book.

Finance Minister Arun Jaitley released the successor book on *Mann Ki Baat* at the National Media Centre, New Delhi, on 2 March 2019. The book is based on the first 50 episodes of the radio show.

Former BJP President Amit Shah, current BJP President J.P. Nadda and Union Ministers Smriti Irani and Piyush Goyal celebrated the success of *Mann Ki Baat* at various booth events. The senior leadership of the BJP actively participated in such programmes through the years.

A collage of live sessions of the 100th episode of *Mann Ki Baat* organised for listener
More than 400,000 such events were held across India and worldwide.

INDIA'S MANN KI BAAT
EVERY INDIAN'S MANN KI BAAT
ONE INDIA ONE FAMILY

Prime Minister Narendra Modi during the recording of *Mann Ki Baat*'s landmark 100th episode, at his Lok Kalyan Marg residence, on 28 April 2023.

The Prime Minister at the Jana Shakti exhibition at the National Gallery of Modern Art Delhi, in May 2023. The show displayed artworks by India's leading artists, focussing on the themes addressed in *Mann Ki Baat*.

Union Minister Amit Shah unveiled a 100 rupee commemorative coin during the National Conclave on *Mann Ki Baat@100* in New Delhi. The event also saw the release of a limited-edition 'Mann Ki Baat India Stamp', by the Indian Postal Department, in celebration of the 100th episode of the iconic radio show.

BJP President J.P. Nadda joined the residents of Honnali, Karnataka, in celebrating the momentous 100th episode of *Mann Ki Baat*.

Union Minister Rajnath Singh and party workers, listened to the 100th episode of *Mann Ki Baat* at the BJP party office.

Grammy award winner Ricky Kej, filmstars Aamir Khan, Raveena Tandon and other prominent panellists attended the day-long national conclave *Mann Ki Baat@100*, in New Delhi.

External Affairs Minister Dr. S. Jaishankar listened to *Mann Ki Baat*'s 100th episode, along with senior diplomats, members of the Indian diaspora and elected representatives from Tri -State region, in New Jersey, USA.

> a very small satellite which is going to be launched into space in the next few months. Tanvi told me about her work very simply in Gujarati. Like Tanvi, about 750 school students in the country are working on 75 such satellites in the Amrit Mahotsav, and it is also a matter of joy that most of these students are from small towns of the country,'

For Prime Minister Modi, questioning every facet of life, extracting answers and showing the right path to humanity is a key scientific driver. Time and again, the Prime Minister has said that science and technology are value-neutral. They don't possess any value in themselves. Any machine will work the way we want it to. What task we want it to perform depends entirely on us. What is truly significant is purpose or 'human objectives' as he calls them. Among the noblest of these is the use of science for the purpose of human welfare. No wonder it became one of the important talking points in the programme.

It is the PM's innate belief in the need for a scientific temperament to be inculcated across all levels of society that has led to several opportunities for innovation in this sector. *Mann Ki Baat,* as a whole, has played a key role in propelling this seed thought forward.

Today, the common man who tunes into the show knows that when the PM speaks of sparking an interest in science, he speaks from both a sense of conviction and action.

11

Swachh Bharat—A Mass Movement

> 'Swachh Bharat has become the dream of each Indian. Some Indians have made it their resolve. Some Indians have made it their aim and purpose. But, each one is connected to it in one or the other way and everyone is making a contribution.'
>
> – Prime Minister Narendra Modi

In the inaugural episode of the iconic radio show, on the occasion of Vijay Dashami, the Prime Minister laid out for the nation an earnest vision of a clean country, and set out on a motivated mission: to ensure the participation of people to realise this vision. This saw the genesis of Swachh Bharat, a bugle call that made us understand that we must take a vow to eliminate dirt and filth from our lives and our nation.

'Yesterday, on 2 October on the eve of Mahatma Gandhi's birth anniversary, more than 1.25 crore countrymen started the Swachh Bharat movement. I had shared one thought yesterday which is that I will nominate nine people and they need to upload their videos of cleaning the nation on social media websites, and nominating nine more people to do the same. I want you all to join me, clean the nation and nominate nine more people to clean it. Then those nine people must nominate nine other people and so on. Eventually, the entire nation will have this atmosphere. I strongly believe that all of you will join hands with me to carry this movement forward.'

Right from the inception of the radio programme, Swachh Bharat—Clean India—has become the dream of every Indian citizen thanks to our leader's focus on it. For us, it has become a personal as well as a national resolve. The purpose of raising awareness about this initiative on a medium of mass communication like radio is that gradually, citizens will become connected to it, in one way or the other, while continuing to make their contribution. Prime Minister Modi often discusses the various innovative efforts in this direction. Acting on one such idea, the Government of India even called upon the people to make short films on Swachhta and send them to the government. A competition was held and the winners were awarded prizes on Gandhi Jayanti. Through a mix of creativity and ingenuity, a new strength was imbued in the Swachhta Abhiyan. New slogans emerged, newer methods came into being, a new inspiration was generated and all this happened only with the great support of the people, according to the PM.

Two years later, he was pleased with the progress that the country had made:

> 'My dear countrymen, we had launched the Swachh Bharat mission two years ago on 2 October, the birth anniversary of our revered Bapu. That day too I had said that cleanliness should become our nature, a duty for every citizen and there should be an atmosphere harbouring a sense of revulsion against filth. Not only this, a cleanliness app, the Swachhta

app, has been launched for people to lodge complaints concerning cleanliness, and also to know about the progress of resolution of these complaints. Government of India has also appealed to the corporate world to come forward in this endeavour. They can sponsor young professionals willing to work for the Swachhta Mission. They can also be sent to various districts as Swachh Bharat Fellows.'

SWACHHTA – A WAY OF LIFE

Swachh Bharat is decidedly one of those ideas that took shape because of *Mann Ki Baat* but progressed into a mass movement beyond it. In the many episodes of *Mann Ki Baat*, this has been interwoven into the subtext. In August 2015, while speaking of the dangerous spread of dengue, we were told that while it is true dengue is dangerous, prevention of dengue is easier as it is directly related to the Swachh Bharat campaign. As an example, we were told that there are several ways of keeping the smallest thing in the household clean by using pure water.

The next month, Prime Minister Narendra Modi highlighted how a listener had written to him saying, 'I want to tell you that, for the Swachhta Abhiyan that you started, you should get dustbins installed on every street and every corner'. In August 2017, the Ministry of Drinking Water and Sanitation organised the Swachh Sankalp se Swachh Siddhi Pratiyogita (From the Resolve of Cleanliness to Attaining Cleanliness Competition) comprising an essay competition, a short film-making competition and a painting competition. Listeners were invited to write essays in various languages or to make a short film that would inspire cleanliness. It could be in any language or it could be silent too. The best entries at the district level and the state level were given prizes. In 2017, Prime Minister Modi also reiterated the resolve to celebrate Gandhi Jayanti as the Swachh Do Aktoobar (Clean 2 October). And to this end, from 15 September, he asked the country to take the mantra, Swachhta Hi Seva (Cleanliness is service) to each and every home.

> ‘Brothers and sisters, it is with great happiness that I wish to tell you, that I am given to understand that under the aegis of the Swachh Bharat Campaign, the Reasi block in Jammu and Kashmir has become completely free of open defecation. I wish to congratulate the people of Reasi block and also the public servants of Reasi block.’

Much later, in Episode 90 that was relayed in June 2022, he told the country of an inspiring story of a group of cyclists who had travelled from Shimla to Mandi carrying the message of cleanliness. The cyclists completed a distance of about 175 kilometres on mountain roads only by cycling. Interestingly, there were children as well as elderly people in this group. ‘If our environment is clean, our mountains and rivers, our seas remain clean, our health also gets better,’ said the PM, praising them and asking other citizens too write to him about such efforts. Again, in the 93rd instalment of the show, he spoke of an effort towards coastal cleaning in the coastal areas of the country which was christened the Swachh Sagar, Surakshit Sagar (Clean Sea, Safe Sea) campaign. This campaign, which started on the 5 July, culminated on 17 September, the day of Vishwakarma Jayanti.

In January 2023, he showed us how our combined efforts towards the goal of cleanliness had led to massive progress. ‘Swachh Bharat Abhiyan has changed the meaning of public participation in our country. If something related to cleanliness takes place anywhere in the country, people always inform me about it. That's how my attention was drawn to a cleanliness campaign started by the youth of Haryana. There is a village in Haryana called Dulheri. The young people there decided that Bhiwani city has to be made exemplary in terms of cleanliness. They formed an organisation called Yuva Swachhta Evam Janseva Samiti. The youth associated with this committee reach Bhiwani at 4 a.m. to run cleanliness drives at different places in the city. These people have so far cleared tonnes of garbage from different areas of the city.'

The genesis and the journey: 'I keep talking about Swachh Bharat to the point of sounding repetitive, because if we have to change mindsets, we will have to do it together and we will have to keep these memories fresh in the minds of the people.'

The real accomplishment of people's participation in making cleanliness a priority is that it was upheld consistently. Take the example of what the PM said in Episode 51, that it made him proud to see the collective efforts that made the Swachh Bharat Mission a successful campaign. He cited the example of Jabalpur, Madhya Pradesh, where over three lakh people came together to work on a sanitation campaign.

Similarly, he dove deeper into our thinking by relating concepts that made the campaign even more resonant—Waste to Wealth was presented as an important dimension of the Swachh Bharat Abhiyan. Kamala Moharana, from Kendrapada district of Odisha, who runs a self-help group that makes many things like baskets and mobile stands from milk pouches and other plastic materials was brought up as someone to be looked up to. 'This is becoming a good source of income for them along with ensuring cleanliness. If we resolve, we can make a huge contribution towards a clean India. At least we all should take a pledge to replace plastic bags with cloth bags. You will see how much satisfaction your resolution will give you and also inspire other people.'

In Episode 54, Prime Minister Modi asked us to think laterally, saying that we have heard of many a prestigious beauty contest, but why not also think about having a shining toilet contest? He apprised us about more than 50 lakh toilets that had participated over a month in this unique contest called; Clean Beautiful Toilet. It was yet another simple competition but it made people focus on their toilets, making them clean and colourful, having them painted and renovated. He appealed to all the sarpanches and village heads to take a lead in the campaign in their respective panchayats and share their clean, beautiful toilet photos using the handle #MyIzzatGhar on social media.

This very concept of izzat was underlined to clean our country and to get rid of open defecation. Due to the unequivocal support from the people, and the mention of it on *Mann Ki Baat,* India quickly moved towards liberation from open defecation as a homage to Bapu. Prime Minister Modi declared:

> ‘In this memorable journey of clean India, listeners also contributed a lot to the *Mann Ki Baat* forum and that is why I'm happy to share the fact that more than five lakh fifty thousand villages and six hundred districts have declared themselves free of open defecation and sanitation coverage has crossed 98 per cent limit in rural India whereas latrines have been provided to nearly nine crore households.’

In Episode 80, while addressing the challenges we were facing due to the onslaught of COVID-19, he touched upon the myriad aspects of cleanliness that needed to be highlighted. He insisted that we should not let the cleanliness campaign diminish even in the slightest. He gave examples to show how efforts by everyone towards nation building results in progress for all of us, along with inspiring us and infusing us with new energy to do something, as well as imparting a new confidence to us and giving a meaning to our resolve. He added that whenever the issues of Swachh Bharat Abhiyan came up, the example of Indore would always be given because Indore had created a special identity of its own in relation to cleanliness, because of which people of Indore were entitled to felicitations.

Indore has remained number one in Swachh Bharat rankings for many years. Prime Minister Modi let us know that Indore was not satisfied with this ranking of Swachh Bharat; the people of Indore always want to move forward, to do something new. Today, Indore is earnest about maintaining its status as a Water Plus city where no sewage is dumped into any public water source without treatment. The citizens have connected their drains to the sewer line. A cleanliness campaign has also been started and due to this, polluted water being dumped into the Saraswati and Kanh rivers has also reduced considerably and an improvement in the quality of water is also visible. At a time when our country is celebrating the Amrit Mahotsav of Independence, the PM reminded us that we should never let the resolve of the Swachh Bharat Abhiyan diminish. The greater the number of cities which were Water Plus cities in our country, the greater would be the cleanliness of our rivers, allowing us to fulfill the values associated with humanity's responsibility towards conserving water.

In this context, Art of Living founder **Sri Sri Ravishankar** tweeted, 'Purity, both external & internal, is essential for progress in life. The #SwachhBharatMission has spread a lot of awareness towards maintaining cleanliness in our country. It's our responsibility to ensure we continue to play our part in keeping our surroundings clean. #SHS2018.'

Former cricketer **Sachin Tendulkar** has also said on social media that, 'I'm proud to be associated with the Swachhta Hi Seva Andolan. Requesting each of you to pledge to keep your surroundings clean and make India truly a @swachhbharat. Share your "Swachhta Hi Seva" moments with me, just use the hashtag.' Other celebrities such as Rajinikanth, Ratan Tata, Ustad Amjad Ali Khan, Akshay Kumar, Anushka Sharma, Anil Kapoor and many more people also joined in.

In Episode 56, the PM conveyed that the Swachhta Abhiyan has a big role to play in our perception. He was delighted to share that our rank had risen to thirty-four on the cleanliness index whereas five years ago, we had been ranked 65th, which was a big jump. If we all tried harder, then, by the 75th year of our independence, we would have carved a place for ourselves amidst the major tourist destinations of the world, he told his listeners.

In October 2019, he once again cited an incredible example of the common citizens doing their bit in creating an outcome that belongs to 125 crore Indians. 'Just imagine the highest battlefield in the world, where the temperature drops from zero to minus 50–60 degrees. Oxygen in the air is also at a miniscule level. Living in the midst of such adverse conditions and challenges is no less than any display of valour. In such a difficult situation, our brave heart soldiers are not only protecting the borders of the country, but are also running a Swachh Siachen campaign in that area.'

On behalf of our countrymen, he commended the Indian Army for this amazing commitment. While expressing gratitude, he recognised that the segregation and management of garbage being done to remove 130 tonnes and more of garbage from the glacier and its fragile ecosystem is a great service. He added that Siachen is an area which is home to rare species like the snow leopard, the ibex and the brown bear. Siachen, as a glacier, is also a source of rivers and clean water. Therefore, running a cleanliness campaign here means ensuring clean water for those who live in low-lying areas and also allowing the use of the water from rivers like Nubra and Shyok.

Earlier that year, in August, the PM invited us to donate toil and sweat through shramdaan during the months of October–November as a karyanjali to Mahatma Gandhi. The idea was to create a mega campaign for ensuring cleanliness in public places with a focus on reducing the impact of plastic.

Noted lyricist and song writer **Prasoon Joshi** says, '*Mann Ki Baat* is such an unprecedented programme through which our Honourable Prime Minister, Mr Narendra Modi, has brought the whole country together. He has made us realise that the things we would hear only in government schemes have real importance in our lives, like in terms of sports, Swachh Bharat and G-20. There is a national pride that has awakened in us and it has brought a sense of responsibility. I want that this programme runs successfully in the upcoming years and it brings us consciousness among ourselves.'

Even Doordarshan began broadcasting a special programme called 'Swachhta Samachar', the cleanliness news, highlighting simple but significant feats achieved by Indian people. In one of the episodes of *Mann Ki Baat,* Prime Minister Modi said that we the people have lent pace to the cleanliness campaign from time to time. Our efforts towards ensuring cleanliness was what, in fact, inspired *Mann Ki Baat*. A journey that began years ago gathered momentum with mass participation, setting newer benchmarks in cleanliness and sanitation. He hailed the movement that advanced from cleanliness to beautification. 'Yogesh Saini is an engineer who left his job in America and returned to serve Mother India. Recently, he has picked up the gauntlet to not just clean up Delhi, but to beautify it. With his team, he began with the garbage bins of Lodi Garden. Through the medium of street art, he has decorated many localities of Delhi with aesthetically appealing paintings.' Through citizens like him, the PM said, we can all experience the beauty and the aesthetics of the Swachhta Abhiyan. It is imperative that the culture of transforming waste to wealth develops in our society. In a way, we have to move ahead on the path of converting garbage to gold.

In the penultimate month of that year, Prime Minister Modi quoted one line from a poem written by Harivansh Rai Bachchan,

> '*Mitti Ka Tann, Masti Ka Mann, Kshan Bhar Jeewan, Mera Parichay.*'

Harivansh Rai used to give his introduction through this line. His son, actor **Amitabh Bachchan**, who has the cleanliness mission running in his veins, had written to the PM adapting his father's lines to say, '*Swachh Tann, Swachh Mann, Swachh Bharat, Mera Parichay*'. He tweeted, 'T 2038 - #MannKiBaat PM @narendramodi acknowledges @NDTV @swachhindia campaign. We are encouraged to do more. @vikramchandra!'

The PM said,

> 'I respectfully bow to Harivansh Rai-ji. I also thank Shriman Amitabh-ji to connect in such a warm manner with *Mann Ki Baat* and for taking forward the Cleanliness Campaign.'

CHAMPIONS OF CLEANLINESS – ONE AND ALL

In December of 2020, *Mann ki Baat* once again focused on the significant deeds that can be accomplished with seemingly simple motivations, especially if they relate to cleanliness. He took the example of Pradeep Sangwan who has been running a campaign called Healing Himalayas since 2016. Sangwan goes to different areas in the Himalayas with his team and volunteers where they clean plastic waste dumped there by tourists. In four years or so, he had cleaned tonnes of plastic from various tourist locations in the Himalayas.

In the landmark 100th episode of the programme, where our PM spoke to the many, many grassroots heroes that he had interacted with over the years, he again mentioned the efforts—the sadhana—of Sangwan. This time, Sangwan had the proverbial last word as he said emotionally, 'At the time of being mentioned on Mann Ki Baat, believe me sir, I was at the stage of almost giving up. But after that a lot of change came in my life and speeded up our work so much which was beyond our comprehension. So, I'm really thankful that you find out about people like us. People who work in such a remote area, we are working in the Himalayan region. We are working at this altitude. You found us here. You brought our work in front of the world. So, it was a very emotional moment for me even then and even today, I feel emotional that I am able to talk to the principal servant of our country. Nothing can be more fortunate for me than this.'

Similarly, Anudeep and Minusha, a newlywed couple from Karnataka decided that they would clean up the garbage that people would leave behind at the Someshwar beach. This was the first resolve that both husband and wife took after marriage. Together they cleaned up a lot of garbage from the beach. Anudeep also shared his resolve on social media. Inspired by his stupendous work, a number of young people joined him. In a matter of a few months, they ended up cleaning more than 800 kilograms of waste from Someshwar beach.

Noted singer Kailash Kher was among those that lauded the PM. He said in a tweet, 'Swachhta as Seva is a great thought as shared by PM in #MannKiBaat'.

In November 2015, Narendra Modi highlighted the proactive role played by the media in spreading the message of a Swachh Bharat and taking it to every household, which was another way of adding momentum to an already-building mass movement.

This is what chairman, Essel Group, Dr Subhas Chandra had to say on the Prime Minister's words for the media: 'The role of the media is to be an effective agent of change, for the larger good of society. We, through Zee Media's multiple platforms, have always been proactive in furthering the cause of a clean India. I was personally delighted, and so was my team, when the Prime Minister lauded our efforts to further the message of cleanliness. We felt duty bound to be a means of conveying such a vital message of national relevance to our viewers. *Mann Ki Baat* has played a positive role in making India cleaner and influencing mindsets, which will eventually help the nation.'

In Episode 81, the PM reminded us of Gandhi-ji and asked the youth of today to commit themselves to the campaign for cleanliness just as the youth of yonder years had committed to the freedom movement. Prime Minister Modi said,

> ‘It was Mahatma Gandhi who turned cleanliness into a mass movement. Mahatma Gandhi had connected cleanliness to the dream of Independence. Today, after so many decades, the cleanliness movement has once again connected the country to the dream of a new India. This is also becoming a campaign to change our habits and we must not forget that this cleanliness is a programme. When the campaign for cleanliness continues generation after generation, cleanliness as a trait gets imbibed by the entire society. And that is why this is not a subject of a year or two, of one government or the other. Generation after generation, with alertness, continually, without being tired or stopping, with high reverence must remain associated with cleanliness and continue the campaign for cleanliness.’

Praising a listener of *Mann Ki Baat*, Shriman Ramesh Patel who had written to him, the PM said that learning from Bapu in this Amrit Mahotsav of our freedom, we should all take the resolve of economic cleanliness too. Just as building toilets enhances the dignity of the poor, similarly, economic cleanliness ensures the rights of the poor and eases their life. He was impressed by another listener of *Mann Ki Baat*, Prabha Shukla from Meerut in UP, who had written to him about cleanliness saying, ‘We all celebrate cleanliness during festivals in India. Similarly, if we make cleanliness a daily habit, then the whole country will become clean.’ He also praised Ramveer Tanwar, the Pond Man from Ghaziabad, who had been in service after completing his mechanical engineering. However, such a sense of devotion to cleanliness got ignited in his mind that he had left his job and started cleaning ponds.

He reminded us in a subsequent episode that the efforts of cleanliness can be fully successful only when every citizen understands cleanliness as his or her responsibility. During Diwali, for instance, we clean our houses, but the garbage inside our houses reaches our roads outside. 'And yes, when I talk about cleanliness, then please do not forget the mantra of getting rid of single-use plastic. Come, let us take a pledge that we will not let the enthusiasm of Swachh Bharat Abhiyan diminish. Together, we will make our country completely clean and keep it clean!'

Echoing this, Dr Ravindra Khaiwal, professor, Community Medicine and School of Public Health, PGIMER Chandigarh said,

> 'When we talk about environment conservation, we know that Hon'ble Prime Minister Modiji had in 2014 started the discussion on this topic. He discussed the Swachh Bharat Abhiyan, how we are creating cleanliness issues in the country, how to keep our surroundings clean and how to segregate waste properly. Single-use plastic got banned from 1 July 2022. The discussion on plastic pollution happened first way back in 2014, where it was discussed how the plastic and microplastics are causing the damage to the environment. When we talk about tiger conservation and biodiversity conservation, then the discussion started in 2018.'

EARLY MESSAGING BUT CONTINUED PROLIFERATION

In the final episode of the year 2022, Prime Minister Modi let us know that there had been many messages and suggestions related to 2022 from all corners of the country. He said that one theme was always there in most people's messages, that of cleanliness and Swachh Bharat. He insisted that the commitment to cleanliness will be fulfilled only with discipline, awareness and dedication. 'We can get a glimpse of that in the Puneet Sagar campaign undertaken by cadets. More than 30,000 NCC cadets participated in this campaign. These cadets cleaned the beaches, removed plastic waste from there and collected it for recycling. Our beaches, our mountains are worth visiting only when there is cleanliness at the place. Many people dream of going to a particular place all their lives ... but when they go there, knowingly or unknowingly, they leave behind waste there. It is the responsibility of every countryman that the places which give us so much joy should not be dirtied by us.'

Through *Mann Ki Baat*, we even came to know about a start-up named Saafwater been started by youth. With the help of Artificial Intelligence and the Internet of Things (IoT), the app was created to give information related to the purity and quality of water in a particular area to the people living in that area. This, he said, was just another step in the ongoing journey of cleanliness: '*Ek qadam Swachhta ki ore*'. Be it the institutions or the government, everyone has an important role, the PM reiterated.

He apprised us of the efficient, saaf methodology being followed in government offices where old files and papers were also being cleaned. Since the government has started changing old practices, files and piles of paper are getting digitised and stored in computer folders. Similarly, special campaigns are also being run in ministries and departments to remove old and pending materials. There are other interesting things that have happened because of this campaign. When this cleanliness drive was started in the postal department, the junkyard there became completely empty. Now this junkyard has been turned into a courtyard and cafeteria. Another junkyard was converted into a parking space for two wheelers. Similarly, the Ministry of Environment converted its vacant junkyard into a wellness centre. The Ministry of Urban Affairs has even installed a Swachh ATM in which people can deposit their garbage and take cash in return. Departments under the Civil Aviation Ministry have started making compost from organic waste. This department is also working to make stationery from waste paper. Till a few years ago, no one even believed in it, but today, Swachhta has become a part of the system. This is the new thinking of the country, which is being led by all the countrymen together, the Prime Minister informed the nation.

The journey that commenced in 2014 was revisited yet again in Episodes 86 and 87 to show how the Clean India Mission had expanded manifold with the passage of time. In Kokrajhar, Assam, a group of morning walkers undertook a commendable initiative under the Clean and Green Kokrajhar mission. All of them delivered a motivational message about hygiene by cleaning the three-kilometre-long road in the new flyover area. Similarly, under the Clean India campaign in Visakhapatnam, the use of cloth bags was being promoted over polythene. People there were also campaigning against single-use plastic products to keep the environment clean. Along with this, citizens were also spreading awareness regarding segregation of waste at home. Here's how noted sand artist Sudarsan Pattnaik hailed the PM's message:

The students of Somaiya College in Mumbai included beautification in their campaign for cleanliness by decorating the walls of Kalyan railway station with beautiful paintings. An inspiring example from Sawai Madhopur in Rajasthan was also quoted by the PM. The youth there had started a campaign named Mission Beat Plastic in Ranthambore, under which plastic and polythene bags had been completely removed from the forests of Ranthambore. This spirit of sabka prayas—everyone's effort—strengthens public participation in the country and when there is public participation, even the biggest goals are easily met.

In an episode of *Mann Ki Baat*, the PM mentioned Swachhgrahi Chandrakishor Patil who lives in Nashik,

Maharashtra. Chandrakishor's resolve regarding cleanliness is truly heart-warming. He stands by the Godavari river and constantly encourages people not to throw garbage in the river. If he sees someone doing so, he immediately stops them. This effort of his raises awareness and inspires others. Similarly, another Swachhgrahi was recognised by the PM—Rahul Maharana of Puri in Orissa. Rahul goes to the pilgrimage sites in Puri early in the morning every Sunday and clears the plastic garbage there. He has cleaned hundreds of kilos of plastic garbage and dirt so far. As per Prime Minister Modi, be it Rahul of Puri or Chandrakishore of Nashik, all of them have taught us a lot, which is that as citizens, we must carry out our duties, whether it is cleanliness, nutrition or vaccination and because such efforts also help us in staying healthy.

He also said that ensuring cleanliness is equivalent to performing sadhana. Some are cleaning near the place they stay, while others are cleaning garbage along their travel route. Many non-governmental organisations and voluntary organisations are also working along with the Swachh Bharat campaign team.

> 'Friends, just as a pilgrimage is important here [Devbhoomi Uttarkhand]; equally important is *teertha sewa* as has been mentioned and I would also say that without *teertha sewa*, a pilgrimage is incomplete. There are many people in Devbhoomi Uttarakhand who are engaged in the sadhana of cleanliness and service. You will be greatly inspired by Shriman Manoj Bainjwal hailing from Rudra Prayag. For the last 25 years, Manoj-ji has taken it upon himself to look after the environment. Apart from running the campaign of cleanliness, he is also engaged in making holy places plastic free. While, Surendra Bagwadi-ji hailing from Guptkashi

> has also made cleanliness his life mantra. In Guptkashi, he regularly runs cleanliness programmes, and, I have learned that he has also named his campaign as *Mann Ki Baat.*'

Other grassroot champions cited by the PM are Champa Devi from Devar village who has been teaching waste management to women of the village. She has planted hundreds of trees and through sheer hard work, has set up a stretch of forest full of greenery. It is through the efforts of such people that the divinity of Devbhoomi and other holy places have been maintained. The PM said, '

> '‘Purity, cleanliness and a pious environment ... we should never forget these and for that, it is imperative that we abide by the resolution of cleanliness’.'

In autumn that year, he spoke of Youth for Parivartan, the team that has been working on cleanliness and other community activities with the motto ‘Stop Complaining, Start Acting’. This team has so far beautified more than 370 places across the city. The campaign of Youth for Parivartan has connected 100 to 150 citizens at every place. Every Sunday, this programme starts in the morning and continues till noon. In this task, not only is the garbage cleared up, the work of painting the walls and making artistic sketches is also carried out. At many places, you can also see sketches of famous people and inspirational quotes by them. He also told us about the Kabaad se Jugaad campaign of Meerut how it is related to the protection of the environment as well as the beautification of the city. The special thing about this campaign was that waste such as iron scrap, plastic waste, old tires and drums got re-used. This campaign is also an example of how to beautify public places at a low cost. He appreciated all the people involved in such campaigns.

In Episode 96 of the show, we got to know of the example that has been set by Sange Sherpa of the Thegu village in Sikkim. For the last 14 years, he has been engaged in the work of environmental protection at an altitude of more than 12,000 feet. He has taken up the task of keeping clean the Tsomgo (Somgo) lake that is of tremendous cultural and mythological importance. With his untiring efforts, he has changed the look and feel of this glacier lake. When Sange Sherpa started this campaign of cleanliness in 2008, he faced many difficulties. Today, one can find huge garbage bins all around the lake. Now, the garbage collected there is sent for recycling. Garbage bags made of cloth are also given to the tourists going there so that garbage is not strewn around. Every year, about 5 lakh tourists reach there to see this very clean lake, we were informed.

In Episode 97 that aired in February 2023, the PM spoke of Vijay, an engineer from Telangana who had written to him about e-waste. Prime Minister Modi went on to talk about 'Waste to Wealth' i.e., 'Kachre se Kanchan' campaign. He reminded us that devices like mobiles, laptops and tablets—the latest devices today are tomorrow's e-waste. Whenever someone buys a new device or replaces an old device, it becomes necessary to ensure that is discarded properly as it can become part of the circular economy of recycle and reuse. He also let us know that about 17 types of precious metals can be extracted from e-waste through different processes. This includes gold, silver, copper and nickel, so utilising e-waste is like making Kachre Se Kanchan. He also encouraged the start-ups that were working on this. 'At present, around 500 e-waste recyclers are associated with this sector and many new entrepreneurs are also being associated with it. This sector has also given direct employment to thousands of people. E-Parisaraa of Bengaluru is engaged in one such effort. It has developed an indigenous technology for extracting precious metals from printed circuit boards.' He also told us about Ecoreco in Mumbai which developed a system to collect e-waste through a mobile app. Attero of Roorkee, Uttarakhand has obtained many patents in the field of recycling worldwide. It has also earned a lot of awards by preparing its own e-waste recycling technology. Tonnes of e-waste is being collected in Bhopal through a mobile app and a website called Kabadiwala. He told us that there are many such examples which are all helping make India a global recycling hub.

In his own words, while appreciating a listener's message, 'Indeed, where there is cleanliness, there is health, where there is health, there is capability and where there is capability, there is prosperity. That is why the country is giving so much emphasis to the Swachh Bharat Abhiyan.'

12

Towards a Healthy and Fit India

> 'I am happy that in the era of evidence-based medicine, Yoga and Ayurveda are now standing up to the touchstone of tests of the modern era.'
>
> – Prime Minister Narendra Modi

Health is wealth—this age-old maxim saw a revival by Prime Minister Modi when he championed the essential way of healthy living in his radio dialogue. The year 2018 saw the launch of the world's biggest health insurance scheme Ayushman Bharat. Not just that, yoga has seen an unprecedented push thanks to *Mann Ki Baat* too. By posting his own yoga videos, Prime Minister Modi inspired the country to come out, exercise and share their fitness videos on social media platforms as part of the fitness challenge. He urged people to tag each other on these posts to spread the challenge to the masses, making it a mass movement. Recognising that the youngsters of India are more in sync with technology, and use social media more than other sections of the society, he called them the flag-bearers of the Fit India movement. The Prime Minister encouraged the youth to persuade even others to participate with them in the Fit India campaign. In an early episode of *Mann Ki Baat* he shared,

> 'My dear countrymen, I want to ask a question, especially to our youth. How many push-ups you can do at once? What I am about to tell you will surely fill you with wonder. Thounaojam Niranjoy Singh, a 24-year-old youth from Manipur, has made a record of 109 push-ups in a minute. Breaking records is nothing new for Niranjoy Singh; earlier also, he had held the record for the most knuckle push-ups with one hand, in a minute. I am sure you will be inspired by Niranjoy Singh and make physical fitness a part of your life,'

In June 2015, Prime Minister Modi shared with his avid listeners that a wave of confidence was creating ripples throughout the country due to the Ayushman Yojana. In his usual style of sharing successes with his extended family—he said,

> 'With the blessing of such families, the blessings of crores of mothers, our country is moving towards development with strength.'

The nation learn how a small department under the government named Ayush which had not received any prominence earlier, save a mention here and there, became the country's pride on International Yoga Day. It was this small department that organised this event in the entire world. Therefore, listeners felt it to be an example of how little things can go a long way; and even a small department can do a great job, if there is a goal.

In the final episode of 2018, Episode 51, Prime Minister Modi shared his pleasure at launching the world's biggest health insurance scheme, Ayushman Bharat. This refrain of pride has run through the course of the radio show spanning 100 episodes. In Episode 96, his quote says it all: *Satyam kim pramanam, pratyaksham kim pramanam*, which means, truth does not require proof; what is evident also does not require proof.

People in India did everything possible to make the first International Day of Yoga a success. Images of the Rajpath were a sight to reckon on that day. Entrepreneurs, film stars, sportspersons and political leaders across party lines lent their support. The PM's radio call delivered on the radio, to each and every Indian to become brand ambassadors of yoga, paid rich dividends.

Yoga guru **Baba Ramdev** says, 'Yoga is the crown jewel in our glorious traditions. It is good for physical as well as mental health. In Narendra Modi, we have a leader who is not hesitant to showcase the power of yoga to the world. He leads from the front. When Narendra Modi talks about yoga on the radio, he is not doing so as the Prime Minister. He is like a fellow citizen urging people to lead a healthier life. It is like a family elder guiding a person. It is great that he has made yoga popular across and outside India.'

FITNESS BEYOND FADS, FASHION, AND FORMULAE

Prime Minister Modi noted early on in his conversations with the nation that when it comes to modern medical science, the most important thing is evidence. The lack of evidence-based research into practices like yoga and ayurveda has always been a challenge, even though they have both been a part of the Indian way of life for centuries. The irony is that while the results are visible, the evidence is not. Through the show we learnt about the path-breaking research at the Tata Memorial Centre in Mumbai, an institute that has earned a name for itself in research, innovation and cancer care. The intensive study revealed that yoga is very effective for breast cancer patients. The centre even presented the results of its research at a prestigious breast cancer conference held in the United States. Some of the world's most prominent experts noticed Tata Memorial Centre's research that regular yoga practice reduced the risk of recurrence and death of breast cancer patients by 15 per cent. This is the first example of testing Indian traditional medicine vis-à-vis the stringent standards of Western methods. Also, this is the first study in which yoga has been found to improve the quality of life in women affected by breast cancer. Its long-term benefits have also come to the fore. The Tata Memorial Centre went on to present the results of its study at the European Society for Medical Oncology conference in Paris as well. The Prime Minister shared the achievement.

> 'Friends, in today's era, the more evidence-based Indian medical systems are, the more their acceptance will increase world wide. This is the thought behind setting up the Centre for Integrative Medicine and Research at AIIMS in Delhi. The centre was established six years ago to validate our traditional medical practices.'

Using latest modern techniques and research methods, the centre has already published 20 papers in reputed international journals. For instance, a paper published in the *Journal of the American College of Cardiology*, describes the benefits of yoga for patients suffering from syncope. Similarly, a paper in the journal, *Neurology*, has explained the benefits of yoga on migraine. Apart from these, studies are underway regarding the benefits of yoga in many other diseases—heart disease, depression, sleep disorders and problems faced by women during pregnancy constitute some of them.

In a recent episode, Prime Minister Modi tied the strings of natural therapies and holistic approaches to fitness by linking yoga with millets—Shree Anna. He said,

> ‘If I ask you, what is common between Yoga Day and our different types of coarse grains such as millets, then you might think ... what is this comparison? If I say that both have a lot in common, you will be surprised. First, the United Nations has decided to observe both International Yoga Day and International Year of Millets accepting India's proposal. Secondly, both yoga and millets play an important role in health. The third thing is more important—a revolution is on the way because of public participation in both campaigns. Just as people have made yoga and fitness a part of their lives by actively participating on a large scale, similarly, people are including millets in their diets on a large scale. People are now making millets a part of their diet.’

In one of the editions, the Prime Minister spoke of his experience at the World Ayurveda Congress in Goa. Delegates from more than 40 countries participated, presenting over 550 scientific papers. He share that around 215 companies from around the world, including India, displayed their products in the exhibition. In this expo, which lasted four days, more than one lakh people enjoyed ayurveda-related experiences. In *Mann Ki Baat*, the PM told us how in the World Ayurveda Congress, he had reiterated the importance of evidence-based research to the ayurveda experts gathered from all over the world. He also insisted that we focus on our traditional treatment methods and share them on social media.

Lauding the efforts of various citizens, the Prime Minister said,

> 'We often say that when every citizen of the country takes a step ahead, our nation moves 130 crore steps forward! And when such things are witnessed first-hand in society, everyone gets elated, derives satisfaction and is infused with motivation to do something in life!'

WELLNESS STARTS AT HOME BUT BENEFITS THE COMMUNITY

Encouraging wellness practices at home and reducing the risk of diseases during the rains, Prime Minister Modi spoke of minor everyday solutions in Episode 67, such as immunity enhancers like the ayurvedic kadha.

> 'My dear countrymen, it is also the season of rains. Last time too, I had said that the risk of diseases arising out of filth increases during this period. Consequently, it leads to overcrowding in the hospitals. I urge you to pay special attention to cleanliness around you and to keep taking immunity enhancers such as ayurvedic kadha. During the times of the corona pandemic, we must protect ourselves against other diseases. We will have to take complete care so we do not have to frequent hospitals.'

Similarly, in the episode aired next year in September 2021, he mentioned the agri-business incubator Medi-Hub TBI which is operational in Anand, Gujarat. Sudha Chebrolu and Subhashree got help from this incubator, with the former even launching her start-up with this help. The PM also shared the inspiring story of one Patayat Sahu from Nandol, Kalahandi, Odisha who planted medicinal plants and was documenting them. Traditionally, natural products beneficial for wellness and health are abundant in our country. That Sahu had planted medicinal plants on one and a half acres of land and had carried out documentation of these medicinal plants too was commendable.

He also drew our attention to an aloe vera village in Jharkhand. The women of Deori village near Ranchi had undergone training in aloe vera cultivation from the Birsa Agricultural School under the leadership of Manju Kachha. After this they started cultivating aloe vera in their village. Not only did this benefit the field of health but the income of these women also increased. They managed a good income even during the COVID-19 pandemic. One of the primary reasons for this was that the companies making sanitisers now, would buy aloe vera directly from them. Over time, a team of about 40 women got involved in this work. In Episode 86 of *Mann Ki Baat*, the PM said,

> ‘Friends, in the last seven years, much attention has been paid to promoting ayurveda in the country. The formation of the Ministry of AYUSH has further strengthened our resolve to popularise our traditional methods of medicine and health. I am very happy that in the last few years, many new start-ups have emerged in the field of ayurveda. The AYUSH start-up challenge started earlier this month. This challenge aims to identify and support the start-ups working in this field. I urge the youth working in this field to participate in this challenge,’

AYUSHMAN BHARAT, SWASTHA BHARAT

Similar confidence has been created in the country through the Ayushman Yojana. While praising the scheme, the PM said,

> 'When the poor come home healthy, with free treatment, they feel they have a new life. They feel confident that the country stands by them.'

In Episode 81, on the occasion of the Pandit Deen Dayal Upadhyay's birth anniversary, inarguably one of the greatest thinkers of the last century, the Prime Minister brought up the idea of health for life, yet again. Pandit Deen Dayal Upadhyay's economic philosophy, his policies that constantly aimed at empowering the society, and the path of antyodaya shown by him, is inspirational, and remains relevant even today. Three years ago, in 2018, again on Pandit Deen Dayal Upadhyay's birth anniversary that the world's largest health assurance scheme—the Ayushman Bharat scheme—was implemented. By 2021, more than two and a half crore impoverished people of the country had availed of free treatment up to Rs 5 lakh under this scheme. Reminding us of the great patriot's philosophy, the PM said,

> 'Once in Lucknow, Deen Dayal-ji had said, 'We derive all good things and good qualities from society itself . We must pay the debt of society; we must think along these lines.' That is, Deen Dayal ji taught us that we take so much from society, from the country. Thus, we should think about how we will repay our debt towards the country.'

In Episode 87, he made the concept even more relatable by introducing Baba Sivanand who was earlier seen during the

Padma Awards ceremony. 'The agility of the 126-year-old was surprising for all, just like it was for me. Before one could bat an eyelid, he started bowing in the Nandi Mudra. I bowed several times and offered my pranaam to Both Baba Sivanand's age and fitness are the subject of discussion in the country today.' He said in a light tone that it wasn't surprising to see people's comments on social media, commenting that Baba Sivanand is fitter than even those who are one-fourth his age!

AYURVEDA TRUMPHS |

In an episode aired in the spring of 2021, the PM spoke of how everyone is wished a hundred years of healthy life in our culture. He announced India would celebrate World Health Day on 7 April every year. With enormous pride, he said that today the Indian collective thought on health, whether it be yoga or ayurveda, is increasingly trending worldwide. Through *Mann Ki Baat,* he talked about a yoga programme that had been organised in Qatar. The citizens of 114 countries participated and made a new world record there. Similarly, the scope of the Ayush industry is growing continuously. He said, 'Six years ago, the market for medicines related to ayurveda was around 22000 crores. Today, the Ayush manufacturing industry is reaching around 1,40,000 crore rupees. This means the possibilities are increasing continuously in this sector. In the start-up world, too, Ayush is becoming a subject of attraction.'

Prime Minister Modi often referred to start-ups in the health sector on the show. But his focus on Ayush start-ups has been singular. He apprised us of a start-up called Kapiva whose meaning is hidden in its name—Ka for Kapha, Pi for Pitta and Va for Vaata, the three doshas recognised by ayurveda. This start-up sells products based on healthy eating habits following our traditions. NirogStreet is another start-up based on a unique concept of the ayurveda healthcare system. Its technology-driven platform connects ayurveda doctors from across the world directly to the common people. More than 50,000 practitioners are associated with it. Similarly, Atreya Innovations, a healthcare technology start-up, continues to work towards holistic wellness. Ixoreal Biomed has not only spread awareness about the use of ashwagandha, but has also invested a significant amount on top-quality production processes. Cureveda has created dietary supplements for holistic life through the confluence of modern herbal research and traditional knowledge, which we learned through the PM in *Mann Ki Baat*.

In Episode 83, Prime Minister Modi shared the story of a beneficiary of the Ayushman Bharat scheme, Rajesh Kumar Prajapati, who underwent treatment with the help of the scheme and has started a new life. The Prime Minister said,

> ‘When we hear this, we too are filled with empathy. It is satisfying and inspiring to take that scheme to the people. In a way, it is just "*Swant: Sukhay*", joy to one's own soul ...’

Rajesh Kumar Prajapati had an ailment of the heart. In his conversation, he shared with the PM, and through him, with us, how he used to have a burning sensation in the chest and was told that he had acidity. He met Amresh Agarwal, who did his angiography and informed him of a blockage in his vein. To assuage his fears about the cost, the doctor asked him to use his Ayushman card. 'He took my Ayush card, and all my treatment has been done with it. This card made for us poor people is very convenient. How can I thank you enough!' said Prajapati.

Similarly, in May 2020, the PM spoke of another Ayushman Bharat scheme beneficiary, Sukhdevi, who also got her treatment done through the Ayushman card. Sukhdevi had attended a meeting in the local school where she and her husband came to know of the scheme. Her husband got the card made in her name.

DIFFERENT STROKES FOR DIFFERENT FOLKS

In September 2021, through *Mann Ki Baat,* we learnt about the Ministry of Ayush's programme to increase children's awareness about medicinal and herbal plants. This was done through a comic book named Professor Ayushman ji. Through this initiative, short stories were told through different cartoon characters. The usefulness of healthy medicinal plants like aloe vera, tulsi, amla, giloy, neem, ashwagandha and brahmi has also been enumerated. Prime Minister Modi said,

> 'Friends, in the current context, growing popularity of medicinal plants and herbal products, India has immense potential. In the past, there has been a significant increase in the export of Ayurvedic and herbal products. I urge scientists, researchers and people associated with the start-up world to pay attention to such products, which not only increase the wellness and immunity of the people, but also help increase the income of our farmers and youth.'

In June 2021, the PM cited a quote from our scriptures on the medicinal properties of plants,

'नास्ति मूलम् अनौषधम्. (*Nasti Moolam Anoushadham)*'

This means, there is no such plant on earth which does not have any medicinal properties! Many trees and plants around us have amazing properties, but we do not even know about them!

On the show, the PM also called out to Paritosh, a friend from Nainital who had sent him a letter writing that he had learnt about the miraculous medicinal properties of giloy and many other plants only after the outbreak of corona. Through the PM, Paritosh urged all the listeners of *Mann Ki Baat* to be aware of the flora around them, and also convey their benefits to others. Ramlotan Kushwaha from Satna, Madhya Pradesh was also praised for a commendable job in building a museum of indigenous plants on his farm. In this museum, he collected hundreds of medicinal plants and seeds. And he has brought them here from far-flung regions. Apart from this, he also grows many types of Indian vegetables every year. People visit this garden, this museum of Ramlotan, and learn a lot from it. The PM said,

> 'Indeed, this is a very good experiment which can be replicated in different regions of the country. I would like that those of you who can make such an effort, should attempt it. This can also open up new sources of income for you. Another benefit will be that the identity of your area will gain wide prominence through the local medicinal plants.'

It was through the medium of *Mann Ki Baat* that the PM reminded us how medicinal herbs had played an important role in the fight against the coronavirus, not just at the national but also at the global level. There is a growing interest in ayurveda and Indian medicine around the world. This is one of the major reasons why Ayush exports have witnessed record growth. It is also a matter of great joy that many new start-ups are also emerging in this sector. In the Global Ayush Investment and Innovation Summit, investment proposals of about 10,000 crore rupees had been received, the PM apprised his listeners in Episode 91 of the programme.

HUM FIT TOH INDIA FIT

The huge success of the Fit India campaign is largely attributable to the consistent push given to it by the Prime Minister on *Mann Ki Baat*. Narendra Modi-ji appreciated the participation of the youth in the campaign. He said that the rising notes of youth participation helped in building up the crescendo of the *Hum Fit toh India Fit* campaign.

Famous artiste Malini Awasthi shared her own fitness mantra and tweeted, 'Scuba Diving at the age of 51! Yes, that's me. Fitness and Health are not determined by age or gender. Thank you, Prime Minister Narendra Modi and Union Minister Rajyavardhan Rathore, for inspiring the Nation for fitness and well-being (sic).'

In Episode 56, the PM mentioned that on 29 August, National Sports Day, the Fit India movement was also being launched across the country. He said, not only do we have to keep ourselves fit but the nation has to be made fit as well. The campaign was all-encompassing—children, women, the elderly and the young were all encouraged to make it their movement. In subsequent episodes, he asked if his listeners still remembered Fit India and reminded us all to build a healthy India. 'Fit India does not mean that if we go to the gym for two hours every morning and evening, it will suffice! All these addictions must avoided to be a part of Fit India. I am sure you will not misconstrue whatever I've said, but rather happily accept my counsel; I will definitely like it,' he said, reminding the youth to abstain from addiction.

He shared the example of the Fit India Plog Run in the September 2019 episode, praising Ripudaman, who had designed the entire programme in a very innovative manner and in a way that would be liked, especially by young people. The Prime Minister said,

> 'Heartiest congratulation to you. And friends, this time on the anniversary of revered Bapu, the Ministry of Sports too is organising a Fit India Plog Run. On 2 October, citizens will plog for two kilometres and it will be held across the country. We heard through the experiences of Ripudaman-ji, how this programme should be organised, and what it should consist of. What we have to do in this campaign that commences on 2 October is that while we jog for 2 kilometres we collect all kinds of plastic waste on the way. Through this endeavour, we shall pay better attention to our health and also take a step towards ensuring protection for Mother Earth.'

By saying so, the Prime Minister raised awareness levels in people about sanitation and cleanliness, along with making them aware of their primary goal—fitness.

Likewise, in October 2019, *Mann Ki Baat* spoke of the Run for Unity event, encouraging running to benefit the mind, body and soul. During Run for Unity, not only did we have to run, he said, running also reflected the spirit of Fit India. 'We also find ourselves connected with Ek Bharat-Shrestha Bharat! And so, not just our body, but our mind and value system get integrated with ushering unity in India to take India to loftier heights!'

Fit India Week was brought to the fore yet again in Episode 56 in November that year. Since he had already sensitised his audience, he took it to the next level by saying that CBSE had taken a commendable initiative of introducing the concept of Fit India Week. Schools could celebrate Fit India Week anytime during December, he let us know. The schools that achieved this ranking could use the Fit India logo and flag. The week could be organised with fitness-related events, such as quizzes, essays, articles, painting competitions, and traditional and local sports, yogasana, dance, sports and games competitions. Students, their teachers and parents could also participate in the Fit India Week. Prime Minister Modi reminded us that Fit India didn't just mean exercising the mind, making fitness plans on paper or merely looking at fitness apps on the laptop, computer or mobile phone. One had to sweat it out, he said. Food habits had to change and the habit of maximising focus activity had to be inculcated. When the poor come home healthy with free treatment ... they feel confident that the country stands by them.

Essentially, he made Fit India a movement that was innate to our temperament, something that became a mass movement and raised awareness.

In Episode 61, he lauded the many events related to Fit India, being organised across the country, such as a pan-India cyclothon. 'Millions of countrymen participating in this cyclothon spread the message of fitness. Efforts to ensure that our new India remains fit are evident at every level, filling us with fervour and enthusiasm.' Over time more than 65,000 schools obtained the Fit India school certificate through online registration. This enabled him to urge the rest of the schools in the country to integrate physical activity and sports with education and to ensure that they became fit schools. Also, concomitantly, he continued to drive the appeal home.

He was overjoyed to see people getting connected to it with a lot of enthusiasm. Many people expressed support for this, wrote to him, sent him letters, and shared their fitness mantra—Fit India—stories on social media.

A gentleman named Shriman Shashikant Bhonsale, sharing his photo by the swimming pool, wrote, 'My weapon is my body, my element is water, my world is swimming.' Rooma Devnath wrote, 'I truly feel happy and healthy through my morning walks. For me, fitness comes with a smile, and we should smile, when we are happy.' Dhawal Prajapati, sharing a photograph of himself trekking, wrote, 'For me, travelling & trekking is Fit India.'

The Prime Minister gave the example of Telangana's mountaineer, Poorna Malavath, who completed the 7-summit challenge and added a feather to her cap. The seven-summit challenge involves climbing seven of most difficult and highest mountain peaks in each of the seven continents. With her indomitable spirit, Purva ascended the highest peak of North America, Mount Denali, and brought honour to the country. 'Poorna is the same daughter of India who had accomplished the amazing feat of conquering Mount Everest at just 13,' he reminded us.

> 'It was heartening to see many eminent personalities encouraging our youth in interesting ways for Fit India. Cine artiste Akshay Kumar has shared a video on Twitter. Even though I have gone through it, you too should view it. It shows him exercising with wooden beads. He has mentioned that

this exercise benefits muscles of the back and the stomach, to a great extent. Another video of his that gained popularity is where he's trying his hand at playing volleyball with others. Many other young people have shared their experiences, having joined the Fit India efforts. I feel movements like these benefit all of us, for the entire country.'

YOGA AS A WAY OF LIFE

Incorporating yoga into our lives is a unique facet of healthy India—one that we as a country can take complete pride in, inspiring others to partake in it.

Just as *Mann Ki Baat* focused on the necessity for a healthy life is cleanliness, similarly, it shone the light on yoga having attained worldwide recognition as a measure of preventive health care, as a guarantee of both fitness and wellness. 'It is the result of our concerted efforts and commitment that yoga has now become a mass movement and reached every house,' the PM said in March 2018.

Tying the concept of Fit India with yoga, he reiterated the significance and the merit of 21 June, International Yoga Day, which has been accepted and welcomed globally. After that every year, he would ask us to prepare for it; not just ourselves, but our cities, villages, neighbourhoods, schools, colleges, every entity should make an attempt to connect with yoga, he said. The immense benefits of yoga in one's holistic physical and mental development have been underlined by the show many times. In a lighter vein, he even mentioned how a video depicting him had been widely circulated highlighting nuances of yoga mudras, 'just the way a teacher does'. He congratulated those who had done the animation for the video. Lalit Jalan, a corporate professional, spoke about the Prime Minister's fitness video and tweeted, 'Truly inspiring!! If within your 24×7 routine for 365 days, without a day break you can devote this time, then no one has any excuse. Adding substantial thrust to my fitness. #HumFitToIndiaFit #fitnesschallenge.'

Critically acclaimed actor Anupam Kher said, 'Prime Minister @narendramodi! You are a #RockStar. What an amazingly inspirational morning exercise video. Thank you for sharing it. Jai Ho.'

On May 22, *Mann Ki Baat* gave a special shoutout to the 8th International Yoga Day. 'This time, the theme of Yoga Day is Yoga for Humanity. I would urge all of you to celebrate Yoga Day with great enthusiasm. Yes! Also, take precautions related to corona. By the way, the situation is now looking better across the world. Because of more vaccination coverage, people are going out more than ever; therefore, many preparations are also being seen all over the world for Yoga Day. The corona pandemic has made us all realise the overarching importance of health in our lives and yoga being a great medium in ensuring the same.' Through the PM's constant insistence on yoga and fitness listeners have experienced physical, spiritual and intellectual well-being. From the world's top business persons to film and sports personalities, from students to common people, everyone has started making yoga an integral part of their lives. The PM shared how some very innovative initiatives were being taken for Yoga Day in the country and abroad, such as the Guardian Ring, in which the movement of the sun is celebrated, welcoming both the sun and yoga from different parts of the earth. Indian missions in other countries would organise yoga programmes at sunrise according to the local time. This yogic journey from the east to west was only one of the interesting takes from the programme. Dr David Frawley, a Padma Bhushan-decorated Vedic scholar, tweeted, 'Brilliant to have a Prime Minister that is a yogi. All political leaders should practice yoga and meditation, and connect with nature every day. Forms the best foundation for a life of karma yoga.'

Considering the Amrit Mahotsav, International Yoga Day was celebrated at 75 major places in the country. On this occasion, too, motivated by the PM, many organisations had prepared to do something unique in their respective fields. Encouraging us to celebrate Yoga Day, the PM asked us to choose the most special place in our city, town or village. This place could be an ancient temple or a tourist centre, or it could be the banks of a famous river, lake or pond, he said. This way, in addition to yoga, the identity of the local area would get reinforced and tourism would also get a boost. 'At present, the 100-day countdown leading to Yoga Day, is also underway; rather, programmes based on personal and social efforts, have already begun three months ago. On these lines, there have been countdown programmes on the 100th day and 75th day in Delhi.' The 50th countdown events were organised in Sivasagar, Assam, while the 25th was organised in Hyderabad.

In yet another episode, yoga was mentioned at the onset. He said,

> 'Today I will tell you about the Indian culture making its mark in Argentina. Our culture is appreciated in Argentina. In 2018, during my visit to Argentina, I participated in a yoga programme, Yoga for Peace. There is an organisation in Argentina – the Hastinapur Foundation. You will be

surprised to hear. Argentina is so far away. And there's a Hastinapur Foundation there too!'

Yoga is among those niche topics that find wholehearted resonance with celebrities. A host of sportspersons across various sports, such as Virat Kohli, Anil Kumble, Tushar Khandker and Devindar Walmiki, tweeted about their own fitness routines. Cinema personalities like Akshay Kumar, Anil Kapoor and others tweeted on the same topic. Many journalists did so as well. Sonu Sood felt that the Prime Minister was an inspiration to everyone else in his attempt to create a fitter, healthier world. He tweeted, 'This is pure bliss sir @narendramodi ji thank you for inspiring the world to take care of their health n stay fitter. Always believed fitness is a baton that has to be passed to the next by every individual. Keep motivating others. #HumFitTohIndiaFit.'

THE HEALTHY INDIA CYCLE AND YOGA CIRCLE CONTINUES

'Shriman Isaak Munda-ji hails from a village in Sambalpur district of Odisha. In his YouTube videos he shows prominently the local dishes, traditional ways of cooking, his village, his lifestyle, family and food habits.'

In July 2021, the PM spoke of a brave young girl called Anvi, who had started practising yoga with her mother and had gone on to become a yoga expert, despite Down's syndrome. He has constantly inspired the listeners of *Mann Ki Baat* to stay connected with ayurveda, yoga and natural medicinal herbs and plants. Seamlessly linking it to modern medicine, he also spoke of the celebration of National Doctors Day on the 1 July. The day, dedicated to the birth anniversary of the great doctor and statesman of the country, Dr BC Roy, should motivate us to stay committed to the cause of fitness, said the PM.

Prime Minister Narendra Modi's own belief can be summed up in a quote that he referenced, 'Hippocrates, one of the most respected persons in the world of medicine, had said, "Wherever the art of medicine is loved, there is also a love of humanity".'

13

Seeding a National Culture of Sport

> 'Sports unites us. Every sporting tournament gives the message that we are stronger and better together.'
>
> – Prime Minister Narendra Modi

Swami Vivekananda once said that he would want the youth to play football on the field than read the Gita. In a nation where cricket is the most popular sport, Prime Minister Narendra Modi used the *Mann Ki Baat* platform in March 2016 to speak of football, a sport that is gaining popularity, particularly among the urban youth. The context was the 2017 FIFA U-17 World Cup hosted by India. Many episodes later, in Episode 98, he harkened back to that episode, veering the conversation to champion traditional sports of India. Soon after, there was a wave to join, enjoy and learn more about Indian sports. Such is the impact and emphasis on seeding a culture of sports in India.

Prime Minister Modi used the radio to convey, rather convincingly, why the FIFA U-17 World Cup was a perfect opportunity for Indian youth since the event would lead to a massive infrastructural upgradation of football facilities that would eventually help youngsters. He added that a World Cup brought excellent sporting infrastructure that had the potential to create more interest in the sport. At the same time, with such a young population, India has great potential for football tournaments, coaches and sporting companies to establish a base here and make the game more popular.

Mega sporting events like the Olympics and the World Cup also bring more tourists to a nation. Sports lovers from across the world converge to catch a glimpse of the games and use the opportunity to travel to other places in the host country. For instance, if a game is played in Delhi, foreign tourists would not miss a visit to the Taj Mahal, Jaipur or the hills. The PM observed during an early *Mann Ki Baat* episode that the World Cup can also become an occasion to draw tourists to India and give economic opportunities to many youngsters.

Making the exercise interactive, the Prime Minister asked youngsters to share their ideas about the World Cup and how to make football more popular on the mobile app. Suggestions came in thousands, and youth participation was laudatory. The nature of the comments was diverse. People were concerned about sports facilities, particularly in sports other than cricket. Some ideas revolved around the need to facilitate the spread of football to all parts of the nation. From unique ways of scouting sporting talent to recruiting them, the Prime Minister promised to send these inputs to the relevant authorities. Years later, these efforts have come to fruition, as the nation has seen glorious achievements in the many global sporting events.

Former cricketer **Sachin Tendulkar** wrote in his tweet, 'Excited to hear about the launch of sports talent search portal on #MannKiBaat, which will enable discovery of India's finest sports talent.'

REORIENTING MINDSETS TO BE MORE SPORTS-ORIENTED

Many initiatives to promote sports—Khel Mahakumbh—and initiatives like Gunotsav have been a part of the PM's ethos of creating a stronger and more holistic education system. The beauty is that all these initiatives were driven by the guiding principle that Jan Bhagidari, or people's participation, would lead to true development and empowerment of the poorest. The Prime Minister spoke of persons with disabilities in the very first, Episode 1 of *Mann Ki Baat*, on 3 October 2014, when he read out a letter from Gautam Pal, who had written that greater civic participation for persons with disabilities shows the gravitas that the PM ascribes to the culture of sports.

Journalist **Boria Majumdar** tweeted, 'On #NationalSportsDay glad to see PM@narendramodi speak about Olympics and Paralympics in the same breath in his #MannKiBaat. It goes a step towards achieving equality and inclusivity in sports in the country.'

In the address, the Prime Minister recalled his interaction with specially-abled athletes when he was the chief minister of Gujarat. This inspired him to involve them in Gujarat's sports extravaganza, Khel Mahakumbh and create separate sporting events for persons with disabilities. He added that when it comes to persons with disabilities, it becomes the responsibility of the entire nation to ensure a change in the mindset and that persons with disabilities are not denied the opportunities they deserve.

The Prime Minister has always emphasised cultivating a culture of sports, sportsmanship and fitness among the people of India, particularly the youth. For him, sports are not merely about a handful of people playing on the field. Instead, it is an arena that showcases the spirit of new India—a young, restless and energetic nation excelling on the world stage.

In Episode 43, the PM devoted a significant part of the *Mann Ki Baat* programme to encouraging the athletes who had won medals at the 2018 Commonwealth Games. In the episode, he mentioned that among the happiest sights when an Indian wins a medal, is when the tricolour is unfurled and the national anthem of India is played. He mentioned table tennis player Manika Batra, Deepak Lather, who became the youngest weightlifter to win, and Anish Bhanwala, the youngest Indian to win gold at such an event. He also spoke with pride about the epic match between Saina Nehwal and P.V. Sindhu, adding that even though only one of India's proud daughters could win, it had made every Indian happy to see that both the competing players were Indians. As a special treat for the listeners, three athletes, Manika Batra, Mirabai Chanu and P. Gururaja, even joined the episode and spoke about competing in the 2018 Commonwealth Games.

While sports tournaments such as the Olympics, the Commonwealth Games and the Asian Games draw enough attention from sports enthusiasts across the world, *Mann Ki Baat* also introduced the importance of para-athletes. The Prime Minister has always prioritised the well-being of persons with disabilities, and several episodes of the show have been spent to appreciate the skills of divyang athletes.

Earlier, during the 49th *Mann Ki Baat* programme on 28 October 2018, he talked about India's stellar performance in the Asian Para Games 2018 in Jakarta. He shared memories of his meeting with para-athletes later at his residence. India, it may be recalled, won seventy-two medals—a historic number in India's Asian Para Games history. Even then, he had shared some inspiring stories of individual athletes, like Narayan Thakur, who is a divyang by birth and had spent time in orphanages.

Ten special children who defeated cancer against all odds saw a special mention in Episode 55 when the PM reminded about certain turns in life that make our hearts swell with joy, chief among these being the achievements of children. He said,

> 'I feel like mentioning a few children today—Nidhi Baipotu, Monish Joshi, Devanshi Rawat, Tanush Jain, Harsh Devdharkar, Anant Tiwari, Preeti Nag, Atharva Deshmukh, Aronyatesh Ganguli and Hrithik Alaamandaa. What I tell you about them will fill your hearts with pride & verve as well. We all know that just the word cancer is more than enough to scare the world. It conjures images of death waiting at the doorstep. But each of these ten children fought against the dreaded disease in a battle for their lives, and also brought glory and laurels to the country. In sports and games, a player becomes a champion after winning a tournament or bagging a medal. This was a rare occasion when the participants were champions even before they had entered the contest ... they were champions in the game of life.'

These ten sports heroes had participated in The World Children's Winners Games held in Moscow, a unique sports tournament meant only for young cancer survivors, who defeated cancer and survived. Sports such as shooting, chess, swimming, running, football and table tennis were organised as part of this tournament. It was commendable that all ten champions of our country won medals in this tournament. Out of these, some players even won more than one medal.

One of the things that the PM regularly does after every big sports tournament is to tweet about individual medal winners, along with a photograph of them. He believes that this creates a positive environment among the fans of the athlete, and at a larger level, motivates more youngsters to pursue sports.

A sportsperson who makes it to this stage does so after putting in a lot of hard work. It's a kind of severe and dedicated tapasya, the PM emphasised in July 2016.

REINTRODUCING SPORTS AS AN ORGANIC PART OF LIFE

In August 2019, Prime Minister Modi touched upon malnutrition using a Sanskrit *subhashit* (a poem or saying with a moral). The lines cited by him were written centuries ago, but carry great relevance, even today –

> 'पृथिव्यां त्रीणि रत्नानि जलमन्नं सुभाषितम् |
> मूढैःपाषाणखण्डेषु रत्नसंज्ञा प्रदीयते ||'

This means there are three gems on this earth—food, water, and pleasing words—but fools consider pieces of rocks as gems. In our culture, much glory has been ascribed to food. We have even converted the knowledge about food into science, he said. Balanced and nutritious food is essential for all of us, especially for women and newborn children, since these two categories are the foundation of the future of our society. Using the medium of the show, he spoke to us of the Poshan Abhiyaan, where holistic nutrition is being made available with the help of modern scientific methods. This is being converted into a mass movement all over the country. People are fighting a battle against malnutrition in innovative and interesting ways, the PM said. He also encouraged participation in the Poshan Abhiyaan celebrated in September across the country.

Again, in Episode 92, he reiterated the many creative and diverse efforts that were being made all over the country against malnutrition,

> 'Efforts for social awareness play an important role in tackling the challenges of malnutrition. I would urge all of you to take part in the efforts to eradicate malnutrition, in the coming nutrition month.'

Good nutrition and participation in sports are intrinsically connected. He spoke of the National Sports Day and the Fit India movement, in August 2019, which created an organic orientation towards a healthier and fitter lifestyle.

In August 2020, he reiterated the efforts being made to celebrate nutrition month, such as having a nutrition monitor (quite like a class monitor) and a nutrition card (like a school report card). He cited the example of the Statue of Unity of Sardar Vallabhbhai Patel in Gujarat, which had a unique nutrition park where one could obtain nutrition-related education along with fun and frolic.

Being an ordinary citizen, whatever affects us has the same effect on him, '... since, I'm just one amongst you,' he said in one of the episodes. Talking about the spirit of great sportsmanship on display in the US Open, he said,

> 'Just see how on the one hand, victory in the U.S. Open victory was being discussed, and on the other, runner up Daniil Medvedev's speech was equally doing the rounds in public discourse, especially on social media. Hence, I heard

the speech and watched the match too. The sheer simplicity and maturity displayed by the 23-year-old Daniil Medvedev touched everyone. It surely stirred me. Moments before this speech, he had suffered defeat at the hands of tennis legend, and 19 times Grand Slam winner, Rafael Nadal. An event such as this would have pushed anyone towards remorse and despair. But in Medvedev's case, there was no sign of even the slightest despair on his countenance.'

The PM discussed how Daniil won hearts with his humility, simplicity and sportsman's spirit, encouraging us to imbibe the same kind of spirit.

'If you haven't heard Medvedev's speech yet, I urge you, especially young friends, to watch this video. It holds much for people across the age and class spectrum to see and learn. These moments go way beyond winning and losing, where victory and defeat cease to be. Life is victory ... This has been beautifully articulated in our scriptures. The wisdom of our ancestors is truly praiseworthy.'

He also quoted one of our ancient texts to reiterate this:

'विद्या विनय उपेता हरति
न चेतांसि कस्य मनुजस्य
मणि कांचन संयोग:
जनयति लोकस्य लोचन आनन्दम.'

This means that when ability and humility amalgamate in a person, whose heart will such a person not be able to win over?

In Episode 57, he touched upon another issue that could be resolved through a commitment to sports and fitness. He spoke of the dangers posed by cigarettes, especially e-cigarettes. He cautioned,

'There is little awareness among people about e-cigarettes. They are also completely unaware of its danger , so sometimes e-cigarettes get sneaked into the house out of sheer curiosity. Kids sometimes pretend to show a magical trick—blowing smoke without lighting a cigarette or striking a match to light it—end up smoking an e-cigarette in the presence of their parents or friends! And, as if a magic show is going on, the family members also respond with applause! There is no awareness! There is no knowledge that once teenagers or our youth get caught in its clutches, they slowly, become hooked and fall prey to this noxious addiction.'

In Episode 59, Prime Minister Narendra Modi welcomed all to *Mann Ki Baat* by addressing the young people of our young nation, especially praising the enthusiasm, patriotism and sense of selfless service that envelops them. He reminded us that every year, the fourth Sunday of November was celebrated as the National Cadet Corps (NCC) Day and that India's NCC was one of the largest uniformed youth organisations in the world. It is a tri-services organisation comprising the Army, the Navy and the Air Force. Being in the NCC means making qualities such as leadership, patriotism, selfless service, discipline and hard work an integral part of one's character; sportsmanship, of course teaches us all of the above too!

In January 2020, the PM congratulated the Government and the people of Assam for being excellent hosts of the Khelo India Games, in the show. On 22 January 2020, the third Khelo India Games concluded in Guwahati. Six thousand players from different states participated in the games. He shared with pride that not only had 80 records been broken during this grand sports festival, but 56 of these had been broken by our daughters. He said,

> ‘These laurels have been recorded in the name of our daughters! I, along with all the winners, congratulate all the participants. I also thank all the people, coaches and technical officers associated with Khelo India Games for organising them successfully.’

Through him, we learnt that the participation of athletes in Khelo India Games is seeing an upsurge year after year, which is a clear indication of the increasing inclination of school children towards sports.

> ‘I wish to tell all of you that in 2018, when Khelo India Games were instituted, 3,500 players took part, but in just three years the number of players has almost doubled to more than 6,000. Not only this, in just three years, through Khelo India Games, 3,200 gifted children have emerged on the sporting horizon!’

It is important to note that many of these children had grown up amidst dearth and poverty. He cited the example of Purnima Mandal of Guwahati, a sanitation worker in Guwahati Municipal Corporation whose daughter Malvika had shown her mettle in football, her son Sujit had represented Assam in Kho-Kho, while her other son Pradeep played hockey for the state.

> ‘Sports mean physical fitness, mental alertness and personality enhancement. What else does one need? Sports, in a way, is a recipe to bring people together.’

In an episode in 2018, he spoke to the athlete and gold medal winner in the Germany World Cross Country, Chhavi Yadav over a phone call. Together, they addressed how sports and games that were once a special part and parcel of every child's summer holidays. Games played in every lane in the neighbourhood, are now fading into oblivion. Sometimes on scorching afternoons and sometimes after dinner, children used to play for hours together, leaving all their worries behind. Some games, from pitthoo to kanche (marbles), kho-kho, lattoo and *gilli-danda*, saw the participation of the whole family. Innumerable games were an inseparable part of children from Kashmir to Kanyakumari, from Kutch to Kamrup, said the PM. The Prime Minister also shared nuggets of knowledge, such as how the games are known by different names in different places. Pitthoo is one such game with many names—some call it lagori, at other places it is called satoriya, saat pathar, dikori, satodiya!

With that, through the show, he presented traditional indoor games of India in a new and attractive avatar. Consequently, those involved with creating these games for the market, the suppliers and start-ups associated with these traditional indoor games grew in popularity, and our pledge to be vocal for local also saw resonance. A avid listener, Snehal Patel took to Twitter to say, '(Prime Minister Modi) refreshed childhood memories ...' Abhijeet Kar opined that not only did the Prime Minister bring back childhood memories, but also made him wonder why he had never pursued sports! Utsav Pansari found it pleasantly surprising that a prime minister was talking about traditional games and bringing a spirit of pride among people towards India's past. This was when he was also encouraging the sport that India reveres as a religion and unites us all—cricket!

Former cricketer **Mohammad Shami** tweeted, 'Thank you so much to Honourable Prime minister for appreciating the performance of the Indian cricket team in australia. Keep supporting us and we are proud to be a part of Indian Cricket Team #TeamIndia #MannKiBaat.'

Cricketer **Virat Kohli** also tweeted, 'Thank you @ narendramodi Sir for all the kind words; your support will always help us strive for better.'

In Episode 103, the PM spoke of a Yoga-practising French woman, Charlotte Chopin. He recalled his recent visit to France, where he met Chopin, who is more than 100 years old,

'She has crossed a century. She has been practising yoga for the last 40 years. She only credits her health to yoga and has become a prominent face of India's science of yoga and its strength in the world.'

ROAD TO TOKYO #CHEER4INDIA

In one of the episodes of *Mann Ki Baat,* Prime Minister Modi once again talked about the importance of striking a balance between sports and academics among the children of the nation. He said,

> 'A few days ago, I had the opportunity to be associated with the inaugural use of the synthetic track of the Usha School of Athletics, run by renowned athlete, P.T. Usha. The more we promote sports, the more we see the spirit of sportsmanship. Sports play an important role in personality development too. There is no dearth of talent in our country. If the children in our family are interested in sports, they should be given opportunities. They should not be forced off the playing fields to be locked in rooms with books. They should

study as well, and if they can do well in their studies, they should certainly do so. But, if they have the potential and the inclination to do well in sports, that should be encouraged and supported by the school, college, family and the people around them. Each one should nurture dreams for the next Olympics.'

In June 2021, he focused squarely on the Olympics—right from the 'Road to Tokyo' quiz about India's performance in earlier games to our preparation for the ongoing Tokyo Olympics and talking to legendary athletes like Milkha Singh (who the country lost during COVID-19). The PM talked about his conversation with the ace sportsman who had represented the country in the 1964 Tokyo Olympics and his sense of commitment, even during his illness. Milkha Singh had promised to boost the morale of our athletes. The Prime Minister said,

> 'When talent, dedication, determination and sportsman's spirit come together a champion is made. In our country most sportspersons hail from the smaller towns and villages. Our team going to Tokyo too has many such players whose life is so inspiring.'

He even spoke about sportspersons such as Praveen Jadhav, the Indian archer who hailed from a village in Satara district of Maharashtra. His parents earned their living as labourers. Another player, hockey talent Neha Goyal also won the Prime Minister's praise. Goyal's mother and sisters had managed the family expenses by working in a cycle factory. He also spoke of Deepika Kumari's life that had been full of ups and downs. Deepika's father drove an auto rickshaw and her mother was a nurse. Deepika was the only female archer from India in the

Tokyo Olympics, the Prime Minister said, and was once ranked world's number one archer. C.A. Bhavani Devi from Chennai is adroit at fencing and became the first Indian fencer to qualify for the Olympics.

While citing the example of Priyanka Goswami, whose father was a bus conductor, Prime Minister Narendra Modi said it was the sight of medals that had always fascinated her. This passion made her participate in the race-walking competition for the first time. She went on to become a champion! Just like our javelin thrower from Banaras, Shivpal Singh, whose entire family had been his motivation since they were associated with the sport. Badminton player **Chirag Shetty** and his doubles' partner, Satwik Sairaj also overcame personal odds and gone on to give their best in the Men's Doubles Badminton Competition. Shetty tweeted, Shetty tweeted, 'Really thankful to our Honourable Minister Shri Narendra Modi for the kind and encouraging words in today's *Mann Ki Baat*. We surely will give our best at the games and make our country proud!'

In one episode, the PM encouraged citizen to send wishes to these players on social media with a #Cheer4India hashtag. Not one to shy away from the ground reality, he said,

> 'Wherever we reach in life, whatever height we attain this connection with the ground, always, keeps us bound to our roots. The joy of success experienced after a period of struggle is something else! Our players going to Tokyo faced scarcity of means and resources in their childhood, but they persevered and endured with fortitude.'

In this episode, the PM encouraged citizens to send wishes to these players on social media with a #Cheer4India hashtag.

In Episode 80 of the show, the PM spoke of Major Dhyanchand and his birth anniversary.

> 'It was Dhyanchand-ji's hockey that brought glory to Indian hockey. Four decades later, almost after 41 years, the youth of India, her sons and daughters, once again infused vitality in our hockey. Irrespective of the number of medals won, no Indian enjoys victory until a medal is won in hockey. And this time, in the Olympics, the medal won for hockey came our way after four decades. You can imagine ... wherever Major Dhyanchand-ji might be ... his heart, his soul must be overflowing with joy.'

Paying this tribute to the hockey legend, the Prime Minister effortlessly tied our sporting past with the present.

In Episode 92 that aired the successive year in August 2022, the Prime Minister brought the focus back to National Sports Day to be celebrated on the birth anniversary of Major Dhyanchand.

> 'May our young sportspersons continue to raise the glory of our Tricolour on global forums. This will be our tribute to Dhyan Chand-ji. Let us all keep working together for the country like this; keep raising the honour of the nation.'

Episode 90 enumerated more winners with humble beginnings, such as Adil Altaf from Srinagar, who won the gold in 70 km cycling. His tailor father left no stone unturned to fulfil his son's dreams. Adil has brought pride to his father and the entire state of Jammu & Kashmir. Gold winner L. Dhanush's father was a carpenter in Chennai. Sangli-girl, Kajol Sargar's father worked as a tea vendor. Kajol would help her father and practice weightlifting as well. Her family and her hard work paid off and Kajol won many accolades in weightlifting. Tanu

Singh of Rohtak also performed a similar kind of miracle. Tanu's father, Rajbir Singh, was a school bus driver. By winning the gold medal in wrestling, Tanu realised her own, her family's and her father's dream.

Whenever the subject of sports and games is touched upon, the entire young generation naturally comes into view. And when we look keenly at the young generation, we notice a sweeping change there. The mind of the youth has transformed And today's young minds, shunning obsolete, age-old methods and patterns, want to do something new altogether, something different. Today's young minds did not want to walk on the readymade well-trodden paths of the past, Prime Minister Narendra Modi said, while encouraging sports among the youth on one of the later episodes of the show.

Encouraging a sportsman spirit while leveraging the concept of sabka prayas, he praised the nation for raising the flag of success in Para sports as well. As a result of the PM's sentiment, today, many people are engaged in promoting fitness culture among the specially-abled at the grassroots level. This imparts a lot of strength to the self-confidence of the specially-abled. In Episode 94, he mentioned the theme Judega India to Jeetega India for the National Games, which he said gave a strong message of unity, apart from promoting India's sports culture. He said,

> 'You will be happy to know that the National Games this time were the biggest ever organised in India. Thirty-six sports were included. Among these seven sports were new and two had been indigenous competitions—Yoga and Mallakhamb. The three teams at the fore in winning

gold medals are the Services team, the Maharashtra team and the Haryana team. Six national records and about 60 national games records were also made in these games. I congratulate all the players, who won medals, made new records and participated in this sports competition. I also wish these players a bright future.'"

NORTH, SOUTH, EAST OR WEST, INDIA IS THE BEST

The Prime Minister expressed his appreciation, in the early days of *Mann Ki Baat,* towards all those people who had contributed to the successful organisation of the National Games held in Gujarat during Navratri. In Episode 97, he spoke of Kashmiri youth who had made cricket even more amazing in the snow. The PM has praised the enthusiasm among the youth regarding sports. Equally, he has bridged the gap between rural and urban India by using the glue of sports. Take the broadcast for Episode 82, where he spoke of Gujarat Police's bike rally from the Lakhpat Fort in Kutch to the Statue of Unity. Similarly, a Tripura Police contingent had organised a bike rally from Tripura to the Statue of Unity, connecting the country from East to West, to celebrate Unity Day. Personnel of the Jammu & Kashmir police too delivered a similar message of unity by taking out a bike rally from Uri to Pathankot.

The Prime Minister also spoke about Ladakh, which is soon going to be home to an astroturf football stadium, being built at the height of more than 10,000 feet. This would be the largest open stadium in Ladakh, where 30,000 spectators could sit together. This modern football stadium would also have a synthetic track with eight lanes. Apart from this, there would also be a hostel facility with one thousand beds.

> 'You will also like to know that this stadium has been certified by FIFA, the foremost football organisation. Such a large sports infrastructure brings great opportunities for the youth of the country. Such an arrangement results in the movement of people from all over the country, promotion of tourism and the creation of many employment opportunities. The stadium will also benefit many youngsters in Ladakh.'

He also spoke about the increasing dominance of Indian players, and the emergence of a new image of Indian sports, in the sporting world. For example, in Khelo India Youth Games, besides disciplines that were a part of the Olympics, five indigenous sports—Gatka, Thang Ta, Yogasan, Kalaripayattu and Mallakhamb—were also included.

The PM struck an emotional chord when he spoke of **Mithali Raj**, one of India's most talented cricketers who recently announced her retirement from cricket. She tweeted, 'Thank You sir @narendrammodi Your words means a lot! Indeed Women's cricket in India is truly arrived! #MannKiBaat.'

Echoing the Prime Minister's sentiments, ace cricketer **Sachin Tendulkar** also tweeted, 'My thoughts resonate with those of our PM @narendrammodi shared on #MannKiBaat regd my fellow Indian women cricketer's exemplary performance.'

In Episode 91, the PM shared stories of PV Sindhu, who had won her first title in the Singapore Open and Neeraj Chopra, who continued his excellent performance and won the silver medal for the country in the World Athletics Championship. He mentioned the Chess Olympiad being organised in India, where more than 180 countries participated. He said,

> 'At the Ireland Para Badminton International our players have boosted the glory of the country by winning 11 medals. Indian players also performed well in the World Cadet Wrestling Championship held in Rome. Our athlete Suraj has done wonders in the Greco-Roman event. He won the gold medal for wrestling in this event after a long gap of 32 years. For the players, this entire month has been full of action.' He also expressed happiness at India hosting the FIFA Under 17 Women's World Cup.'

In his endeavours to appreciate sports and sportspersons, one of the Prime Minister's strongest allies has been the *Mann Ki Baat* platform, through which he has undertaken numerous efforts to make sports a mass movement and to encourage sportspersons who shine on the world stage. Prime Minister Modi clearly understands that when major tournaments come to India, it is a win-win scenario for our people. For one, sporting infrastructure is significantly enhanced. Secondly, our citizens get an opportunity to watch matches and it is also a boost for tourism and other economic activities. Thus, he has used this platform to create awareness and enthusiasm around sports tournaments.

Addressing the Sports Minister's Chintan Shivir in Manipur in late April 2023, he said that no sports talent should remain untapped and that quality sports infrastructure was the right of all. This shows, yet again, his unmistakable commitment to transporting the nation to its sporting best. He has set the goal for us, as a nation, to set our eyes on creating and fostering a culture that thrives on sports.

SECTION III

India's Civilisational Unity in Its Splendid Diversity

14

A Cultural Renaissance

'India's diversity, which others once thought was a burden to India, has proven to be the priceless power of India. A strong testimony of its power.'

– Prime Minister Narendra Modi

From felicitating our cultural festivals to honouring our national heroes, to imbuing the fabric of India with multihued shades of the country, Prime Minister Modi has done a fantastic job in re-acquainting us with our own rich and diverse cultural heritage. Whether it was his own visit to the Amarnath shrine or motivating us to inculcate a 'back to our roots' approach, he has been at the forefront of each and every journey, real and metaphoric.

When it comes to showcasing Indian culture to the world, many citizens have remarked that Prime Minister Modi is among the most culturally rooted political leaders and one of the most passionate leaders India has seen. Festivals and festive gatherings, such as rath yatras and pilgrimages, are an important feature of India's rich history and cultural tapestry. Celebrating societal harmony and brotherhood, worshipping and conserving nature, rejoicing in the victory of good and taking heart from it, or even encouraging introspection and forgiveness—many such themes that are embedded in our festivals have been a recurring feature in the Prime Minister's addresses through the radio.

In Episode 68, he said,

> 'There is a coincidence attached with the return of the idol of Mata Annapurna ... World Heritage Week was celebrated only a few days ago. World Heritage Week provides a wonderful opportunity to lovers of culture to revisit the past and to know about the history of these important milestones ... National Museum is working on introducing around ten virtual galleries—isn't this interesting? Now, sitting at your home, you can tour National Museum in Delhi. It is important to take our cultural heritage to the maximum number of people, and the use of technology as a medium can contribute to the conservation of this heritage.'

In 2015, the Amarnath Yatra saw the greatest number of pilgrims, when compared to the last four years. In Episode 55 of *Mann Ki Baat*, Prime Minister Modi spoke of the month of Saawan, and how it symbolises the surreal pilgrimage of the Amarnath Yatra. He told the listeners,

> 'A total of 3,00,000 pilgrims have had the darshan of the holy Amarnath shrine from 1 July till now. In 2015, the number of devotees who performed this pilgrimage over 60 days has been crossed over by the number of pilgrims in mere 28 days this year!'

But he didn't just stop there. He used the occasion to convey his gratitude to the people of Jammu & Kashmir for their hospitality. He said that the Yatra wouldn't have been a success in the truest sense, had it not been for the locals and the warmth they showered on the pilgrims. Within a span of a month-and-a-half of the commencement of the Chardham Yatra in Uttarakhand that year, more than 8 lakh devotees had partaken of the darshan of the Kedarnath shrine. This was a record number of pilgrims post the apocalyptic events of 2013.

With that, he appealed to all listeners to visit tourist spots within our country whose scenic beauty is a wonder to behold during the monsoon. There are no better ways to witness this nation's beauty and people's sentiments and no better teachers than tourism and pilgrimage, he said.

While extending his felicitation, he also seamlessly melded the concept of spiritual integration with national integration, highlighting how 15th August could be celebrated both as a folk festival and a people's festival. It is during the pious month of Saawan that many devotees perform the Kanwar Yatra, and many observe fasts and eagerly wait for festivals like Krishna Janmashtami and Nag Panchami. It is during this season that the festival of Raksha Bandhan, which symbolises the bond between a brother and sister, also falls. Therefore, he implied, our national celebration too should be all-encompassing.

FROM THE STARS TO THE SANDS

In December 2019, the Prime Minister spoke of our connection with the twinkling stars in the sky being as old as our civilisation. He talked about how there are magnificent observatories (Jantar Mantars) in many places in India which are worth seeing, and how these observatories have a connection with astronomy. Referring to the prodigious talent of Aryabhata, who expounded in great detail about the solar eclipse, and also explained the lunar eclipse from both philosophical and mathematical standpoints, the Prime Minister spoke about the inherently informed sensibility that ties everything back to our cultural heritage.

Mathematically, what Aryabhata expounded in the fourteenth or fifteenth century was carried forward by Maadhav of the village of Sangam in Kerala, who used calculus to determine the position of planets in the universe. The night sky was not merely something that whetted curiosity. It was an important source for mathematicians and scientists. He concluded,

> 'A few years ago, I had unveiled a book called *Pre-modern Kutchi Navigation Techniques and Voyages*. This book, in a way, is the diary of Maalam. Maalam was a navigator, and whatever he experienced professionally he recorded in his diary. Even in the modern age, the very same "Maalam's volume" exists as a collection of ancient Gujarati manuscripts. It describes ancient navigation technology, and "Maalam's volume" repeatedly references the sky, the stars, the speed of the stars, and clearly describes how the direction is determined in sea voyages with the help of stars; it is stars that navigate us towards our destination.'

In August 2019, the Prime Minister touched upon yet another aspect of our heritage, by appealing to our sense of pride through our tourist places. He reiterated,

> 'On 15th August, I urged all of you from the ramparts of the Red Fort to visit at least 15 places within a span of the next 3 years, 15 places in India. Witness and observe. Do take the family and spend some time there.'

Our country is diverse, and opening ourselves to its diversity can truly enrich our lives, he said. Not only does visiting new places help people come back with renewed energy, enthusiasm, zeal and inspiration, it also expands their thinking. Later, in November 2019, in Episode 59, this sentiment was echoed by a listener, Tarannum Khan, who said: Sir, in your messages you have told us that every Indian citizen should visit 15 places in three years. Would you like to tell us what places we should visit? And what was the one place that made you feel good, rather best?

The Prime Minister responded that he had always had a certain fondness for the Himalayas.

In Episode 51, he focused on yet another amazing site for tourism that had a deep connection with our Indian heritage.

> ‘In honour of Sardar Vallabhbhai Patel who bound the entire country with the thread of unity, India witnessed the coming up of the tallest statue in the world, Statue of Unity.’

He reiterated the significance of the Statue of Unity across various episodes.

> ‘The distinction of having the world's highest statue fills every Indian with pride; the head of every Indian is held high. You will be happy to note that in a year, more than 26 lakh tourists visited the Statue of Unity.’

This means that an average of 8,500 people witnessed the grandeur of the Statue of Unity every day. The homage paid to Sardar Vallabhbhai Patel by these visitors reflects the reverence and devotion that Indians have for him in their hearts. Besides, the fact that it houses many other sites of attraction such as Cactus Garden, Butterfly Garden, Jungle Safari, Children's Nutrition Park and Ekta Nursery, which are all constantly evolving and providing a fillip to the local economy, becomes yet another reason for us to celebrate our heritage. Sardar Patel integrated the nation with the thread of unison. This mantra of unity is like a sacrament in our lives. In a diverse country like ours, we should adhere to this mantra on all paths, at every bend and at every pit stop.

> 'Our nation has always been very proactive and alert in strengthening unity and communal harmony in the country. If we look around us, we will find many examples of individuals who have been working ceaselessly to foster communal harmony. But sometimes it so happens, that the efforts of the society and its contribution get wiped from our collective memory.'

In the same episode, the Prime Minister also paid homage to Guru Gobind Singh-ji, whose birth anniversary is celebrated on 13th January. The Prime Minister said in his moving tribute to the tenth Sikh guru,

> 'Guru Gobind Singh-ji was born in Patna. For most of his life, his work was centred in North India and he sacrificed his life in Nanded, Maharashtra. His birthplace was Patna, karmabhoomi was North India and his last moments were spent in Nanded. In a way, all of India received his blessings. A glimpse of his lifespan reflects a glimpse all of entire India.'

Guru Gobind Singh-ji was bestowed with a quiet and simple personality, but whenever an attempt was made to suppress the voice of the poor and the weak, or injustice was done to them, then Guru Gobind Singh-ji raised his voice firmly for the poor and the weak and therefore he said, 'It is when I make sparrow fight hawks, it is when I make lions out of wolves, it is when

I make one fight with one hundred thousand that I am called Gobind Singh.'

THE FIBRE OF UNITY

In Prime Minister Modi's messages, there is a strong undercurrent of his unambiguous commitment to the spirit of unity and inherent secularism. Referring to the landmark Allahabad High Court verdict on Ram Janmabhoomi in September 2010, he said it was heartening to see the restrained, balanced and mature public response to the verdict and he praised his listeners for it. The Prime Minister said,

> 'On the one hand, the machinations went on to generate tension for a week or two, but, when the decision was taken on Ram Janmabhoomi, the government, political parties, social organisations, civil society, representatives of all sects and saints gave restrained and balanced statements. There were attempts to reduce the tension in the socio-political environment. But I remember that day vividly. And whenever I do that, I get happy that the dignity of the judiciary was very proudly honoured and no allowance for any heated discourse or tension was made anywhere. These incidents should always be remembered as they give us a lot of strength. That day, that moment, instils in us all a sense of duty. It is an example of how the voice of unison can bestow strength upon our country.'

In Episode 59, he again lauded the harmony in the nation.

> '130 crore Indians once again proved that, for them, national interest is supreme. The values of peace, unity and goodwill are paramount in our country. When the verdict on Ram

> Mandir was announced, the entire country embraced it with open arms. They accepted the verdict with ease and with peace. Today, through the *Mann Ki Baat* programme, I would like to appreciate and thank my countrymen.'

In the truest sense, this verdict has also proved to be a milestone for the judiciary in our country. After this historic verdict of the Supreme Court, the country did move ahead on a new path, with a new resolve, replete with new hopes and aspirations.

Similarly, in Episode 52, he expressed how pleased he was that the Government of India was a partner in the restoration of many Buddhist temples, which also includes the centuries-old magnificent Ananda Temple in Bagan, Myanmar. The Prime Minister said that Lord Buddha's teachings show the world the way to get rid of hatred with compassion. 'I hope people spread the teachings of Lord Buddha all over the world and believe in the principles of compassion. I wish all of them an auspicious Buddha Purnima. I seek blessings from Lord Buddha for the entire world, so we can fulfil our responsibility to build a peaceful and compassionate world based on his teachings.'

In Episode 33, the Prime Minister said:

> 'I convey my hearty greetings to all fellow Indians and everyone across the world, especially the Muslim brethren at the advent of this auspicious month of Ramzan. Prayer, spirituality and charity are accorded the highest priority during Ramzan. We, Indians, take pride in our diverse communities and faith.'

Even outside the ambit of *Mann Ki Baat*, the Prime Minister attests to the spirit of secularity as a definitive Indian trait. Lauding Hazrat Imam Hussain, he tweeted,

> 'We recall the sacrifices made by Hazrat Imam Hussain (AS). His courage and commitment to justice and human dignity are noteworthy.'

Often through the show, the Prime Minister has said that our civilisation, culture and languages preach the message of unity in diversity to the entire world. In Episode 59, he spoke of how we belong to a country in which

> 'The taste of the water changes after every couple of kilometres, the dialect changes every few miles. Hundreds of languages have blossomed and flourished in our country for centuries. At the same time, we are also concerned about the possible extinction of these languages and dialects.'

In the context of languages, the Prime Minister spoke about the people of the Rang community who inhabit Dharchula in the Pithoragarh district of Uttarakhand. The community speaks Ranglo, but the number of people who can speak the language had been dwindling. Saddened by this fact, one fine day, some members of the community got together and resolved to save their language. In no time, other people from the Rang community joined in, and everyone in this 10,000-strong community resolved to contribute to saving their language–be it an 84-year-old elderly man Diwan Singh or a 22-year-old youth Vaishali Garbyaal. Social media helped as well, and people started posting stories, poems and songs.

> 'Friends, another important thing to note is that the United Nations has declared 2019 as the "International Year of Indigenous Languages". That means, efforts are being made to conserve those languages which are on the verge

> of extinction. A hundred and fifty years ago, the father of modern Hindi, Bharatendu Harishchandra had also said, 'The progress of one's language is the source of one's overall progress. All progress is meaningless if one's mother tongue is neglected.' That means, no progress is possible without the knowledge of one's mother tongue.'

The Prime Minister heartily lauded the initiative of the Rang community to save their language.

In the same episode, the Prime Minister recalled the words of Mahakavi Subramania Bharati. Towards the end of the 19th century, the great poet had said:

> मुप्पदु कोडी मुगमुडैयाळ
> उयिर् मोइम्बुर ओंद्रुडैयाळ
> इवळ सेप्पु मोळी पधिनेट्टूडैयाळ
> एनिर्सिन्दनैओंद्रुडैयाळ

Meaning, Mother India has 30 crore faces but one body. She speaks 18 languages but thinks as one.

In Episode 60, the Prime Minister spoke of luminaries who had elevated our cultural heritage indubitably,

> 'Swami Vivekanand-ji had observed, "My faith is in the younger generation, the modern generation; out of them will come my workers". Referring to the youth, he had remarked, "The value of youth can neither be ascertained nor described!" Youth is the most valuable phase of one's life. Your life and future entirely depends on the way you utilise your youth. According to Vivekanand-ji, young people are the ones full of energy and dynamism, possessing the power to usher in change. I am of the firm belief that for India, this decade will not only be about the development and progress

of the youth; it will also prove to be about the country's progress, harnessing their collective might. This generation will play a major role in modernising India; I feel it beyond any doubt. On the birth anniversary of Vivekanand on 12 January, and the occasion of National Youth Day, every young person should give a thought to this responsibility, taking on some resolve or the other for this decade.'

Speaking of the rock in Kanyakumari where Swami Vivekanand-ji had entered a meditative state, or spiritual 'Antardhyan', the Prime Minister said that, at that place, one naturally experiences a surge of inner energy, a sense of positivity and the resolve to contribute something to the country.

He spoke also of our Vice President's visit to the Desert Festival held in the Rann of Kutch, Gujarat.

'When our Hon'ble President and Vice President are visiting such important tourist destinations in India, it is bound to inspire our countrymen. I urge you to travel and visit these places as well.'

BHARAT'S CULTURAL ODYSSEY

In June 2015, the Prime Minister spoke of the world becoming increasingly curious about India.

'The world wants to know about the values, the rituals and the heritage of India. It is our responsibility that without any artificiality we share our legacy and introduce ourselves to the world. We can only do this when we ourselves are proud of our traditions.'

The month of March 2021 saw the celebration of Azadi Ka Amrit Mahotsav, to commemorate 75 years of India's independence. The PM said,

> 'The Amrit Mahotsav had begun from the day of the Dandi Yatra and will continue till 15 August 2023. Programmes in connection with Amrit Mahotsav are being held throughout the country consistently; people are sharing information and pictures of these programmes from a multitude of places. Amrit Mahotsav will be filled up with similar inspiring drops of nectar ... and then the elixir that will flow will inspire us till a hundred years of the Independence of India ... it will elevate the country to newer heights, begetting a fervour to do something or the other for the country.'

From a competition on patriotic songs and loris (lullabies) to rangoli-making during Amrit Kaal, a month that saw a renewed sense of glory in everything Indian.

The great thing about *Mann Ki Baat* is that it makes good on its promises; for the lullaby competition, the first prize was won by B.M. Manjunath of Chamrajnagar district in Karnataka for his lullaby *Malagu Kanda* written in Kannada. Dinesh Gowala, a resident of Kamrup district in Assam, won the second prize; his lullaby referred to the popular craft that the local artisans use to make clay and pot vessels.

Just like songs and lullabies, the rangoli competition also turned out to be quite popular. The participants made many a beautiful rangoli, each one better than the last. In this competition, Kamal Kumar from Punjab came through as the winner. He made a beautiful rangoli of Netaji Subhash Chandra Bose and Amar Shaheed Veer Bhagat Singh. There were some other stunning entries as well. Sachin Narendra Avsari-ji of Sangli, Maharashtra, depicted the massacre of Jallianwala Bagh and the bravery of Shaheed Udham Singh in his rangoli. Gurudutt Vantekar, a resident of Goa, made a rangoli on Gandhiji while Malathi Selvam of Puducherry depicted many great freedom fighters in her rangoli artwork. The winner of the patriotic song competition, T. Vijay Durga is from Andhra Pradesh.

In Episode 58, we found ourselves connected with Ek Bharat Shrestha Bharat through the agency of the Prime Minister's mike. In August 2021, on the occasion of Vishwakarma Jayanti, we welcomed another new facet of our heritage. Bhagwan Vishwakarma is considered a symbol of the creative power behind the genesis of the world and therefore the foremost skill-maker. In the light of this, Prime Minister Modi said that whether it is sewing and embroidery, software or satellite, all this is a manifestation of Bhagwan Vishwakarma. Even though skill is being recognised in a new way in the world today, our sages and seers have emphasised on skill and scale for thousands of years. They have interlinked skill, talent and ability with faith, thereby making it a part of the philosophy of our lives. Our Vedas have also dedicated many *sookta* to Bhagwan Vishwakarma. Whichever great creations are there, whatever new and big works have been done, our scriptures ascribe them to Bhagwan Vishwakarma. In a way, it represents the thought that all development and innovation in the world happens only through skills. This is the very sentiment behind celebrating the birth anniversary of, and worshipping, Bhagwan Vishwakarma. And this has been quoted in our scriptures too: 'विश्वम कृत्-सन्म कर्म व्यापारो यस्य सः विश्वकर्मा', which means that the one who takes all efforts in the process of creating and building is a Vishwakarma.

The Prime Minister never misses a chance to talk about how our lives go on because of many such skilled people around us; be it an ironsmith, a potter, a carpenter, an electrician, a house painter, a sanitation worker or someone who repairs mobiles and laptops. All of them are known only because of their skill.

In Episode 93, he spoke of the Swachh Sagar, Surakshit Sagar campaign, which started on the 5 July and culminated on the 17 September, the day of Vishwakarma Jayanti. The International Coastal Clean-up Day also fell on the same day. This campaign, which was part of Azadi Ka Amrit Mahotsav, lasted for 75 days. It is said that public participation in it was a sight to behold. During the Ganpati immersion in Kakinada, people were told about the harm caused by plastic.

> ‘About 5,000 young friends from the NSS collected more than 30 tonnes of plastic. Within three days in Odisha, more than 20,000 school students took a pledge that they would inspire their family and people around them for the Swachh Sagar, Surakshit Sagar initiative. I would like to congratulate all the people who took part in this campaign.’

In India, it is customary to chant the following shlok while bathing:

> *Gange cha yamune chaiva Godavari Saraswati, Narmade Sindhu Kaveri Jale asmin sannidhim kuru*

By talking about this shlok in September 2021, the Prime Minister drew attention to the fact that, at our homes, the elderly in the family would make children memorise this shlok that led to aastha, or faith, towards the rivers in our country. This, in turn, would establish an emotional connect with rivers. It would result in nurturing a harmonious credence towards the very river that embodies the mother. It was a way to instil sanskaar, Prime Minister Modi said.

Likewise, speaking of global peace and unison, in Episode 82, the Prime Minister said that we belong to a land where people believe and pray:

> *Vanas-Patayah Shanti-VishwedDevah Shanti-Brahma Shantih,*
> *Sarvag-Wam Shantih Shanti-Reva Shantih Sa Ma Shanti-Redhi* ||
> *Om Shantih Shantih Shantih* ||

Reminding us that India has always worked for world peace and the country has been a part of UN peacekeeping missions continuously since the 1950s, he said that India is also playing a leading role in working closely with World Health Organization (WHO) to popularise Yoga and AYUSH. In March 2021, WHO announced that a Global Centre for Traditional Medicine would be set up in India.

On another cultural tangent, in Episode 83 we came face to face with the 'Janajati Gaurav Saptah' celebrating the contribution of our tribal communities in attaining freedom. Various programmes were held across different regions of the country, to celebrate the Saptah. In the Andaman & Nicobar archipelago, people from tribal communities such as Jarwa and Onge vibrantly displayed their culture. The Prime Minister also mentioned miniature writer Ram Kumar Joshi, from the Una district of Himachal Pradesh, who, on tiny postage stamps, had drawn outstanding sketches of Netaji Subhash Chandra Bose and former Prime Minister Lal Bahadur Shastri. He also conveyed information on a memorable *Dastangoi*, a storytelling programme. In that, memories of the indomitable courage and sacrifice of Rani Durgavati have been rekindled. Another such programme took place in Kashi, where a three-day festival was organised in honour of illustrious luminaries such as Goswami Tulsidas, Sant Kabir, Sant Ravidas, Bharatendu Harishchandra, Munshi Premchand and Jaishankar Prasad. In different periods, all of them played a major role in fostering the development of a rich cultural and national legacy. In the 98th episode, the Prime Minister also spoke very fondly of his regard for Lata Mangeshkar–Lata Didi.

In Episode 75, the Prime Minister greeted his fellow citizens on Easter, saying,

> ‘Symbolically, Easter is associated with a new beginning of life. Easter is a symbol of the resurrection of expectations. On this holy and auspicious occasion, I greet not only the Christian Community in India but also Christians globally.’

In another edition of *Mann Ki Baat*, Prime Minister Modi shared the story of the people of Jalaun who worked to revive the Noon River, as an example of Sabka Prayas. Mrs Jyotsna had written a letter to the Prime Minister about this. Sonal Mansingh, the world-renowned Odissi exponent, said,

> ‘Many don’t even know that the Ramayana is extremely popular in Southeast Asia. The Prime Minister talking about such things on *Mann Ki Baat* was good to hear. He has been a global ambassador for Indian culture, showcasing its depth and variety to global leaders. He has made India’s ancient culture a powerful tool in increasing our nation’s global

appeal. It is heartening to have a culturally rooted Prime Minister who takes Indian culture to the world, be it yoga or Ramayana, be it getting global leaders to visit beautiful temples or witnessing Varanasi's Ganga aartis with them.'

As early as Episode 11 of *Mann Ki Baat*, the Prime Minister had spoken about the strength of charity, or the power of giving on the festival of Akshaya Tritiya. He reminded us that Jain traditions like Akshaya Tritiya happen to be important days in the life of the first Tirthankara Lord Rishabhdev. The followers of Jainism celebrate it as a festival, and people like to initiate auspicious projects on this day. This day also marks the birth anniversary of Lord Basaveshwara.

'It has been my good fortune that I have had the opportunity to learn and connect with reminiscences of Lord Basaveshwara and his messages repeatedly. I extend many felicitations to all the followers of Lord Basaveshwara in our country and the world on his birth anniversary.'

The holy month of Ramazan too was ongoing and the Prime Minister gave his best wishes saying,

'This time, we should pray more than ever before so that prior to the celebration of Eid the world is rid of Corona and we celebrate Eid with enthusiasm and gaiety like we did. I am confident that during these days of Ramazan, by adhering to the guidelines of the local administration, we will reinforce our fight against Corona.'

VARIED COLOURS OF UNITY

In Episode 70, Prime Minister Modi paid obeisance to Maharishi Valmiki and extended his heartiest greetings to the citizens of India on the occasion of Valmiki Jayanti. Maharishi Valmiki's lofty ideals continue to inspire millions of people and provide them strength, he said. He further added that Maharishi Valmiki continues to be a beacon of great hope for millions of the impoverished and Dalits, instilling them with hope and trust.

> ‘Maharishi Valmiki emphasised positive thinking—for him, the spirit of service and human dignity was of utmost importance. Maharishi Valmiki's conduct, thoughts and ideals are the inspiration and guiding force for our resolve for a New India. We will always be grateful to Maharishi Valmiki for composing an epic like Ramayana to guide the future generations.’

In Episode 66, calling deshbhakti intrinsic to the culture of India, he transported us 101 years back to 1919, when the Jallianwala Bagh massacre took place. He spoke with great reverence and humility about Shahid Veer Bhagat Singh and extolled his virtues. He said,

> ‘Can you imagine that an empire, which ruled over a huge chunk of the world and about which it was often said that the sun never sets on this empire, such a powerful empire was terrified of this 23-year-old? Shaheed Bhagat Singh was as much a fighter as he was a scholar, a thinker. Bhagat Singh, along with his revolutionary friends, without caring for their own selves, carried out such daring acts, which had a huge bearing on the country attaining freedom. Another appealing aspect of Shahid Veer Bhagat Singh's life is that he appreciated the importance of teamwork. Be it his devotion

towards Lala Lajpat Rai or his camaraderie with fellow revolutionaries such as Chandra Shekhar Azad, Sukhdev and Rajguru, amongst others, personal accolades were of no importance to him. He had a single mission for as long as he lived, and he sacrificed his life for that mission–that mission was to free India of injustice and British rule.'

EK BHARAT SHRESHTA BHARAT

In Episode 70 in the context of the Statue of Unity, the Prime Minister asked us to constantly use our creativity and love to bring out the beautiful colours of Ek Bharat, Shrestha Bharat even in the smallest of our tasks.

Two months later, he spoke of a Yuva brigade that had transformed an ancient Shiva temple named Veerbhadra Swami in Srirangpatna in Karnataka into a sight to behold.

Distraught after seeing some tourists post a video of this forgotten temple on social media, this Yuva brigade decided to renovate it. They removed the thorny bushes, grass and plants that had come up in the compound of the temple. They repaired and re-constructed wherever required. Seeing their good deed, the local people too extended a helping hand. Some offered cement, others offered paint, yet others came up with many other such contributions. All these youths had different professions and would remain busy during weekdays, so they would take out time during weekends to help renovate the temple. They arranged for an electricity connection for the temple and got doors installed, thus restoring the old grandeur of the temple. Passion and firm commitment are two means through which people can achieve every goal, the Prime Minister told the listeners.

Speaking with much regard for Ustad Bismillah Khan, the Prime Minister drew our attention to the Ustad Bismillah Khan Yuva Puraskar, which is conferred on emerging, talented artists in the field of music and performing arts. These also include artists who have breathed new life into those instruments whose popularity was decreasing with time.

In his address telecast in February 2018, Prime Minister Modi spoke about Nari Shakti, a very significant aspect of our continued heritage and legacy.

> ‘The idea of perfect womanhood is perfect independence.’ This idea of Swami-ji from about 125 years ago expresses the importance of woman power in Indian culture. Today, it is our fundamental duty to ensure the participation of women in every field of life, be it social or economic. We are part of a tradition where men are identified through women, like Yashoda-nandan, Kaushalya-nandan, Gandhari-putra. Today, our woman power has shown inner fortitude and self-confidence–the Indian woman has made herself self-reliant. Not only has she advanced herself, she has carried forward the country and society to newer heights. After all, our dream of ‘New India’ is one where women are strong and empowered and are equal partners in the development of the country.’

In another instalment of *Mann Ki Baat*, he spoke of Lokmanya Tilak who had started a great tradition of celebrating the Sarvjanik Ganeshotsav with the basic aim to inculcate the spirit of unity, enhance awareness in society and promote the culture of togetherness.

> ‘We must think of new ways to steer community Ganesh festivals in consonance with the sentiments of Tilak-ji.’

Similarly, he spoke of Sister Nivedita as one of the most influential women of India. She revived the pride of Indian culture and worked to unite people by awakening national consciousness, said Prime Minister Modi who has always been an avid proponent of Indian culture, celebrating its unique gifts proudly and promoting India's soft power worldwide. Foreign leaders and heads of state who visit India have found themselves being taken to enthralling cultural hubs like Varanasi to witness the Ganga aarti or visiting architectural marvels such as the Swaminarayan Temples in various states. These have come as a whiff of fresh air, taking Indian culture to the world through powerful images.

In Episode 88, he conveyed his heartfelt wishes to the diverse audience, congratulating them on the amalgamation of Eid, Akshaya Tritiya and the festival of Vaishakh Budh Purnima.

He said, 'All these festivals stand for restraint, purity, charity and harmony. Celebrate these festivals with great joy and harmony.'

In a prior episode that aired during the Covid-19 pandemic, he had similarly extolled the virtue of joy with restraint while wishing the citizens on the occasion of Eid, Sharad Poornima, Valmiki Jayanti, followed by Dhanteras, Diwali, Bhaidooj, Chatth Puja and finally the birth anniversary of Guru Nanak Dev.

In fact, the first *Mann Ki Baat* address was aired on the day of Vijaya Dashami in 2014. The first words spoken on *Mann Ki Baat* were the Prime Minister's Vijaya Dashami greetings to the nation. Since Vijaya Dashami is a festival of the victory of good over evil, taking cue from the message of a citizen, Narendra Modi appealed to everyone—including himself—to try and eliminate ten bad habits.

Deriving the essence of festivals and inspiring people to apply it in their daily lives has become an important thread running through the various episodes of *Mann Ki Baat*. It is indeed through the vehicle of *Mann Ki Baat* that the Prime Minister has shepherded, preserved and promulgated the tapestry of our rich cultural heritage.

15

Honouring Our Unsung Heroes

> 'Stories of the valour and patriotism of our heroes should be told and re-told to our newer generations in ways more than once.'
>
> – Prime Minister Narendra Modi

We are often too busy with our daily routines to appreciate our culture, our history and our heritage. As we now enter the Amrit Kaal, it is imperative that we do not undermine the contributions made by our unsung heroes. This is an ideal era, and *Mann Ki Baat* has become the perfect vehicle to express our appreciation and celebrate those who have contributed immensely to the edifice of New India.

In Episode 103, the Prime Minister inspired the nation to continue to honour its Brave. He said,

> 'Friends, amid Amrit Mahotsav and the Independence Day celebrations, we will launch the Meri Mati Mera Desh campaign to honour our martyred Bravehearts. In the memory of these luminaries, special inscriptions will be installed in lakhs of village panchayats of the country. The Amrit Kalash Yatra will also be organised across the country under this campaign.

> The Amrit Kalash Yatra, carrying soil in 7500 urns from every corner of the country, will reach Delhi, the country's capital. Also onboard are saplings from different parts of the country. Amrit Vatika will be built near the National War Memorial by fusing the soil and saplings that would arrive in 7500 urns. This Amrit Vatika will also become a grand symbol of Ek Bharat Shresth Bharat. I had talked about "Panch Prana" for the next 25 years of Amrit-kal, from Red Fort last year. By participating in the Meri Mati Mera Desh campaign, we will also take an oath to fulfil these "five resolves".'

Addressing this particular concern and its effective resolution through the medium of the radio show, eminent scholar, historian, actor and filmmaker, **Dr Chandraprakash Dwivedi** says, 'I remember that the *Mann Ki Baat* programme began from the day of Vijayadashmi in 2014. We use the phrase *Mann Ki Baat* regularly in our daily conversations, but as soon as the Prime Minister used the phrase *Mann Ki Baat*, the entire meaning transformed. For the first time, the Prime Minister of India used radio as a medium to communicate with the people of the nation directly. We all know that Doordarshan reaches all parts of the country, but radios reach is even further than that. Radio reaches almost 90 per cent of the population of India. To use this platform for connecting with the people living in remote rural areas of the country to convey his message, to talk about India, to talk about the issues of the people, to talk about the solutions regarding the problems faced by the people; this was a wonderful experiment by the Prime Minister.'

In India, a large part of our history was lost to the whims and fancies of a select few. An entire era was lost; nobody remembered it, no one appreciated it, no one spoke of those times, and no one mentioned those people. They were the unsung heroes, and despite their supreme sacrifice, they were 'unwept, unsung and unhonoured'. *Mann Ki Baat* changed all that, one hero at a time.

Congratulating the country right after Republic Day in Episode 52, Prime Minister Modi said,

> 'This great land, India, has given birth to innumerable great men, men whose deeds for the sake for humanity have been extraordinary, truly unforgettable. Our country is Bahuratna Vasundhara, the land of myriad gems. One among them was Netaji Subash Chandra Bose. On 23 January, the country celebrated the birth anniversary of Netaji in an uncommon, special manner. On this occasion, I was fortunate to get an opportunity to inaugurate a museum dedicated to heroes who fought in India's freedom struggle ... Every inch and every brick of these museums is redolent with the fragrance of our glorious history. Tales of valour of the heroes of our freedom struggle emanating from every nook and corner of these museums inspire us to delve deeper into our history.'

In fact, the year 2014 served as a pivotal moment in the history of our country. History is not being rewritten but through the agency of the radio programme, it is being retold to include those who were missed, those who were forgotten and those who were diminished.

Prime Minister Narendra Modi has often talked about the people and the events that were forgotten. *Mann Ki Baat* has brought a change in the way we look at our unsung heroes.

LEST WE FORGET . . .

'जननी जन्मभूखमश्च स्वगाघदखप गरीयसी' is a quote from the Ramayana. It means 'Mother and Motherland are superior to any heaven.'

Those who fought for the country and laid life for the honour of the country are to be worshipped, but the history of the valiant has often been lost to the sands of time, and to our ignorance and unfamiliarity. Take one such example: the Prime Minister often speaks about Lachit Borphukan, the legendary Ahom General who fought the Mughal Army and helped in defeating them in the battle of Saraighat. Not much was known about this son of the soil, but the Prime Minister set the ball rolling. At the closing ceremony of the year-long celebrations marking the 400th birth anniversary of Lachit Borphukan, in Delhi, Prime Minister Modi said, 'New India is rectifying the mistakes of past decades and honouring its unsung heroes.' The intent of the Prime Minister to celebrate our heroes across the length and breadth of India found great resonance with the listeners. In Episode 70, he hailed a listener from Bihar who had contacted him through the NaMo app,

> 'Jai Ram Viplava, a resident of Munger, has written to me about the Tarapur Martyr Day. On the 15 February 1932, the Britishers mercilessly killed several brave young patriots. Their only crime was that they were raising the slogan of "Vande Mataram" and "Bharat Mata Ki Jai". I bow to those martyrs and remember their courage with reverence.'

Likewise, requesting all his young friends to write about our freedom fighters, in as many languages as possible, he often hails the contribution of Rani Gaidinliu of Nagaland, Rani Chenamma of Kittur, Rani Lakshmibai of Jhansi and Bhagwan Birsa Munda. All their stories reverberate through time and echo far and wide. They find repeated mentions in the speeches of the Prime Minister and various episodes of *Mann Ki Baat*. History in India is no longer Delhi-centric, and the stories of heroes of India are revered across India.

In a letter discussed during Episode 53, a keen listener had written about Birsa Mundaji and Jamsetji Tata bringing laurels to the state of Jharkhand. The Prime Minister picked up from there and further added that Bhagwan Birsa Munda made us aware of our existence and identity, and the farsighted Jamsetji Tata created great institutions for the country. He compared and contrasted the two to drive home the point of celebrating the identity of being Indian.

Similarly, in Episode 91, he remembers Tirot Sing, chief of the Khasi tribe. The story of Tirot Sing is awe-inspiring. He fought with native weapons, such as a sword and shield. He was shot at by the British and had to hide in a cave and tend to his wounds. He was finally captured by the British in January 1833 and deported to Dhaka where he breathed his last in 1835. Tirot Singh fiercely opposed the British conspiracy to control the Khasi Hills and destroy our culture. The contribution of these warriors to the fight for Indian independence is awe-inspiring.

OUR UNSUNG HEROES

Maine vachan diya bharat maa ko
Tera sheesh nahi jhukne dunga.

– Excerpt from the Poem by Prime Minister Modi

Narendra Modi not only takes inspiration from these national heroes, he urges the future generations to read about them and inculcate the spirit of nationalism. He elucidated in Episode 68 of the show,

> 'The more my young friends learn about Sri Aurobindo, the more they will learn about themselves, enriching themselves. The state of inner consciousness in which you are, where you are engaged in trying to achieve the many resolves, amid all this you will always find a new inspiration in Sri Aurobindo; you will find him showing you a new path. Just as at present when we are moving forward with the campaign "Vocal for Local", Sri Aurobindo's philosophy of Swadeshi shows us the path,'

The venerable mentions of brave Indian warriors further continued when he honoured the legendary hero Alluri Sitarama Raju, by unveiling his 30 ft statute in Bhimavaram, West Godavari, in July 2022.

Prime Minister Modi said,

> 'Freedom struggle is not just a history of a few years, few areas, or of a few people.'

He added that he was fortunate to tread on the sacred land where Sitarama Raju had fought many a valiant battle against the British and laid down his life at the young age of about 27 years.

The beauty of the way our Prime Minister conveys his own impassioned tribute to our heroes is that he does not follow a prescribed syllabus when he speaks about them. From legends to folklores, he takes everything into account, trying not to leave anyone behind in this great revolution of revisiting our actual history.

Dr Chandraprakash Dwivedi, who was the screenwriter for the popular Indian TV show *Chanakya*, says, 'Whenever the Prime Minister mentions an "unsung hero" from some remote area who has not been noticed by the people and who does not get any coverage in the mainstream media, it shows how organised the entire administration of the Prime Minister is. And this would not be possible if the Prime Minister himself does not gather information about people from across the nation. For instance, just recently he talked about the late Bismillah Khan sahib.

'This changes the context as now people start acknowledging the unsung heroes who are working for social development. The Prime Minister talks about both ordinary and extraordinary personalities, such as artists, sportspersons and weavers. When the name of any person is mentioned, not only does the entire nation get to know about them, but the life of that person also witnesses positive change. The Prime Minister himself says that it was an ordinary gesture that resulted in extraordinary changes in the nation.

'It gives me immense pleasure to see the Prime Minister assume the role of an elder person in the family. Sometimes he assumes the role of a father, sometimes of a grandfather and sometimes of a friend. He teaches you that scoring good marks in examinations is not a big deal. I remember one of his statements: "It is not important that life should be successful, what matters is that life should be meaningful." I understood the meaning of this very well. I tell my friends that earlier I used to think differently–that we want to be successful in our lives and we had different criteria for success, like being materialistically prosperous and having a big house. However, this one sentence from the Prime Minister made me and millions of people think about what is successful and what is meaningful.'

Finding meaning in the small gestures of our leader is an important aspect of the radio show. In our growing-up years, we have at times ignored and at times missed the contributions made by inspiring heroes, the pillars on which our nation stands. The Prime Minister often mentions important dates such as birth and death anniversaries; this he does to make us aware of the historical heroes. His intention is not just knowledge dispensation but also character building. His true appreciation of the highest sacrifices made by our soldiers has been mentioned incessantly in the programme. This conscious effort on the part of our Prime Minister has been praised by many.

Filmmaker **Ashoke Pandit** said, 'In Episode 66 of *Mann Ki Baat* relayed in September 2020, the PM said about Veer Bhagat Singh, "Bhagat Singh, along with his revolutionary friends, without caring for their own selves, carried out such daring acts, which had a huge bearing on the country attaining freedom. Another appealing aspect of Shahid Veer Bhagat Singh's life is that he appreciated the importance of teamwork. Be it his devotion towards Lala Lajpat Rai or his camaraderie with fellow revolutionaries such as Chandra Shekhar Azad, Sukhdev and Rajguru, amongst others, personal accolades were of no importance to him. He had a single mission for as long as he lived and he sacrificed his life for that mission. That mission was to free India of injustice and British rule.'

A unique feature of *Mann Ki Baat* is that our Prime Minister often speaks about the soldiers of our armed forces who have time and again laid down their lives to protect the honour of their motherland with pride and regard.

Here the Prime Minister interweaves nationalism with teamwork. He not only appreciates the sacrifices made by revolutionaries, but he also stresses the nationalist fervour that was generated in the country, which is now being regenerated through him.

OF WRITERS AND PHILOSOPHERS

Mann Ki Baat is not only about the valiant heroes who died fighting for the country, it is also a movement where the Prime

Minister lauds the efforts of people who were instrumental in nation-building. His conversation does not miss out on the essence of the moral fabric, which is interwoven in the form of simple stories of such people.

In Episode 70, he spoke about the Valmiki Jayanti celebrations. He said,

> 'Maharishi Valmiki's lofty ideals continue to inspire millions of people and provide them strength. He is a beacon of great hope for millions of impoverished and Dalits, and instils hope and trust in them.'

The objective was to communicate and celebrate the ideals of Maharishi Valmiki. His qualities of positive thinking, the spirit of service and human dignity are encouraged to be adopted.

In Episode 52 of *Mann Ki Baat*, while sharing the news of the demise of Shri Shiva Kumar Swami of Tumakuru, Prime Minister Modi spoke about Jagadguru Basaveshwara, a 12th-century philosopher, poet and social reformer in the Shiva-focused Bhakti movement, saying that like Bhagwan Basaveshwar, 'Kayakave Kailas', meaning discharging one's duties with due diligence and perseverance, is akin to being in the abode of Bhagwan Shiva, that is, Kailash Dham, and Swamiji was very much inspired about this thought. It has been a conscious effort on the part of the Prime Minister to make people aware of the diligent discharge of duties.

The Prime Minister seems to have a natural flair for picking up the best qualities of those whom he mentions, and he stitches these qualities into a narrative that serves the purpose of overall nation-building.

In Episode 71 of *Mann Ki Baat,* released in February 2021, the Prime Minister shared a quote of **Sant Ravidas**: '*Ekai maati ke sab bhaande, sab ka ekau sirjanhaar, Ravidas vyapai ekai ghat bheetar, sab ko ekai ghadai kumhaar.*'

It means all of us are earthen vessels of one clay; all of us have been coiled and shaped by the One. Sant Ravidas spoke of the social ills that had plagued the country. Prime Minister Modi, while quoting Sant Ravi Das, envisions the self-same principles of equality which he shares as a part of the social revolution.

REFORMING OUR SOCIAL LANDSCAPE

Mann Ki Baat also serves as a stage to share the immense contribution of social and political reformers who ensured that the freedom we got was duly preserved. In Episode 53, Prime Minister Modi spoke about Moraraji Desai, our former Prime Minister. He said,

> 'Morarji Desai was born on 29 February. All of you know that this day comes just once in four years. A simple, peace-loving personality, Morarji Bhai was one of the most disciplined leaders. In independent India, the record of presenting the budget the maximum number of times is held by Morarji Bhai Desai. Morarji Desai steered the course of the country through some difficult times when the very democratic fabric of the country was under a threat. To save democracy, Morarji Desai flung himself into the movement against the imposition of Emergency. For this, he had to pay a heavy price in his old age. The government of that time arrested and incarcerated him. But when the Janata Party won the general elections in 1977, he became the Prime Minister of the country. During his tenure, the 44th constitutional

amendment was introduced. This was important because the 42nd amendment, which was brought during the Emergency and curtailed the powers of the Supreme Court and implemented provisions that stood to violate our democratic values, was struck down. The 44th amendment made it mandatory that the proceedings of Parliament and Legislative Assemblies were made public through the newspapers. This amendment restored certain powers of the Supreme Court and declared that the fundamental rights granted under Articles 20 and 21 of the Constitution could not be abrogated during the Emergency.’

Even though Morarji Desai was the Prime Minister of India, not many people remember him as a savior of democratic principles in India.

On another occasion, Prime Minister Modi spoke about Pandit Deendayal Upadhyaya whose birth anniversary coincided with the transmission of *Mann Ki Baat* on 25th September 2022. The Prime Minister said,

> ‘Deendayal Upadhyaya-ji was a brilliant humanist, thinker, and a great son of the country. The more the youth of any country take pride in their identity and honour, the more their original ideas and philosophies attract them.’

COUNTLESS STORIES AND ENDLESS CONTRIBUTIONS

The Prime Minister’s use of storytelling to praise our unsung heroes makes it a delight for us as listeners. There are countless stories, and those countless stories have endless contributions. In Episode 56, the nation heard the story of Nandalal Bose whose artwork adorns our Constitution and lends to it a new, unique identity. Prime Minister Modi said, 'The very commitment and reverence of Nandalal Bose has made him, along with the Constitution, immortal.' In his address in Episode 71, he also remembered Dr Salim Ali who did exceptional work in the field of bird-watching.

Unsung heroes not only include people who have sacrificed their lives for the country but also common people who make it their daily mission to contribute to society. Such people do not care for laurels and applause but work constantly towards their mission of bringing positive change to the country.

In Episode 72 of *Mann Ki Baat*, Prime Minister Modi spoke of Amresh Samant, an engineer who planted micro-forests which are protecting many villages, and Marimuthu Yoganathan, a bus conductor in Coimbatore, Tamil Nadu, who while issuing tickets to the passengers of his bus also gives a sapling free of cost. He further talks of Sikari Tissau of the Karbi Anglong district in Assam who has been documenting the Karbi language for the last 20 years. Then, he spoke of Bijay Kumar Kabiji who toiled for 12 years for a 25-acre mangrove forest on the outskirts of the village. A single person who can change the way society functions is a motivation for us. The idea of the programme was to awaken the conscience of the nation to contribute selflessly towards society.

In Episode 85 of *Mann Ki Baat*, the Prime Minister spoke of Padma Awards. He said,

> 'There are many names among the recipients of Padma Awards, about whom very few people know. These are the unsung heroes of our country, who have done extraordinary deeds in ordinary circumstances.'

People have started calling the Padma Awards People's awards. Common people who are doing yeoman service for the country are now being appreciated. This is now a ritual. Conferring the Padma honour on unsung heroes has made us realise that real hero-worship is when common people contributing to society are lauded.

In Episode 51 of *Mann Ki Baat*, Prime Minister Modi mentioned Dr Jayachandran, who was called 'Makkal Maaruthuvar'. He said,

> 'Dr Jayachandran was known for his efforts towards making the most economical treatment possible available to the poor. People tell us that he would be ever ready and eager when it came to the treatment of patients. In the case of elderly patients, he would even bear the cost of their travel. On the betterindia.com website, I have read about many of his endeavours that serve as an inspiration to society.'

In the same episode, the Prime Minister also spoke about Sulagitti Narasamma from Karnataka. Sulagitti Narsamma was a midwife, who aided pregnant women during childbirth. In Karnataka, especially in remote places, thousands of women availed her services. She too was honoured with a Padma Shri.

Such tales may not be classified as tales of valour but they appreciate the efforts of people who bring about a societal change. Be it our soldiers or our freedom fighters. Kathak exponent **Shovana Narayan** spoke about *Mann Ki Baat* at the completion of the 100th episode. She said, 'It has become a tool for awakening and knowledge sharing.' The Padma Awards, according to her, have changed a lot in recent times and now people from villages and the four corners of India who have contributed immensely to the social and economic upliftment of the country find themselves being mentioned in the radio programme. Prime Minister Modi has brought to the forefront the contribution of such people who previously were not spoken about.

In Episode 65, the Prime Minister spoke about the importance of telling our students the tales of past. He said,

> 'It is imperative for today's students to remain familiar with the heroes of our freedom struggle. Only then can students get apprised about the history of our freedom struggle.'

Here the Prime Minister aims to sensitise the new generation and make them aware of our collective past. It is expected that the architects and builders of new India have their roots intact. The overarching concept is to revise, remind and revive the tales of our heroes so they no longer remain unsung. It is to ensure that the new generation does not forget to respect, revere and regard the contributions of those men and women who helped create the India we have now.

In Episode 81, Prime Minister Modi said, 'There is another interesting information–more than 5,000 upcoming writers are searching for tales of the struggle for freedom.' He spoke of how the youth of India has taken the lead in writing about the unsung heroes of the freedom struggle whose names do not appear on the pages of history and who were not even discussed during the last 75 years. He said,

> 'I appeal to all the listeners; I appeal to all those connected with the field of education. You, too, should motivate the youth. You, too, should come forward. It is my firm belief that during the Amrit Mahotsav of Independence, the people who are writing history will make history as well.'

The information is encouraging, it is an attempt to call on the youth and people at large to contribute to bringing forth the stories of unsung heroes. To learn and relearn, to sing and to tell the poems and stories of valour.

JAN BHAGIDAARI FOR OUR UNSUNG HEROES

The Prime Minister speaks a lot about the 'Amrit Kaal' in *Mann Ki Baat*. He said in Episode 78,

> 'The country has also set many collective goals in the Amrit Mahotsav. Like, we have to revive the history related to our freedom fighters by remembering them,'

A disorder, disruption and disarray has happened in the way history is being read and retold, in the way heroes are recognised, honoured and celebrated. *Mann Ki Baat* has been instrumental in creating an awareness in the masses to be mindful of our past, thankful for our present, and hopeful for our future.

16

Small Details That Make India Big and Beautiful

> 'The world was not cognizant that India has an inherent potential of strong culture and values, a bond of thoughts deeply embedded in mind and soul; and that is—India is a mother of all democracy.'
>
> – Prime Minister Narendra Modi

In March 2021, through the medium of the seminal Episode 75, Prime Minister Modi readily expressed how overwhelmed he was with the phenomenal experience it had been to watch our society, learn its overtly minor but remarkable achievements more minutely and realise our full potential and strength. During the preceding Episode 76, he said one had gone through a multitude of subjects in *Mann Ki Baat*. At times, there was a reference to rivers or to the peaks of the Himalayas or to matters pertaining to deserts; sometimes, the idea was to soak in innumerable stories of service to humanity; in some episodes, he had touched upon inventions in technology and in others, he had shared the story of an experience of doing something novel in an unknown corner.

All of these, he said, had transported him into a space of positivity and optimism for the future.

> 'You see, whether it's about sanitation or a discussion on conserving our heritage [or a] reference to making toys, what is it that was not there? Perhaps the sheer number of topics that we touched upon would turn out to be countless. During all this, from time to time, we paid tributes to great luminaries whose contribution to the building of India has been unparalleled; we learnt about them. We also spoke on many global matters; we've tried to derive inspiration from them. There were many points that you told me; you gave me many ideas. In a way, in this "Vichar Yatra", journey of thought and idea, we kept walking together, connecting and adding something new throughout.'

Interestingly, Prime Minister Modi has been a strong proponent of things that perhaps none of his predecessors would even have the time to think about, let alone enact.

> 'My dear countrymen, World Sparrow Day was celebrated just a few days ago. Sparrow, that is, goraiya, [which] at places is also known as chakali, chimni or ghanchirika. Earlier, goraiya would be found chirping on the boundaries of the walls of our houses or the neighbouring trees. Today, we are required to make efforts to save it. My friend hailing from Benaras, Indrapal Singh Batra has initiated a novel effort in this direction that I would like to certainly tell to the listeners of *Mann Ki Baat*. He has turned his own house into a home for the goraiya.'

Praising Batra, the Prime Minister told us that the former had got wooden nests made in his house where the goraiya could dwell easily. As a result, many homes in Benaras joined in this campaign, which in turn led to the creation of a wonderful natural environment in the houses. By discussing it, the PM encouraged all of us to make efforts, big and small, for the conservation and protection of nature, environment, animals and birds.

> 'When there are no major challenges to face in one's life, the best of one's personality also fails to surface—hence always keep on challenging yourselves.'

It was through *Mann Ki Baat* that we got to know of many things that would normally escape our attention. In December 2020, ahead of the solemn occasion of Republic Day, the Prime Minister told us about *Gaganyaan,* for instance. Our pledge to take an Indian into space through the Gaganyaan mission was emphasised by him as a historic achievement in the field of science and technology for India in the 21st century. He introduced us to the four candidates who have been selected as astronauts for this mission. All of them are pilots of the Indian Air Force who symbolise India's skill, talent, ability, courage and dreams. 'Our four friends are about to go to Russia in a few days for their training. I am confident that this would script another golden chapter in India–Russia friendship and cooperation. They will be trained for over a year. After that, the responsibility of carrying the hopes and aspirations of the nation and soaring into space will rest on the shoulders of one of them.' As of March 2023, the astronauts selected for *Gaganyaan* mission had completed the first semester of crew training comprising 39 weeks of training activities. The *Gaganyaan* project envisages a demonstration of the capability of human space flight by launching the selected astronauts into an orbit of 400 km for three days. The flight will culminate with their landing in Indian waters.

Praising the all-encompassing reach of the programme, aeconomist **Bibek Debroy** said, 'There are certain principles on which the Prime Minister has built his philosophy of governance, and these are in terms of two standard expressions: ease of living and ease of doing business. Almost every initiative that you can think of—and there are several of those—is either under the umbrella of ease of living or ease of doing business. In addition, there is an emphasis on the environment, Mission LiFE being an example. India was the first country to emphasise on the use of renewable energy, particularly solar energy, to this extent. There has been a great deal of digital success which enabled us to withstand the effects of COVID-19 much better. These are themes that will occur during G20 meetings [since] India is now the president of the G20. I think future episodes of *Mann Ki Baat* will continue to emphasise on Sabka Prayas, the environment, Mission LiFE, making India a more liveable country, the Zero Defect Zero Effect scheme and so on.'

In Episode 66 of the show, the Prime Minister had spoken of an entirely different but equally awe-inspiring achievement. During the COVID-19 pandemic, when everyone was isolated in their homes and when two-yard social distancing had become imperative, families had a chance to bond. Ensuring that every moment is filled with joy when one is spending so much time together is a challenge, yet adherence to certain values and traditions—the Sanskar Sarita—brought many families closer. This is manifested in the art of storytelling. The Prime Minister reminded us of the time when every family invariably had an elderly member who would tell stories, infusing a new inspiration, a new energy in the household. He said that while we may not realise it, there is tremendous significance in the mores and conventions set by our ancestors through the art of storytelling.

> 'Stories express and bring to the fore the creative and sensitive facets of human beings. If the power of stories is to be felt, one has to just watch a mother telling a story to her little one either to lull her to sleep or while feeding her a morsel. I spent a major part of my life as a parivrajak, an ascetic. Wayfaring was my life. Every day it used to be a new place with new people, new families. But whenever I visited a family, I would make it a point to speak to the children. At times, I would playfully ask them to tell me a story. Surprisingly, they would reply saying, 'No uncle ... not a story ... We'll tell you a joke!'

India has had a rich tradition of storytelling or Qissagoi, and proud denizens of the land have nurtured the tradition of *Hitopadesha* and *Panchtantra* in which, through an imaginary world of animals, birds and fairies woven into stories, lessons on prudence and wisdom are expounded easily. Similarly, the tradition of 'katha' has many manifestations in India. The ancient form of religious storytelling, Kathakalakshepam, where myriad folk tales are presented is one such art form in Tamil Nadu and Kerala; Villu Paatu, which comprises a fascinating confluence of story and music and combines with a vibrant tradition of Kathputli, that is, puppetry, is another such. The Prime Minister mentioned a website, *Gathastory.in*, run by Amar Vyas, along with other colleagues. After completing his MBA from IIM Ahmedabad, Amar Vyar went abroad but later returned to India and now lives in Bengaluru. Like him, Vaishali Vyawahare Deshpande is also making stories popular in Marathi. Srividya

Veer Raghavan of Chennai is also engaged in popularising and disseminating stories related to our culture, while two websites named Kathalaya by Geeta Ramanujan and The Indian Story Telling Network are also doing commendable work in this field, we were told. During the show, the Prime Minister even spoke to Aparna Athare and other members of the Bengaluru Storytelling Society who shared their experiences enthusiastically. 'I got a chance to educate thousands of children through the medium of stories. And this story I was referring to ... I had heard it from my grandmother. But when I saw the joy on the children's faces while listening to the story, what do I say to you ... Such smiles, so much happiness there ... and that was the moment I decided that storytelling would be a goal of my life, sir,' revealed Athare.

Episode 67 took listeners on a journey into spirituality, yoga and ayurveda, practices which have attracted the whole world. Many of our indigenous sports that also attract attention the world over were mentioned by the Prime Minister. For instance, Mallakhambh is gaining popularity in many countries. 'When Chinmay Patankar and Pragya Patankar decided to teach Mallakhambh out of their home in America, little did they know how successful it would be. Mallakhambh training centres are running at many locations across America. A large number of American youth are joining and learning Mallakhambh. Be it Germany, Poland or Malaysia, Mallakhambh is becoming popular in around 20 other countries.'

The Prime Minister also spoke of how our country has many forms of martial arts that he encouraged his young friends to know more about.

One such unique learning story was that of a person with a novel passion, that of sharing the joys of reading and writing with others. Pon Mariyappan from Thoothukudi, also known as the Pearl City, runs a hair salon but he has converted a small portion of his salon into a library. He said,

> ‘If a customer, while waiting for his turn, reads something from the library and writes about it, Pon Marriyappan, offers him a discount. Isn’t that interesting?’

FROM CHERRY BLOSSOMS TO KASHMIRI SAFFRON, BHARAT HAS IT ALL

In Episode 68, the Prime Minister mentioned yet another interesting project. He told us about an island named Svalbard in the north of Norway where invaluable heritage data has been archived and stored so that no disaster, natural or manmade, can affect it. It is a matter of pride that the heritage of Ajanta caves is also being digitised and preserved as part of this project. A full view of the caves of Ajanta shall be on display. Along with the digitised and restored paintings, it will also have important documents and quotes related to them. Taking us from Norway to the beautiful Meghalaya, he spoke of how pictures of cherry blossoms had gone viral on the internet.

> ‘You might be thinking that when I am referring to cherry blossoms I am talking about Japan’s distinct identity, but it’s not so. These are not pictures of Japan. These are pictures of Shillong in Meghalaya. These cherry blossoms have further enhanced the beauty of Meghalaya.’

He reminded that 12 November marked the commencement of the 125th birth anniversary celebrations of Dr Sálim Ali, an ornithologist who had done illustrious work in the field of birdwatching. This has also attracted bird watchers of the world towards India. The PM said,

> ‘I have always been an ardent admirer of people who are fond of bird watching. With utmost patience, for hours together from morn to dusk, they can do bird watching, enjoying the scenic beauty of nature; they also keep passing on the knowledge gained to us. In India too, many bird watching societies are active. You too should connect yourselves with this subject. Amid the hectic routine of my life, recently in Kevadia, I also got a memorable opportunity to spend time with birds. Time spent among birds will bond you closer to nature, it will also inspire you towards the environment.’

Praising the Prime Minister's small, sweet gestures, **Anand Mahindra** tweeted, ‘You'd never expect to hear a leader in a national address advise small acts of kindness in the summer heat. @PMOIndia redefining leadership.’

In Episode 69, the PM introduced the Kashmiri saffron. Saffron has been associated with Kashmir for centuries. Kashmiri saffron is mainly grown in places like Pulwama, Budgam and Kishtwar. In May 2020, Kashmiri saffron was given a geographical indication (GI) tag. Through this, a step was taken towards making Kashmiri saffron a globally popular brand. Kashmiri saffron is globally famous as a spice that has many medicinal properties. It has a strong aroma and its colour is deep. Moreover, its threads are long and thick, which enhances its medicinal value. More importantly, it represents the rich cultural heritage of Jammu and Kashmir. Strengthening the efforts to build an Atmanirbhar Bharat, the Prime Minister mentioned Abdul Majeed Wani, a resident of Shar area of Tral in Pulwama who is selling his GI-tagged saffron with the help of the National Saffron Mission at the Trading Centre in Pampore through e-trading. It is because of *Mann Ki Baat* that we know that the next time we decide to buy saffron, we should think of doing so from Kashmir. The Prime Minister said,

> 'The warmth of Kashmiri people is such that it imparts a unique, distinct flavour to the saffron.'

When it comes to unearthing lesser-known facts about India and Indians, the radio show is all encompassing. Take Episode 70, where we learnt how the protection of environment can open avenues of income. The Prime Minister shared,

> 'For centuries, a type of paper called Mon Shugu has been made in a hilly region of Arunachal Pradesh. The locals here make the paper from the bark of a plant named Shugu Sheng, hence trees do not have to be cut to make it. Besides, no chemical is used in making this paper, thus it is safe for the environment and for health too. There was a time when the paper was exported, but with modern techniques, large amount of paper started getting made and the local art was pushed to the brink of closure. Now, a local social worker, Gombu, has made an effort to rejuvenate this art. This is also giving employment to tribal brothers and sisters there.'

He spoke also of news from Kottayam, Kerala that makes us realise our responsibilities. A divyang, NS Rajappan is incapable of walking, but this has not affected his commitment to cleanliness. For the past several years, he has been going by boat into Lake Vembanad and taking out the plastic bottles thrown into it by people. The Prime Minister made us think of how great Rajappa's initiative towards cleanliness and protecting the environment is. Taking inspiration from Rajappan, we too should, wherever possible, make our contribution towards these ends.

Taking us on a journey to San Francisco, the Prime Minister also gave due credit to the four women pilots from India who took command of a non-stop flight from San Francisco in the US to Bengaluru in India. Travelling more than 10,000 kilometres, the flight ferried more than 250 passengers to India. He also drew our attention to the fact that on the 26 January parade, two women officers of the Indian Air Force created history. He didn't pause there; instead, the Prime Minister took us to Jabalpur in Madhya Pradesh where some tribal women working in a rice mill on daily wages collectively started their own rice mill. One of them, Meena Rahangadale, formed a self-help group by bringing together all the women and raising capital from their savings. Under the aegis of Aajeevika mission, the shortfall was sourced as a loan from the bank. The PM said:

> 'Now see, these tribal sisters bought the same rice mill in which they once worked. Today, they are running their own rice mill. Within this very period, this mill has also earned a profit of about Rs 3 lakh. With this profit, Meena-ji and her colleagues are arranging to repay the bank loan and then seeking avenues to expand their business. Such amazing efforts have taken place in every corner of the country to counter whatever circumstances COVID-19 created,'

FROM SANSKRIT TO *SANSKRITI*

Episode 81 hearkens to the period of Amrit Mahotsav and highlights a campaign to disseminate the untold stories of the history of freedom. For this, more than 13,000 people registered in 14 different languages. Significantly, a host of NRIs from more than 20 countries also expressed their wish to join this campaign.

Speaking of the growing global interest in Indian culture, the Prime Minister mentioned Serbian scholar, Dr Momir Nikich, who has compiled a bilingual Sanskrit–Serbian Dictionary. More than 70,000 Sanskrit words included in this dictionary have been translated into Serbian language. It was endearing to learn that Dr Nikich learnt Sanskrit language at the age of 70 by reading the articles of Mahatma Gandhi. The Prime Minister also mentioned 93-year-old Professor J. Gendedharam of Mongolia who, in the last four decades, has translated about 40 ancient Indian texts, epics and compositions into Mongolian language. From there, he brought us back to Goa, where the efforts of Sagar Mule in reviving the ancient tradition of Kaavi paintings were lauded.

The Prime Minister told the listeners,

> ‘The Kaavi form of painting covers the ancient history of India in itself; “Kaava” means red soil. In ancient times, red clay was used in this art. During the Portuguese rule in Goa, the people who migrated from there introduced the people of other states to this wonderful painting form. With the passage of time, this painting was on the verge of being forgotten. But Sagar Mule-ji has infused a new lease of life to this art.’

In February 2021, the endeavour of Babita Rajput of the village of Agrotha in Madhya Pradesh was praised by the Prime Minister. Close to her village, there had once been very large lake which had dried up. She mobilised the women of the village and built a canal to bring water to the lake. Through this canal, rainwater started flowing directly into the lake. Now it remains filled with water. Similarly, Jagdish Kuniyal of Uttarakhand decided to solve the water crisis through tree plantation. Along with fellow villagers, he planted thousands of trees over the entire area.

FROM LESSER KNOWN TO WELL-LOVED HEROES

About the extraordinary impact of ordinary facts that the Prime Minister presents, **Bibek Debroy** says, 'Earlier I worked in NITI Aayog and now I am Chairman of Economic Advisory to the Council of Prime Minister. What has struck me is the moment you move away from an elite crowd, *Mann Ki Baat* resonates even more deeply. That is why *Mann Ki Baat* is such a great success. There have been isolated instances when a Prime Minister has spoken to the country, but those have generally been in emergencies or when a national catastrophe has struck. I don't think a Prime Minister has ever, anywhere in the world, continuously talked to the citizens, sharing their thoughts and problems, or asking for suggestions. And that's the reason *Mann Ki Baat* is such a great success. It shows governance involving citizens: Sabka Prayas.'

In Episode 75, Bijay Kumar Kabiji from Kendrapada on Odisha's sea coast where high tides and cyclone cause havoc at times, was mentioned. Bijoy felt that if anything can stop this environmental devastation, it is only nature. Toiling for 12 years, he raised a 25-acre mangrove forest on the outskirts of the village towards the sea. Today, this forest is protecting this village. An engineer, Amresh Samant, has done similar work in the Paradip district of Odisha by planting micro-forests, which are protecting many villages today. Similarly, we heard of Marimuthu Yoganathan who works as a bus conductor in Coimbatore, Tamil Nadu and while issuing tickets to the passengers of his bus also gives them a sapling free of cost. In this way, he has helped plant innumerable trees.

In November 2021, the Prime Minister observed how on social media the picture of a flying boat in Meghalaya had become viral. This boat, which seems to be floating in the air, is actually moving on the river water. The water of the river is so clear that we can see its bed and the boat seems to be floating in the air. A few months before this, the Prime Minister hailed all those who perform Kalpvaas on the banks of River Ganga or other rivers for an entire month. This tradition of remembering rivers and paying homage to them is inherent to Indian culture, just like bathing early morning is akin to a cerebral pilgrimage.

There are many states in our country, and there are many areas where people have preserved the colours of their natural heritage. These people have made a conscious effort to live in harmony with nature, and their efforts have been recognised in *Mann Ki Baat*. Episode 59 introduced Ramesh Sharma from Nagaon who made us aware of the Brahmaputra Pushkar held between 4 and 16 November, with people from all corners of the country participating.

The Prime Minister said,

> 'My dear countrymen, Pushkaram, Pushkaraalu, Pushkaraha—have you ever heard these terms? These are the different names for festivals organised for 12 different rivers across the country. One river every year, which means it would recur near that particular river after 12 years, and this festival is held sequentially a near 12 different rivers spread across the country. It lasts for 12 long days. Just like the Kumbh festival, this festival also encourages the concept of national unity. It echoes the philosophy of Ek Bharat Shreshtha Bharat (One India Best India). Pushkaram is a festival in which the greatness of the river, the glory of the

river, the importance of the river in our lives—all these are brought forth.'

In Episode 63, Kamegowda-ji from Karnataka, an ordinary 85-year-old farmer possessing an extraordinary personality was introduced by the Prime Minister. He beamed,

'You will be surprised to know that an octogenarian like Kamegowda-ji has dug 16 ponds till now through his hard work and the sweat of his brow. It is possible that the ponds he has constructed may not be very big but then his effort is huge. Today, the entire area has got a new lease of life on account of these ponds.'

In another edition the same year, he spoke of a heart-touching effort at Coimbatore in Tamil Nādu.

'We have seen wheelchairs for humans, but daughter Gayatri in Coimbatore, along with her father, made a wheelchair for a suffering dog. This sensitivity is inspiring and can happen only when a person is filled with kindness and compassion towards all life forms. In Delhi NCR and other cities of the country, in winters, many people are doing a lot for the care of shelterless animals. They arrange for food, water, sweaters and even beds for those animals. Some people arrange food for hundreds of such animals every day. Such efforts should be commended.'

Prime Minister Modi went on to praise several noble efforts, including one in Kaushambi, Uttar Pradesh, where prison inmates are making covers from old and torn blankets to protect cows from the cold. Besides Kaushambi, these blankets are collected from jails of other districts and then they are sewn and sent to cow shelters. He encouraged us, his listeners, to commend such acts of care and imbibe a sense of service to others.

In Episode 23, the Prime Minister spoke of Bharat Ratna Mother Teresa as an exemplary beacon of hope. She was canonised—accorded sainthood on 4 September 2016—because of her selfless service. The PM said,

> 'Though Mother Teresa was born in Albania, and her mother tongue was not English, she transformed her life and did everything to be able to serve the poor. It is quite natural for us Indians to feel proud of her.'

NOBLE ACTS STRENGTHEN THE SENSITIVITY OF THE SOCIETY

In Episode 70, Prime Minister Modi shared how happy he had felt upon reading about a local vegetable market in Boinpalli of Hyderabad deciding that it will not throw away the leftover vegetables but would instead generate electricity from them. 'You may have hardly heard of generating electricity from waste vegetables—this is the power of innovation. Today, in the Boinpalli vegetable market, wealth is getting created from what was once a waste. Nearly 10 tonnes of waste is collected daily, which is collected in a plant where 500-units of electricity are generated every day, along with 30 kilos of bio fuel. The vegetable market is illuminated with this electricity and the bio fuel that is generated is used to cook food in the market canteen—isn't it a wonderful effort!'

Similarly, praising the innovative thinking of farmers across the country in another episode, he mentioned awareness around chia seeds. The Prime Minister told us that Harishchandra of Barabanki in UP had begun the farming of chia seeds. This was a huge step towards augmenting his income and contributing to the self-reliant India campaign. The Prime Minister also mentioned Murugesan from Madurai who has made a machine that uses the waste of bananas to make ropes. This is eco-friendly and good for waste management, while simultaneously being a source of additional income for farmers. In fact, many experiments of creating wealth from agricultural waste are being run successfully in the country. It is because of programmes like *Mann Ki Baat* that we know of them.

In Episode 75, he talked about Chalkhal, a method that involves digging a big pit to collect water. Bharti, a farmer from the hills of Ufrainkhal in Pauri Garhwal, Uttarakhand, went ahead and got more than 30,000 such water tanks constructed. This monumental work of his is inspiring many people.

From villages to urban areas to foreign lands, *Mann Ki Baat* hasn't failed to touch upon the contributions of common citizens. Take the case of Mayur Patil, who, along with his friends in 2017, developed pollution-reducing technology for the buses of the Regional Transport Corporation. Their innovative endeavour had managed to reduce emissions by 40 per cent in these buses.

In Episode 57, the Prime Minister mentioned how Sister Mariam Thresia worked for the good of humanity in her short lifespan of 50 years and became a noble example worthy of emulation. The Prime Minister said,

> 'It is a matter of pride for every Indian that, on 13 October 2019, His Holiness Pope Francis will declare Sister Mariam Thresia a saint. Whatever task Sister Mariam Thresia undertook and accomplished, she did so with utmost dedication and devotion. She rendered service in the fields of education and social service. She had built many schools,

> hostels and orphanages and, throughout her life, remained devoted to this cause. She also founded the Congregation of the Sisters of the Holy Family, which continues to follow the path shown by her. I pay heartfelt tributes to Sister Mariam Thresia and congratulate the citizens of India for this achievement.'

When it comes to enumerating the lesser-known facts about our citizens, our nation or our past, Prime Minister Modi has been vociferous. Notably, he has also often expressed his heartfelt thanks to each and every listener of *Mann Ki Baat* for making it a success, enriching it and staying connected with it. Take the momentous Episode 100, where he repeated his firm faith:

> 'I would also like to express my gratitude to those who don the mantle of *Mann Ki Baat*—the people of India, people who have faith in India. All this has been possible only because of your inspiration and strength.' The vichar yatra that he called *Mann Ki Baat* is indeed all about unfurling uncommon facts and lauding small, unrelated but meaningful individual contributions consistently.'

17

Diaspora Relations That Transcend Boundaries

> 'The world is seeing India with a ray of hope and our diaspora can play a crucial role in further spreading it. The Indian community does not settle abroad to enter into politics or take a seat in the global politics. Wherever they go, they think and act towards benefit of the society.'
>
> – Prime Minister Narendra Modi

Vasudhaiva Kutumbakam—the world is a family—is not just a parable that the Prime Minister uses for platitudinal enunciation. From the very inception of *Mann Ki Baat* to the most recent episodes, where our pride at India's G-20 Presidency has been factored in, he has upheld the view that humanity and nobility as the predominant trait of our nation are at the uppermost niche of our foreign policy.

In January 2019, PM interlaced ancient African and Indian thoughts together to emphasise the universal unity of mankind through adages like *Ubuntu*—which means that 'I am what I am because of who we all are'—in Zulu and *Vasudhaiva Kutumbakam*, showing how aligned we are across mankind.

Over the years, people from India and USA have built upon each other's ideologies. The famous American author and philosopher, Henry David Thoreau, expounded on the concept of non-violence, which was further espoused across continents and practised by the Father of the Nation, Mahatma Gandhi. Thoreau's teachings came back to his own country when Martin Luther King Jr. emulated Mahatma Gandhi's methods in the American Civil Rights Movement. Mahatma Gandhi's vision is what inspired President Obama as well as Prime Minister Modi in their programmes of community organisation and the Swachh Bharat Mission respectively.

Not just our rich diasporic community—considered by the PM to be an important extension of the great Indian family—but even foreigners who have embraced and owned Indian culture have always been mentioned with pride on the radio show. One such incident is seen in the interaction between Prime Minister Modi and **Sedu Dembele**, a citizen of Mali. In Episode 66 an unfamiliar but warm voice said: 'Namaste, brothers and sisters, my name is Sedu Dembele. I am from Mali, a country in West Africa. I had the opportunity to attend the Kumbh Mela, the largest religious festival in India, in February. It is a matter of great pride for me. I felt good on being a part of Kumbh Mela and got to learn a lot about the culture of India by observing. I request that we be given the opportunity to visit India once again, so that we can learn more about India. Namaste!'

The PM responded by telling us that Sedu Dembele is a teacher in a public school in Kita, a town in Mali, and teaches English, music, painting and drawing. Mali, a large and landlocked country in West Africa, far away from India, has produced Dembele who is also called Hindustani Babu, and he takes great pride in being called so. Every Sunday afternoon, he presents an hour-long radio programme in Mali titled *Indian Frequency on Bollywood Songs*! He has been presenting it for the last 23 years. During the course of this programme, he renders his commentary in French as well as in Mali's lingua franca known as Bombara, and does it in quite a dramatic fashion. He has a deep-seated love for India. Another reason for his profound association with India is that he was also born on 15 August. The PM said,

> 'Sedu-ji has started another two-hour programme now at 9 pm every Sunday, in which he narrates the story of an entire Bollywood film in French and Bombara. Sometimes, while relating to an emotional scene, he, along with his listeners, cry together! Sedu-ji's father had introduced him to Indian culture. His father worked in a cinema theatre where Indian films were also played. On this 15th August, through a video in Hindi, he greeted the people of India on Independence Day. Today, his children sing the national anthem of India with great ease! You must watch both of these videos and feel their love for India. When Sedu-ji visited the Kumbh Mela, he was part of the delegation that I met. His passion for India, affection and love are indeed a matter of pride for all of us.'

Later, stressing on the spirit of unity as being integral to self-reliance, the PM said that the one who is rooted in the ground, stays firm during the course of the biggest of storms. Our unity across the seven seas is what makes India and Indian culture unique and resonant.

> 'The whole world is looking at India as a hub of investment, innovation and development.'

India has always been at the forefront of humanitarian efforts. In June 2015, through the medium of the show, the PM informed us how the world had seen India saving people from Yemen to Afghanistan. At that time, in the crisis of Nepal's worst earthquake, we promptly sent help to Nepal as well. When people wanted to open a bank account under the government's new scheme of Jan Dhan Yojana, we saw how people working in banks helped them to do so and connected millions of Indians to banks. All this is possible only because of the international imprint we have been able to create.

Even celebrations that are singularly Indian have a bigger universal appeal. In Episode 58 of the programme, the PM recited a shlok:

Shubham Karoti Kalyanam, Aarogyam Dhansampadaa Shatrubuddhi Vinashaay, Deepajyoti Namostute

It means: It is light that ushers in joy, health and prosperity into our lives, dispelling negative thought, bringing in positivity.

> 'I salute the divine flame respectfully. To make this Diwali memorable, what could be a better way than an attempt to let light spread its radiance, encouraging positivity, with a prayer to quell the feeling of animosity? These days, Diwali is celebrated across many countries. And notably, it is not limited to Indian communities; even governments, citizens and social organisations wholeheartedly celebrate Diwali with gaiety and fervour. In a way, they nurture a microcosm of India at their respective places.'

By saying so, the Prime Minister encouraged festival tourism in India, a concept that has its own exciting attractions. Our

India, the country of festivals, possesses limitless possibilities in the realm of festival tourism. It must be our endeavour to welcomingly include people of other states and other countries when we celebrate Holi, Diwali, Onam, Pongal or Bihu, spreading the festivals' true spirit. In India, every state, every region is replete with distinct festivals, generating a lot of interest in people from other countries. Hence, the Indian diaspora has a significant role to play in promoting festival tourism in India, he informed us.

In Episode 67, he said that when we take pride in our own Indianness, the world's curiosity around it also grows. Just like our spirituality, our practices of yoga and ayurveda have also attracted the whole world. Many of our indigenous sports also attract attention the world over. He cited the example of mallakhambh which is gaining popularity in many countries.

> 'When Chinmay Patankar and Pragya Patankar decided to teach mallakhambh out of their home in America, little did they know how successful it would be. Mallakhambh training centres are running at many locations across America. A large number of American youth are joining and learning mallakhambh. Be it Germany, Poland or Malaysia, mallakhambh is becoming popular in around twenty other countries. And now, its World Championship has also been started, which brings together participants from many countries.'

Ancient India had many such sports which were known to bring about extraordinary growth within oneself; they would add new dimensions to our mind and body balance. However, young people of the new generation are not that acquainted with olden concepts, but through the radio show, the PM has been able to put the spotlight on them. Take Episode 72 where he spoke of how the whole world is now drawn to ayurveda and natural health products from India.

> 'In such a situation, the demand for products like honey is increasing rapidly. I wish more and more farmers of our country to join bee farming along with their traditional farming. This will lead to an increase in the income of the farmers too and will also sweeten their lives!'

The divine teachings of the Vedanta and the Gita are also inspiring the whole world. In Episode 68 that aired in November 2020, Prime Minister Modi told us how India's culture, our shastras and our spiritual knowledge has always been a centre of attraction for the entire world. So many people have come to India to discover and study our shastras and have ended up staying back forever, whereas some of them returned to their respective countries as carriers of our culture. He said,

> 'I got an opportunity to know about the work of Jonas Masetti, also known as Vishwanath. Jonas teaches the Vendata and the Gita to people in Brazil. He runs an institution named Vishwavidya, situated in the hills of Petropolis, an hour's drive from Rio de Janeiro. Jonas, after studying mechanical engineering, set up his own stock trading company. Later, he was drawn towards Indian culture and texts, especially the Vedanta. From stocks to spirituality, it has truly been a long journey for him. Jonas studied Vedanta philosophy in India, staying at the Arsha Vidya Gurukulam in Coimbatore for four years. Jonas has another specialty—he is using technology to propagate his message. He regularly conducts online

programmes. He also does a daily podcast. During the last seven years, through his free open courses on the Vedanta, Jonas has taught over a lakh and a half students.'

Jonas is not only doing great work, he is doing it through a language understood by a large number of people. People are increasingly curious about how Vedanta philosophy can be of help to them during times of hardship such as Covid, and luminaries like Masetti are guiding them, the Prime Minister said, congratulating Jonas on his efforts while wishing him well for his future endeavours.

He also talked about a piece of news that had caught his attention.

> 'A newly elected MP in New Zealand, Dr Gaurav Sharma took the oath of office in one of the ancient languages of the world—Sanskrit. Through the medium of *Mann Ki Baat*, I extend best wishes to Gaurav Sharma-ji. All of us wish he attains newer achievements in the service of the people of New Zealand. Wherever there will be talk of world peace, India's name and contribution will be written in golden letters.'

Sufism can truly reflect the great teachings of Islam, as its message was of love, liberalism and peace, Prime Minister Modi mentioned in one of the popular episodes. Their choice of words, their way of talking, the generosity of the Sufi tradition, its sublimity, its lyricism, one could experience it all. He insisted that it has become imperative to present Islam in its true form to the world. The Sufi tradition, which is associated with love and generosity, can take this message far and wide and will thus benefit, not only humanity, but also Islam. He strongly advocated that regardless of the faith one follows, we should definitely experience Sufism once.

Similarly, he has also spoken of various Buddhist scholars from across the globe, who came together in Bodh Gaya to discuss issues relating to humanity at a global level. Underlining India's importance in the world sphere, in Episode 82, he said that a unique feature related to the United Nations is that Indian women have played a large role in increasing the influence and strength of the United Nations. He said,

> 'In 1947-48, when the Universal Declaration of UN Human Rights was being drafted, it was being inscribed in that declaration that "all men are created equal". But a delegate from India had objected to this and then it was written in the Universal Declaration that "all human beings are created equal".' This was in consonance with India's age-old tradition of gender equality. Did you know that Smt. Hansa Mehta was the delegate because of whom this became possible? At the same time, another delegate, Smt. Lakshmi Menon had strongly put forth her views on the issue of gender equality. And not only this, in 1953, Smt. Vijaya Lakshmi Pandit became the first woman president of the UN General Assembly.'

Prime Minister Modi said that India has always been one for world peace. We are proud of the fact that India has continuously been a part of UN peacekeeping missions since the 1950s. India is also playing a leading role in addressing issues related to poverty alleviation, climate change and labour upliftment. Apart from this, India is working closely with the World Health Organisation to popularise yoga and AYUSH. In March 2021,

WHO announced that a Global Centre for Traditional Medicine would be set up in India.

Not just our present achievements but our history too, that make us who we are today, has been mentioned with great ardour by Narendra Modi. In one such instance, he narrated how former Prime Minister Atal Behari Vajpayee had done us proud.

> 'In 1977, he made history by addressing the United Nations in Hindi. Today I want to play an excerpt of Atal-ji's address for the listeners of *Mann Ki Baat*. Listen to Atal-ji's resounding voice—"Here I am not thinking about the supremacy and prominence of nations. The esteem and advancement of the common man are of greater importance to me. Ultimately, the only criterion to measure our successes and failures is whether we strive to assure justice and dignity to the entire humanity, virtually every man, woman and child." Friends, these words of Atal-ji's show us the way even today. India's contribution in making this earth a better and safer planet is a big inspiration for the entire world.'

'In different episodes, Modi-ji has acknowledged the work done by individuals or groups towards public interest and celebrated them. This news does not often make its way to the headlines. By appreciating works done for water harvesting and conservation, environment protection, public health, education, community service, entrepreneurship, ayurveda, yoga, cleanliness, organ donation, etc., the Hon'ble Prime Minister has inspired us all. I see this as a step towards making the nation a sensitive society, where everyone is concerned about others and takes care of them. It would be better if the G20 nations work to create a joint public broadcast on the lines of the *Mann Ki Baat* programme to fulfil the goal of one earth-one family-one future,' says **Samir Jain**, vice-chairman and managing director, Bennett, Coleman & Co. Ltd.

Episode 68, broadcast in November 2021, was an occasion for much joy. The PM shared a heart-warming piece of news at the very beginning of *Mann Ki Baat*:

> 'Every Indian will be proud to know that a very old idol of Devi Annapurna is returning to India from Canada. This idol was stolen from a temple in Varanasi and smuggled out of the country around a hundred years ago, somewhere around 1913. I express my gratitude to the Government of Canada and to all those, for this large-heartedness, who made this propitious deed possible. Mata Annapoorna has a very special relationship with Kashi. The coming back of her idol is pleasing for all of us. Just like the idol of Mata Annapurna, a lot of our invaluable heritage has suffered at the hands of international gangs. These gangs sell them at a very high price in the international market. Now, not only are they being subjected to heavy restrictions; India has also increased her efforts for the return of the stolen objects. Because of such efforts, India has been successful in bringing back lots of such idols and artifacts in the past few years.'

There was also a beautiful coincidence attached with the return of the idol of Mata Annapurna as the World Heritage Week was celebrated only a few days prior to its return. The World Heritage Week itself provides a wonderful opportunity to the lovers of culture to revisit the past and to know about the history of these important milestones. Whether it is our revered idols or venerated texts and epics, *Mann Ki Baat* has been at the forefront of highlighting those things which truly matter.

Sonal Mansingh, the renowned Bharatnatyam and Odissi exponent, says, 'Many don't even know that the Ramayana is extremely popular in Southeast Asia. It was good to hear the Prime Minister talking about such things. He has been a global ambassador for Indian culture, showcasing its depth and variety to a number of global leaders. He has made India's ancient culture a powerful tool in increasing our nation's global appeal. It is heartening to have a culturally rooted prime minister, who takes Indian culture to the world, be it yoga or the Ramayana, be it getting global leaders to visit beautiful temples or witnessing Varanasi's Ganga aartis with them.'

In Episode 86, talking about Indian culture and our heritage, Prime Minister Modi introduced two people in *Mann Ki Baat*,

> 'These days, two Tanzanian siblings, Kili Paul and his sister Nima, are in the news a lot on Facebook, Twitter and Instagram, and I'm sure you too must have heard about them. They have a passion, a craze for Indian music, and for this reason, they are very popular. Their technique of lip sync shows how hard they work at it. Recently, a video of him [Kili Paul] singing our national anthem *Jana Gana Mana* on the occasion of Republic Day went viral. A few days ago, he also paid a soulful tribute to Lata didi by presenting her song. I really appreciate these two siblings Kili and Nima very much for their wonderful creativity. A few days ago, he has also been honoured at the Indian Embassy in Tanzania. The magic of Indian music is such that it fascinates everyone.'

In one of the episodes, the PM seamlessly blended experiences of cricket and Krishna bhakti, taking listeners from Perth to Vrindavan. First, he spoke of Perth in Australia where there is an art gallery called Sacred India Gallery. This gallery has been set up in the beautiful region of Swan Valley and it is the result of the efforts of an Australian resident, Jagat Tarini Dasi. He said,

> 'Jagat Tarini-ji is actually an Australian ... born and brought up there, but she came to Vrindavan and spent more than thirteen years here. She says that though she returned to Australia ... came back to her own country ... but she could never forget Vrindavan. That's why, in order to stay spiritually connected with Vrindavan, she created Vrindavan in Australia itself. Making her art a medium, she set up a marvellous Vrindavan. People who come here get an opportunity to view myriad artefacts.'

Through the Sacred India Gallery, many people get to see glimpses of the most famous pilgrimage centres of India—the traditions and culture of Vrindavan, Navaadweep and Jagannathpuri. Here, many an artwork related to the life of Bhagwan Shrikrishna has been exhibited. There is an artefact as well that displays the Govardhan Parvat held aloft by Bhagwan Shri Krishna on his little finger, with people of Vrindavan taking refuge beneath. This remarkable endeavour on the part of Jagat Tarini was lauded vociferously by the Prime Minister.

He went on to say,

> 'I was just referring to the subject of Vrindavan, built at Perth, Australia. There's an interesting history as well ... in that Australia shares a bond with our Jhansi, Bundelkhand. Actually, when the Queen of Jhansi Laxmibai was fighting a legal battle against East India Company, her lawyer was John Lang. John Lang was originally a resident of Australia. Staying in India, he fought Rani Laxmibai's case. All of us know of the huge contribution of Jhansi and Bundelkhand in our fight for freedom. Veeranganas, bravehearts such as

> Rani Laxmibai and Jhalkaribai hailed from here ... this region has given to the country legendary sportspersons like Major Dhyanchand too.'

The International Day of Yoga is celebrated today with great fervour across the world. But it would not be incorrect to say that the PM and *Mann Ki Baat* played a huge role in according it the great importance it deserves.

In Episode 59, the PM even expressed that he had never thought that there would be an opportunity in his life to touch the hearts of so many young people around the world. He was referring specifically to his recent visit to Bhutan. 'Just last week I went to Bhutan. I have seen this that whenever I have had the opportunity to go anywhere in the world as Prime Minister—and, of course, the credit also goes to International Yoga Day—people invariably spend close to five-seven minutes asking questions on yoga.'

In Episode 85, the Prime Minister said,

> 'Today I will tell you about the Indian culture making its mark in Argentina. Our culture is very much liked in Argentina. In 2018, during my visit to Argentina, I participated in a yoga programme called Yoga for Peace. There is an organisation in Argentina—the Hastinapur Foundation. This foundation is involved in the propagation of Indian vedic traditions in Argentina. It was founded forty years ago by a lady, Professor Aida Albrecht. Professor Aida Albrecht is going to turn ninety today. How her association with India happened is also very interesting. When she was eighteen years old, she was first introduced to the power of Indian culture. She also spent a lot of time in India. She studied the Bhagavad Gita and Upanishads in depth. Today the Hastinapur Foundation

has more than forty thousand members and about thirty branches in Argentina and other Latin American countries.'

The PM also talked about the Hastinapur Foundation that published more than hundred Vedic and philosophical texts in Spanish. The ashram, with twelve enchanting temples, has idols of many gods and goddesses as well as a site built for advaitwadi dhyan practice.

Baba Ramdev has said, 'Yoga is the crown jewel of our glorious traditions. It is good for physical as well as mental health. In Narendra Modi, we have a leader who is not hesitant to showcase the power of yoga to the world. He leads from the front. When Narendra Modi is talking about yoga on the radio, he is not doing so as the Prime Minister. He is doing so as a fellow citizen who is urging people to lead a healthier life. It is like a family elder guiding a person. It is great that Narendra Modi made yoga popular across and outside India.'

Janayitri Brahmanda, a yoga teacher from Netherlands, tweeted, 'Shri Narendra Modi is going to teach the world some yoga! Thank you so much for this great initiative ... I wish there would be more world leaders like you. Namaste. We keep on practising with you here in Holland! #FitIndia #MannKiBaat #ModiBestWorldleader.'

Prime Minister Modi said that there is hardly any major world leader who has not discussed yoga with him and this has been his own personal experience all over the world. The great part was that this interest in India had transitioned into something even bigger and new that he too was experiencing.

'Whoever I meet or wherever there is a chance to talk, the focus is on wildlife, discussions about the environment, the tiger, the Asiatic lion, the evolution etc., and I am amazed how interested people are in nature.'

Episode 85 spoke about another facet of our national culture—the promotion of khadi in Mexico and ayurveda in Kenya. The latter was expounded upon quite diligently by the Prime Minister:

'A few days ago, I had a meeting with my friend and former Prime Minister of Kenya, Raila Odinga. This meeting was interesting but also very emotional. Since we are very good friends, we also discuss freely. While both of us were in conversation, Odinga-ji told me about his daughter. His daughter Rosemary had a brain tumour and she had to undergo surgery. However, one side-effect of this was that Rosemary almost lost her eyesight; she stopped seeing. You can imagine what must have happened to the daughter ... and we can also guess the condition of the father, we can understand his feelings. There wasn't any major country in the world where he had not tried his best to get his daughter treated. But he didn't find success and, in a way, gave up hope. There was an atmosphere of despair in the entire household. Meanwhile, someone suggested that he come to India for ayurveda treatment. He came to India, started getting his daughter treated at an ayurvedic hospital in Kerala. The daughter stayed here for a long time. The effect of this ayurvedic treatment was such that Rosemary's eyesight returned to a great extent. You can imagine, as if a new lease of life was given and light came back into Rosemary's life. Odinga-ji was emotional while telling me this, and he wishes that the knowledge and science of ayurveda should be brought to Kenya too. The type of plants that are used in it will be cultivated by them and he will do his best to get more people to benefit from it.'

Through the PM, we got to know of a matter of great joy; that our land and rich traditions came together to alleviate great suffering from someone's life. Indeed, lakhs of people across the world are reaping similar benefits from ayurveda. Prince Charles from Britain is also one of the big admirers of ayurveda. Whenever the PM meets him, he definitely mentions ayurveda. He is also aware of many ayurvedic institutions of India. We got to know this through *Mann Ki Baat*.

Dr Nimesh Desai says, 'He has very efficiently conveyed information about various issues to people. On the topic of yoga, I find it interesting that some people now call yog in English yoga, just like Ram became Rama and Krishn became Krishna. This is similar to what happened with turmeric, a battle which we won ten-fifteen years ago. The medicinal benefits of turmeric have been acknowledged in India for centuries by our ancestors. It got repackaged in the West and returned to India. The same is happening with yoga.

'I personally believe it very firmly that just doing some asanas and mediation is not merely yoga. The yogic way must become the way of life. It should start with yama-niyama, then comes pranayama, as per the eight stages of Patanjali. I agree with what the Prime Minister says that if we want to promote awareness about health and well-being in an individual and society, yoga must be made the way of life.'

Through the medium of the radio show, Prime Minister Modi informed that in the last seven years, a lot of attention has been paid to the promotion of ayurveda in the country. The formation of the Ministry of AYUSH has further strengthened our resolve to popularise our traditional methods of medicine and health.

> 'I am very happy that in the last few years many new start-ups have emerged in the field of ayurveda. The AYUSH Start-up Challenge was started earlier this month. The goal of this challenge is to identify and support the start-ups working in this field. I urge the youth working in this field to take part in this challenge. Our ancestors coined the idea that the world is one family.'

Our G20 presidency is actually a continuation of the mark that we have been leaving on the world, be it through our foreign diplomacy, our political leadership, or our continued emphasis on the idea of one world, one humanity.

In April 2015, India earned accolades from various countries for saving citizens of nearly 48 countries of the world from the conflict in Yemen. Be it the citizens of the US, UK, France, Russia, Germany or Japan, we helped citizens of every country. This shows our spirit of wanting to serve people, irrespective of their caste, creed or religion. The world has experienced first-hand the old saying of India, *Seva Parmo Dharma*, meaning the greatest service to humanity is to serve others. Our Ministry of External Affairs, our Air Force and our Navy have played a commendable role in rescuing people from all kinds of conflicts, and that has left an indelible imprint on the consciousness of the world.

Of the reach and relevance of *Mann Ki Baat*, Kerala Governor, **Arif Mohammed Khan** says, 'The 100th episode of *Mann Ki Baat* is going to be completed soon and I believe that the show has been like a *marham*—a therapy. The one thing that is communicated uniformly through all the episodes in a powerful way is the way in which India is trying to improve the standard of living of its common people. It provides answers to how we can fulfil the dreams of our heroes of independence struggle, how we can better the standard of living of common people. How should India re-enact that role of being the epicentre of knowledge in the world—a role it had played before its decline—is the central theme of *Mann ki Baat*. And since the PM is concerned about it, government policies and programmes are moving in the same direction to attain this goal.

'And whatever the PM is saying, I think that has given confidence to the common man. He is stressing on the fact that we have this capacity, that we will be able to reach our goals. This is important because it is not enough to just have a goal, but equally important to fill people who are going to achieve the goals with enthusiasm. That excitement, vision, perseverance to a large extent is resonating with what the PM is saying about our capabilities of becoming supreme once again, and it is becoming stronger by the day.'

So, when we became the leaders of the G20 Presidency, it hardly came as a surprise that the PM took this big moment to bring attention to yet another common citizen of the land. In Episode 95, he said,

> 'Friends, I want to start today's programme by referring to a unique gift. There is a weaver in Rajanna Sircilla district of Telangana, Yeldhi Hariprasad Garu. He has sent me this G20 logo woven with his own hands. I was surprised to see this wonderful gift. Hariprasad-ji is such an expert in his art that he attracts everyone's attention. Hariprasad-ji has also sent me a letter along with this handwoven G20 logo. In it, he has written that it is a matter of great pride for India to host the G20 summit next year. Amid the joy of this achievement for the country, he has prepared this logo

of G20 with his own hands. He has inherited this wonderful talent of weaving from his father and today he is engaged in it with full passion.'

Actually, the G20 represents two-thirds of the world's population, three-fourths of world trade and 85% of the world's GDP. Hosting the presidency is a unique achievement for us, the people of India. 'Imagine ...,' said the PM, '... India is going to preside over such a big group, such a powerful group, three days from now i.e., from the 1st of December. What a great opportunity has come for India, for every Indian! This becomes even more special because India has been awarded this responsibility during Azadi Ka Amrit Kaal.'

He has asked us, his listeners, to look at the G20 as an excellent opportunity to focus on global good and world welfare. Whether it is peace or unity, sensitivity towards the environment or sustainable development, India has solutions for all challenges that arise from these. He reiterated the Sanskrit shloka,

Om Sarvesham Swastirbhavatu. Sarvesham Shanti Bhavatu.
Sarvesham Purnambhavatu. Sarvesham Mangalambhavatu.
Om Shanti: Shanti: Shanti: ॥

The theme that we have given—One Earth, One Family, One Future—shows our commitment to Vasudhaiva Kutumbakam.

The G20 presidency is a unique opportunity to open India to the world, and the world to us. Many programmes related to G20 will be organised in different parts of the country. During this period, people from different parts of the world will get a chance to visit our states, which will enable us to showcase the diverse and distinctive colours of our culture to the world.

'You also have to remember that the people coming to the G20 summits, even if they come now as delegates, are tourists of the future. I urge all of you, especially my young friends to do one more thing. Like Hariprasad Garu, you too must join the G20 in one way or an other. The Indian logo of G20 can be made, can be printed, in a very cool way, in a stylish way, on clothes. I would also urge schools, colleges and universities to create opportunities for discussions, debates and competitions related to G-20. If you go to the G20.in [now G20.org] website, you will find many things to suit your interest.'

In Episode 93, referring again to the G20 summit events, he happily announced that in every corner of the country, wherever the G20 summit would be held, nutritious and tasty dishes made from millets would be included, such as bajra-khichdi, poha, kheer and roti, as well as ragi-based payasam, puri and dosa. Similarly, health drinks, cereals and noodles made from millets would also be showcased in millets exhibitions at all G20 venues. Similarly, the PM informed us that Indian missions around the world are also making a lot of effort to increase the popularity of Indian dishes, especially those made from millets.

> 'You can imagine that this effort of the country and the increasing demand of millets in the world is going to give strength to our small farmers. It gives me great joy to see that the variety of new things that have started being made from millets today are being liked equally by the younger generation. I also congratulate the listeners of *Mann Ki Baat* for such a wonderful start to the International Year of Millets and for relentlessly taking it forward.'

Noted ad-man and lyricist **Prasoon Joshi** says, 'The common man used to feel that these schemes are not related to them, but our Honourable Prime Minister chose radio as a medium and made us realise that even G20 can impact our lives. A nationalistic pride has awakened in us and it has instilled a sense of responsibility. I wish that this programme runs successfully in the coming years and strengthens our consciousness.'

In conclusion, quoting the *Yajur Veda*, Prime Minister Modi said,

> 'May peace prevail all around, in all the realms, in the water, in the air, in space, in the fire, in the wind, in medicines, in vegetation, in gardens, in all of creation. May peace prevail in each soul, each heart, in me, in you, in every particle and everywhere in the universe.'

18

Promoting Incredible India

> 'There are no better ways to witness this nation's beauty and people's sentiments and no better teachers than tourism and pilgrimage.'
>
> – Prime Minister Narendra Modi

We have said this in a previous edition of this book—for a country that boasts of immense natural beauty, beautiful hills, seas, pristine rivers, deserts and a cultural diversity that is perhaps unparalleled across the world, India's tourism sector has not reached its full potential.

Earlier though, there was a sense of regret within the Indian people that Indian facilities were somewhat lacking along with there being a perception of a lack of cleanliness in India. Connectivity too was perceived as another problem. However, Prime Minister Modi, using the platform of *Mann Ki Baat* changed our perception by saying that over and above what governments can do, people also needed to chip in and do their bit to make India more tourism-friendly.

During Episode 8, when he talked about the advent of the holiday season and invited people to share their photos of Indian travel destinations using the hashtag #IncredibleIndia, little did he know the impact it would have.

This simple request from the Prime Minister flooded the Internet with breath-taking images of India, images that even citizens of India had never seen. Just a few hours after the show aired, we Indians shared images of the country that showcased its beauty from all over; some also shared their travel stories. The PM, much to the delight of his fans, responded to some of the tweets later in the day, and even retweeted lots of wonderful images.

The nature of images varied and they were an eclectic mix, encapsulating India's enchanting beauty. Someone shared a beautiful view of the Teesta river, which originates in North Sikkim. Kaushal Inamdar shared an image of the Golden Temple in Amritsar, the holy shrine of the Sikhs. He also added that he was listening to the divine singers inside the temple. Yogesh shared pictures of magnificent Hampi in Karnataka and called his experience truly wonderful and blissful. Kaustubh Khare shared a beautiful image of the seventeenth century Sindhudurg Sea Fort in Konkan, which was once the pride of the Maratha navy.

This campaign caught the attention of people worldwide. Tahseen Shaukat, who was the country head of Ten Sports in Pakistan at that time, shared images of Udaipur in Rajasthan, a destination very popular among both Indian and foreign tourists. A Vietnamese youngster, whose Twitter handle goes by the name of @tienqueen, shared photos from all over India and expressed his admiration for India. Several photos made their way to an album created on the PM's Facebook page.

Chetan, a 27-year-old youngster from Khanna in Punjab, shared this: 'I saw a photo of Pandharpur on the Prime Minister's Facebook page. I had heard about the place but the photo tempted me to go visit and I actually visited it. Pandharpur is not a place that many people outside the local areas visit, but the #IncredibleIndia album did the trick.'

In the seminal Episode 100, Prime Minister Modi referred to our incredible nation and said,

> 'Be it our natural resources, be it rivers, mountains, ponds or our pilgrimage sites, it is very important to keep them clean. This will help the tourism industry a lot. Along with cleanliness in tourism, we have also discussed the Incredible India movement often. Through this movement, for the first time, people came to know about such places, which were just in their neighbourhood. I always say that before going abroad for tourism, we must visit at least 15 tourist destinations of our country and these destinations should not be from the state where you reside ... they must be from any other state outside your state.'

#INCREDIBLEINDIA IS MORE THAN TOURISM, IT IS A PILGRIMAGE

In Episode 50 of the show, the PM appealed to all to visit those tourist spots within our country whose scenic beauty gets enhanced manifold during the monsoons. There is no better way to witness this nation's beauty and no better teacher than tourism and pilgrimage, he said.

In January 2019, he also spoke of mine-tourism.

> 'In this context, I would like to specially congratulate Coal India. Western Coalfields Limited at Savaner near Nagpur, where there are coal mines, has developed an eco-friendly mine-tourism circuit. Generally, we do not think of coal mines as places worth visiting. Pictures of mines make us wonder

what it must be like out there. We even have a saying, "Coal blackens your hands", and hence, people tend to stay away from coal mines. But Western Coalfields Limited has made these same coal mines a destination for tourism. Though this is only the beginning, nearly ten thousand people have already visited this eco-friendly mine-tourism site at Savaner near Nagpur. This in itself gives us an opportunity to see something new.'

So saying, he hoped that when we, the citizens of India, set out on a journey during our forthcoming holidays, we would contribute something to cleanliness too. Over the course of the programme, it became clear that greater awareness about cleanliness had been created in the country and people were making an effort to keep tourist destinations litter-free with both tourists and local residents chipping in. There may have been instances where it was most likely not being done scientifically, but it was being done, nevertheless.

Episode 70 of *Mann Ki Baat* described how the regional office of the Ministry of Tourism had started an Incredible India weekend getaway in the villages of Bengal at the beginning of the month. Through this campaign, the handicraft artisans from West Midnapore, Bankura, Birbhum, Purulia and East Bardhaman had organised handicraft workshops for visitors. The total sale of handicrafts during the Incredible India weekend getaways was very encouraging for the handicraft artisans.

People also got an opportunity to make our art forms popular across the country by employing novel methods. The PM cited the example of Bhagyashree Sahu of Rourkela, Odisha, a student of engineering, who had learnt and mastered the art of Pattchitra; to the extent that she now even conducts workshops to teach this art form.

> 'A few days ago, on the birth anniversary of Subhash Babu, Bhagyashree paid him a unique tribute done on stone. I wish her all the best for her future endeavours. A lot new can be learnt and done through art and colours.'

In January 2019, the PM congratulated Coal India for a spectacular effort on tourism that they had undertaken. Western Coalfields Limited at Savaner near Nagpur, where there are coal mines, had developed an Eco-friendly Mine-Tourism Circuit. It had made the coal mines a destination for tourism. He said,

> 'Though this is only the beginning, but nearly ten thousand people have already visited this Eco-friendly Mine-Tourism. This in itself gives us an opportunity to see something new.'

In Episode 101, the Prime Minister talked about how the nation had come together to celebrate its rich heritage, richly referencing the Kashi-Tamil Sangamam, the Saurashtra-Tamil Sangamam and even the Kashi-Telugu Sangamam held in Varanasi to give strength to the spirit of Ek Bharat, Shrestha Bharat. He went live on air with Gyamar Nyokum, a citizen from Arunachal Pradesh and Vishakha Singh from Bihar. Gyamar said, 'Modi-ji, our institution NIT told us about the Yuva Sangam and that we could participate in it. I learned that this is a very good program, which could enable one to contribute a lot to the vision of Ek Bharat Shreshtha Bharat. I will also get a chance to learn something new. I then enrolled in it right away. My experience was very enjoyable, very good'.

As usual, Prime Minister Modi spoke of public participation being a key cornerstone of the many initiatives being taken to boost tourism. He spoke of Isaak Munda who hails from a village in Sambalpur district of Odisha and who in his social videos prominently presents the local dishes of his area, the traditional ways of cooking, his village, his lifestyle, family and food habits. Of course, there are many more like him. In October 2017, Prime Minister Modi shared with his listeners the story of the transformation of Chandrapur Fort in Maharashtra by an NGO called Ecological Protection Organisation. He appreciated the two-hundred-days long non-stop campaign, where people performed the task of cleaning the fort. Overwhelmed to see the before and after photographs, he congratulated the team of the Ecological Protection Organisation, as well as the people of Chandrapur. He appreciated the toil, resolve and determination of the people associated with this mission and remarked,

> ‘Just by seeing these pictures your disappointment will transform into hope. This mammoth effort of bringing about cleanliness is a wonderful example of fostering aesthetics, cooperation and continuum. Forts are symbols of our heritage. And it is the duty of all countrymen to keep our historical heritage safe and clean.’

The medium of the radio has played a vital role in ensuring that the address was heard across the nation. Says **Shehryar Khan**, ‘There were people who would sometimes miss the programme when it was originally broadcast but then the PMO did a wonderful job of podcasting the episodes and making them available to people all the time. So, all the episodes even today if somebody wants to watch them or hear them they can do that in their own way, just at a click of a button on their smartphones. So, this programme was a great experience for AIR and it also created a bridge between the audio-visual broadcast platforms of India and the world.’

FROM 15 PLACES TO MANY MORE

The Prime Minister once said in a popular episode of *Mann Ki Baat*,

> 'My dear countrymen, you will remember that on 15 August, I had, in my address, said from the ramparts of the Red Fort that by 2022, you should visit 15 tourist destinations in India. At least 15 places and if possible, make a programme to stay over there for an overnight or two-night stay. You should observe, understand and experience India. We have so much diversity. And when holidays come in the shape of Diwali and allied festivals, people do travel and that's why I urge you to visit any 15 such places in India.'

Much later he continued to insist that we commit to making India tourism-friendly as well as economically viable for the local populace. In Episode 57, he let us know that the World Tourism Day had just been celebrated and certain reputed tourism agencies of the world which rank standards of travel and tourism had shown that India had displayed a lot of improvement in the Travel and Tourism Competitive Index.

> 'And you will be delighted to know that today our rank is 34 on this index whereas five years ago we were ranked 65th, which in a way is a big jump. If we tried all that harder, then by the 75th year of our independence, we would have carved a place for ourselves amidst the major tourist destinations of the world.' And all this, he said had been possible due to the cooperation of our citizens and especially because the understanding about importance of tourism had increased among the people. The Swachhta Abhiyan also had a big role to play in all of this.'

Seeing immense tourism potential wherever apt in Episode 78, he drew our attention to 31 October 2018, as the day when the Statue of Unity, was dedicated to the nation and the world in memory of Sardar Saheb. It is the tallest statue in the world. It is double in height compared to the Statue of Liberty located in the US. The distinction of having the world's highest statue in their country fills every Indian with pride; the head of every Indian is held high. Through the PM we also got to know that more than 26 lakh tourists had visited the Statue of Unity by then. That meant that an average of eight and a half thousand people had witnessed the grandeur of the Statue of Unity every day since its inauguration. The reverence and devotion for Sardar Vallabhbhai Patel in our hearts were reflected in the form of this homage paid to him. Besides the statue, the site houses many centres of attraction such as a cactus garden, a butterfly garden, a jungle safari, a children's nutrition park and the Ekta nursery, all of which are constantly evolving and providing a fillip to the local economy. The need to ensure the convenience and comfort of visiting tourists has created many innovative opportunities for employment for the villagers residing close to the statue. He spoke of one such initiative, where many villagers are providing facilities like home stays to visitors. All hosts are professionally trained in the technique of running a home stay. The locals have even started the cultivation of dragon fruit which has become a major source of livelihood for the people there.

> ‘Friends, for our nation and the constituent states, as well as for the tourism industry, this Statue of Unity can be a subject of research. We are all witness to the fact that within a year this place has developed as a world-famous tourism destination. People arrive there from the country and abroad. And one after the other, ancillary services like transport, lodging,

guides and eco-friendly services are getting inducted by themselves in this area. A large economy is developing and people are generating facilities as per the requirement of the tourists. The government is also playing its role.'

As Indians, we are all imbued with pride because the Time magazine has included the Statue of Unity in its list of 100 important tourist destinations around the world. Reiterating that we must all devote some time to visit the Statue of Unity, the PM also appealed to every Indian who takes out time to travel to 'visit at least 15 tourist destinations in India with their family and experience a night stay at whichever place you go.'

The response from his listeners has also been heartening. Priyanka Pandey—a 23-year-old resident of Siwan, Bihar who was also a student of Hindi literature—had said in January 2021 that she had visited the residence of Dr Rajendra Prasad,

'Priyanka-ji wrote on the Namo App that she was highly inspired by my suggestion of visiting 15 domestic tourist places in the country and hence on 1 January, she started for a destination which was very special. The place was 15 kilometres away from her home; it was the ancestral residence of the country's first President Dr Rajendra Prasad-ji. Priyanka-ji has beautifully mentioned that this was her first step in the realm of acquainting herself with the country's great luminaries. There, Priyanka-ji came across many books written by Dr Rajendra Prasad and many historical photographs as well. Really Priyanka-ji, this experience of yours will inspire others too.'

BRINGING TECHNOLOGY WITHIN THE AMBIT OF TOURISM

In Episode 56 of *Mann Ki Baat*, the PM spoke of how whoever he meets or wherever there is a chance to talk, the focus is always on wildlife or the environment, the Tiger. He said he was amazed at how interested people were in nature.

He spoke of a programme that the Discovery Channel planned to broadcast in 165 countries in their respective languages.

> 'Today, when there is a global churning of thought on environment, global warming and climate change, I do hope that in such circumstances, this episode of Discovery Channel will help greatly in familiarising the world with the message from India, the traditions of India and the empathy for nature in India's trail of glorious traditions.'

He also expressed his belief that people must want to know the steps being taken in the direction of climate justice and clean environment by India.

Referring to the Discovery Channel interview, he shared how people were curious and would ask, 'Modi-ji, you were speaking in Hindi and Bear Grylls does not know Hindi, so how did you carry on such a fast conversation between the two of you? Was this episode edited later? How many times did the shooting happen for this episode and how it happened? They ask with great curiosity.' He decided to unravel the secret.

> 'Well, in a way it is no secret at all! The reality is that technology was used extensively in my conversation with Bear Grylls. Whenever I spoke immediately there was a simultaneous translation into English for Bear Grylls who had a small cordless instrument in his ear. So, I used to speak in Hindi but he heard it in English and because of that the

communication became very easy and this is the amazing aspect about technology.'

After the broadcast of this show, a large number of people started talking about the Jim Corbett National Park. The PM encouraged us to visit sites associated with nature, wild life and animals. He reiterated how we must try and visit the north-east part of India at least once in our lifetime and experience the glorious abundance of nature that exists there.

'You will be left wonderstruck! Your horizons will expand. On 15 August, I urged all of you from the ramparts of the Red Fort to visit at least 15 places within a span of the next 3 years, 15 places within India and for 100 per cent tourism, visit these 15 sites! Witness and observe. Do take the family and spend some time there.'

Our country is full of diversity and this wide range of diversity also teaches a person and enriches their life, the PM said in another successive episode of the show. Not just does tourism give a fillip to our imagination, one tends to often come back with renewed energy, enthusiasm, zeal and inspiration with a longing to return to certain places again and again.

'The concern and care for the environment in India seems natural. Last month I had the privilege of releasing the tiger census in the country. Do you know how many tigers there are in India? The tiger population in India is 2967. At the time I was releasing the data on tigers, I also remembered the Asiatic lion of the Gir [forest] in Gujarat. I had the charge of the Chief Ministership of Gujarat at a time when the habitat of lions in the forests of Gir was shrinking. Their number was decreasing. We took several innovative steps, one after the other in Gir. In 2007, it was decided to deploy female guards. There were improvements in the infrastructure to increase tourism. Whenever we talk about nature and wildlife, we only talk about conservation. But we now have to move beyond conservation and think about compassion.'

Our scriptures have provided great guidance with respect to this subject.

> निर्वनो बध्यते व्याघ्रो, निर्व्याघ्रं छिद्यते वनम |
> तस्माद् व्याघ्रो वनं रक्षेत्, वनं व्याघ्रं न पालयेत् ||

That is, if there are no forests, tigers are forced to venture into the human habitat and they get killed, and if there are no tigers in the forest, then man is likely to cut the forest and destroy it, so in fact the tiger protects the forest, the forest does not protect the tiger. This great truth was explained by our forefathers in a fitting manner. Therefore, we need to not only conserve our forests, flora and fauna, but also to create an environment wherein they can flourish properly, the PM advised us.

In Episode 71, he praised Dr Salim Ali who has done illustrious work in the field of bird watching. Speaking of his own love for the avian world, he said that in India many bird watching societies are active. He said,

> 'Amid the hectic routine of my life, recently in Kevadia, I also got a memorable opportunity to spend time with birds. Time spent among birds will bond you closer to nature, it will also inspire you towards the environment.'

In fact, many avid listeners of the show were able to discern that in one of the episodes, the pecking of a peacock could be heard in the backdrop. We have also seen many photographs of the PM feeding peacocks effortlessly.

GLOBAL APPEAL, LOCAL DELIGHTS

Going back to Episode 52 of *Mann Ki Baat*, the tweets it sparked on tourism contained a varied and eclectic mix of images. The nature of images varied and was an eclectic mix, encapsulating India's enchanting beauty. In Episode 60, the PM shared a matter of great joy that our Vice President had visited the desert festival held annually in the Rann of Kutch, Gujarat in order to inaugurate it. 'When our Hon'ble President and Vice President are visiting such important tourist destinations in India, it is bound to inspire our countrymen. I urge you too to travel and visit these places.'

Episode 75 was about the Maritime India Summit which had hosted many programmes including some that sparked an interest in tourism. The PM said,

> 'At this summit, I had talked of developing tourism facilities around the light house complexes in the country. Guru Prasad-ji has shared experiences of his travel in 2019 to two light houses—the Chennai light house and the Mahabalipuram light house. He has shared very interesting facts which will astonish even the listeners of *Mann Ki Baat*. For example, the Chennai light house is one of those select light houses of the world which have elevators. Not only this, it is also the only light house in India which is within the city limits. It has solar panels, too, for electricity. Guru Prasad-ji also talked about the Heritage Museum of the light house, which brings forth the history of marine navigation. Giant wicks of oil lamps, kerosene lights, petroleum vapour and electric lamps that were used in olden times are exhibited at the museum. Guru Prasad-ji has also written in detail about the oldest light house of India, the Mahabalipuram light house. He said that right next to this light

house is the Ulkaneshwar temple, built hundreds of years ago by the Pallava king, Mahendra Verman I.'

The PM said that these light houses are unique in terms of tourism. Because of their grand structures, they have always been centres of attraction for people. We got to know that to promote tourism, 71 light houses had been identified in India too. It has been decided that in all these light houses, depending on their capacities, museums, amphitheatres, open air theatres, cafeterias, children's parks, eco-friendly cottages and landscaped gardens will be built. Speaking of a specific light house, the PM mentioned the one at Jinjhuwada in Surendra Nagar district of Gujarat. This light house is special because now the sea coast is more than a hundred kilometres away from where this light house is located. One can find such stones too in the village which indicate that there must have been a busy harbour here in the past. That means, earlier the coastline was up to Jinjhuwada.

Speaking to how the show has connected every Indian with each other and with the country, **Samir Jain** says, 'Today we have 4G and 5G connectivity as well as the Internet of Things. Even then, radio is still the one medium which reaches even the last person in the most remote rural area of India, in the snow clad mountains to the soldiers posted on the border. By sharing his ideas and sentiments with the people on radio through *Mann ki Baat*, Modi-ji has strengthened his place in the hearts of the people. As a student of journalism and mass communication, I thank the Prime Minister for reminding us the potential of radio broadcasting. *Mann ki Baat* is the voice of every Indian's heart.

In just 23 minutes in a month, you get a glimpse of what people think, what they do, what they want, and what are the new things they are doing. This is the first radio broadcast of the world which reaches such a vast population.'

In Episode 91, the PM mentioned that he had received a letter from a listener of *Mann Ki Baat*, Ashish Bahl from Himachal Pradesh, who had told the PM about the Minjar Mela of Chamba.

> 'Actually, the inflorescence of the maize plant is called minjar. When flowers bloom on the maize, the Minjar Mela is celebrated and in this fair, tourists from all over the country come from far and wide to take part. Incidentally, the Minjar fair is also going on at this time. If you have gone to visit Himachal, you can go to Chamba to see this fair. They say *Chambe Ek Din Ona Kane Mahina Raina*, that is, those who come to Chamba for a day, they stay back here for a month after seeing its beauty.'

In the same episode he said that fairs have always been of great cultural importance in our country since fairs connect people and their hearts. When the kharif crops ripen after the rains in Himachal Pradesh in September, in the areas of Shimla, Mandi, Kullu and Solan, Sari or Sair mela is celebrated. Likewise, in Jagra fairs, Bisu songs are sung after invoking the deity of Mahasu. This awakening of Mahasu Devta takes place in Himachal at Shimla, Kinnaur and Sirmaur and simultaneously, in Uttarakhand.

He also reiterated that there are many traditional fairs of tribal societies in the different states of our country, some of which are associated with the tribal culture, while others are organised to celeberate tribal history and heritage. 'For example, if you get a chance, you must visit the four-day Samakka-Saralamma Jatara fair in Medaram, Telangana. This fair is called the mahakumbh of Telangana. The Saralamma Jatara Mela is celebrated in honour of two tribal women heroes—Samakka and Saralamma. It is a big centre of faith for the Koya tribal community, not only in Telangana, but also in Chhattisgarh, Maharashtra and Andhra Pradesh. The Maridamma fair in Andhra Pradesh is also a big fair connected with the beliefs of the tribal society. The Maridamma fair runs from Jyeshtha Amavasya to Ashadh Amavasya and the tribal society here associates it with Shakti upasana (worship). Here, in Peddhapuram, East Godavari, there is also a Maridamma temple. Similarly, the people of Garasiya tribe in Rajasthan organise the Siyawa ka Mela or Mankhan Ro Mela on the Vaishakh Shukla Chaturdashi.'

The Mawli mela of Narayanpur of Bastar in Chhattisgarh is also very special, he said. He also mentioned the famous Bhagoria mela of Madhya Pradesh which had started in the times of Raja Bhoj. Then the Bhil kings, Kasumara and Balun organised these events for the first time in their respective capitals. Ever since then, these fairs are being celebrated with equal enthusiasm. Similarly, many fairs like the Tarnetar and Madhopur fairs are very famous in Gujarat. Fairs are, in themselves, a great source of energy for our society, our life. In modern times, these old links to the society are very important to strengthen the spirit of Ek Bharat-Shreshtha Bharat.

He encouraged our youth to visit such fairs and share their pictures on social media with a specific hashtag if they wanted. 'Through this, other people will also get to know about those fairs. You can also upload photos on the website of the Ministry of Culture. In the next few days, the Culture Ministry is going to start a competition, where, those who send the best pictures of the fairs will also be rewarded. So do not delay, visit the fairs, share their pictures, and maybe you will get rewarded too.'

The PM's insistence on encouraging tourism is seen throughout the run of the show. Take Episode 95, where he said that the people coming to the G-20 as delegates today, are tourists of the future. He urged all citizens, in their individual as well as collective capacities, schools, colleges and universities to create opportunities for discussions, debates and competitions related to G-20.

In the episode, marking a significant milestone for *Mann Ki Baat,* NESCO DG Audrey Azoulay participated in the show thanking the PM and India for their immense contribution towards furthering the education and preservation of culture. Prime Minister Modi said,

> 'You must remember, once we had discussed Indian forms of education through story telling with story tellers from across the country. I have an unwavering belief that the biggest change can be brought about by collective effort. This year, where we are moving forward in the Azadi Ka Amritkaal, we are also presiding over the G-20. This is also one of the reasons why our resolve to enrich diverse global cultures along with education has become stronger.'

In the next episode, he spoke of the Namami Gange campaign as one that sees continuous participation from the people. In this campaign, Ganga praharis and Ganga doots play a big role and spread awareness through planting of trees, cleaning of ghats, conducting the Ganga aarti, organizing street plays, and painting and poetry competitions. A lot of improvement can be seen in India's river biodiversity due to this campaign. There has been a significant increase in the number of different species of the hilsa fish, the Gangetic dolphin and turtles. With Ganga's ecosystem becoming clean, other livelihood opportunities are also increasing. The PM discussed the Jalaj Ajeevika Model, which was prepared keeping biodiversity in mind. Due to this, boat safaris for tourists have been launched at 26 locations.

> 'My dear countrymen, when the power of our resolve is strong, even the biggest challenge becomes easy. The example of this has been set by Sange Sherpa-ji of Thegu village of Sikkim. For the last 14 years, he is engaged in the work of environmental protection at an altitude of more than 12,000 feet. Sange-ji has taken up the task of keeping clean the Tsomgo (Somgo) lake that is of cultural and mythological importance. With his untiring efforts, he has changed the look and feel of this glacier lake. When Sange Sherpa-ji started this campaign of cleanliness in the year 2008, he had to face many difficulties. But within no time, along with the youth and villagers, the panchayat also started offering full support in this noble work. Today, if you go to see the Tsomgo lake, you will find huge garbage bins all around there. Now the garbage collected here is sent for recycling.'

There, garbage bags made of cloth are also given to tourists so that garbage is not strewn around. About 5 lakh tourists reach Tsomgo lake every year to see this very clean lake. Alluding to another popular Indian destination—Goa—the PM said that as soon as the name of Goa is mentioned naturally the first things that come to mind are the beautiful coastline, the beaches and popular Goan food. But Prime Minister Modi was talking of something different that happened in Goa. The Purple Fest was organised in Panaji from 6 to 8 January 2023, which was a unique effort in which more than 50,000 divyang brothers and sisters had participated. The PM told us that Miramar Beach had become one of the most accessible beaches in Goa for our divyang brothers and sisters.

'Along with a cricket tournament, table tennis tournament and a marathon, a Deaf-Blind Convention was also organised here. There was also a unique bird watching programme along with the telecast of a film. Special arrangements had been made for this, so that all our divyang brothers and sisters and children could enjoy it to the fullest.'

From Episode 56 of *Mann Ki Baat,* where we got to know of how the festival of Onam is celebrated in Kerala to Episode 97 about the Purple Festival, Prime Minister Modi has showcased our festivals in their full glory and has talked of them becoming great attractions for tourism. Be it festivals like Navratri in Gujarat, the Durga Utsav in Bengal, or the Eid-ul-Zuha festival celebrated around the country, as per Prime Minister Modi, all these could become tremendous tourist attractions. In the new India, he also asked us, to transform all festivals into times of ensuring cleanliness of our households and the areas in our vicinity.

In the words of the Prime Minister,

'This is nothing new for us, but it is important to convert it into a social character. Public cleanliness must be insisted upon not just in our homes but in our villages, towns, cities, states and our entire country. Can you too, being a tourist, lay stress on cleanliness at tourist destinations? I am confident that our youth will definitely help me in this task.'

SECTION – IV

Statistics and Numbers

19

100 Episodes, 100 Crore Listeners

> 'Our education should be such that it takes us from *aham* (I) to *vayam* (we) ... our education should be such that it can help us connect the *swa* (self) with *samashti* (the world) ...'
>
> – Prime Minister Narendra Modi

Mann Ki Baat is not just a paradigm shift; it is an example of how democracies can set new paradigms, where the voice of the people—through both formal and informal means—is always a critical factor. To assess the extent of the social transformation that has taken place over the last 100 episodes of *Mann Ki Baat*, several institutes have conducted incisive research on how people have connected with the topics raised and the significant impact of the show—in terms of viewership, duration, citizen sentiment across themes such as Beti Bachao Beto Padhao, tourism, sports, etc.

These studies show that *Mann Ki Baat* has had several far-reaching, positive effects that were perhaps not apparent initially. Take the fact that the popularity of AIR has revived thanks to the programme. Or that RJs are getting more recognition as mass media communicators, or that the show's repeated emphasis on service-oriented themes such as 'share', 'make', 'campaign', 'opportunity', 'resolve', 'service', and 'work' have influenced the society's conscience as a unit. (*IFC, Appendix: Methodology.*)

We examine and summarise four such studies that explore the multipronged and comprehensive coverage that *Mann Ki Baat* has espoused and received.

1) PROFESSOR BHUVANESH PAREEK OF IIM-B

The 100-episode analysis by Professor Bhuvanesh Pareek of Indian Institute of Management, Bangalore (IIM-B) shows some interesting insights into the show, both expected and unexpected. The analysis was conducted using NLP tools. Let's take a deep dive into the individual outcomes.

Communication during COVID-19 pandemic

The first interesting outcome of Professor Bhuvanesh Pareek's analysis was that during the COVID-19 pandemic, when panic amongst people was high, the Prime Minister's communique to the nation through special addresses apart from the regular *Mann Ki Baat* episodes, had a significant impact on his listeners. His insistence on directly communicating with citizens was crucial in keeping negative sentiments at bay.

Average Covid Panic Index 2020-22 (*Figure 1*) features India amongst the top 15 countries out of 200+ countries with the lowest panic index during 2020-22. It was in the same range as Western countries like USA and Canda.

FIGURE 1: Average Covid Panic Index over Quarters

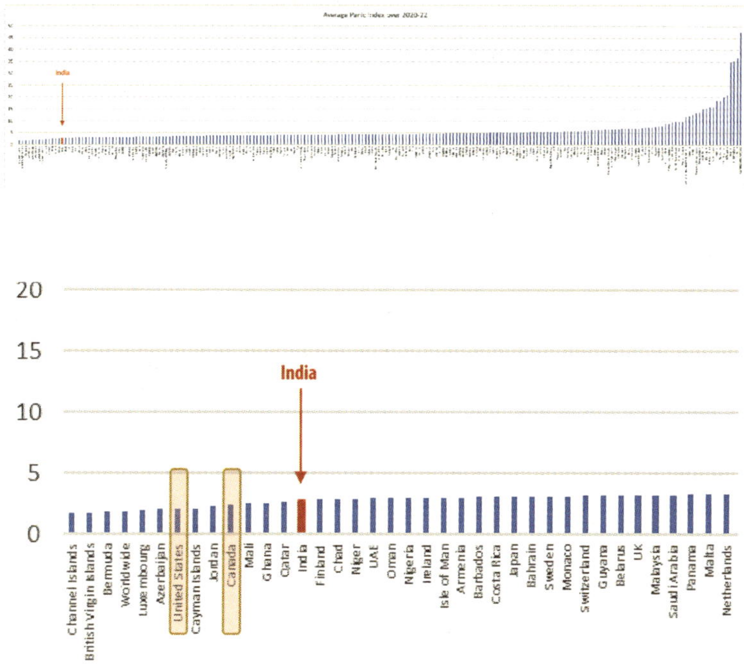

An assessment of the *Average Covid Panic Index* on a quarterly basis gives the second key takeaway which is that the Prime Minister's address to the nation led to a steady decline in the panic index. This is especially true of the phases when the concern over the pandemic was organically high, such as during the first covid wave and the Delta wave, and at the start of the vaccination programme when competing views about the different vaccines abounded. By Q4 of 2022, the panic index in India had nosedived to a very low level. (*Figure 2*)

FIGURE 2: Panic Index over quarters and India's performance

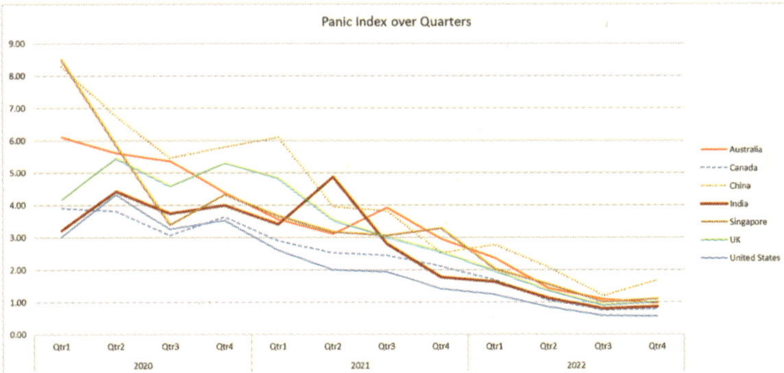

Addressing the nation in challenging times

FIGURE 3: The PM's address to the nation and its effect on mitigating panic

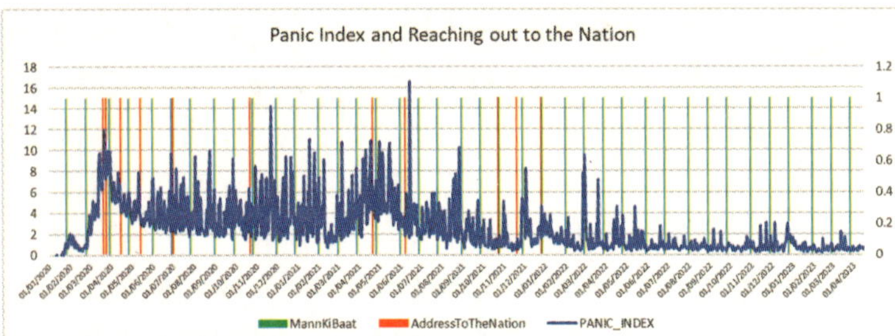

The third key takeaway is regarding the crucial timing of the PM's address to the nation and its role during the COVID-19 crisis. As the various waves hit the country during the pandemic, citizens were naturally concerned. However, their worry was mitigated main due to the regular address by the Prime Minister through many forums, including *Mann Ki Baat*. Whenever the panic index was high, the Prime Minister made it a point to address the nation, which resulted in the relay of accurate and relevant COVID-19 information that was highly effective in neutralising the panic levels.

As is evident from Figure 3, while *Mann Ki Baat* is a continuous monthly radio address (green bar), the Prime Minister also reached out to the nation (red bar) outside of the programme at key inflection points during the entire duration of the COVID-19 crisis.

Whenever there was a change in the nature of the pandemic or its concomitant aspects, there was always an additional address by the Prime Minister. As an example, during the Delta wave in 2021, the panic levels rose, as did the frequency of the Prime Minister's addresses (*Figure 3*). The panic index never surged beyond reasonable levels, primarily due to the Prime Minister's consistent approach of reaching out to the people on time.

During the pandemic, the entire country was worried, and media coverage of the issue was intense. However, frenzied panic was avoided, as fake news was combatted through timely and correct information disseminated by the nation's trusted steward. The crucial role played by the official communication in keeping fake news at bay and ensuring that people's negative sentiments did not convert into panic can be ascertained from Figure 4.

FIGURE 4: Effective combating of fake news

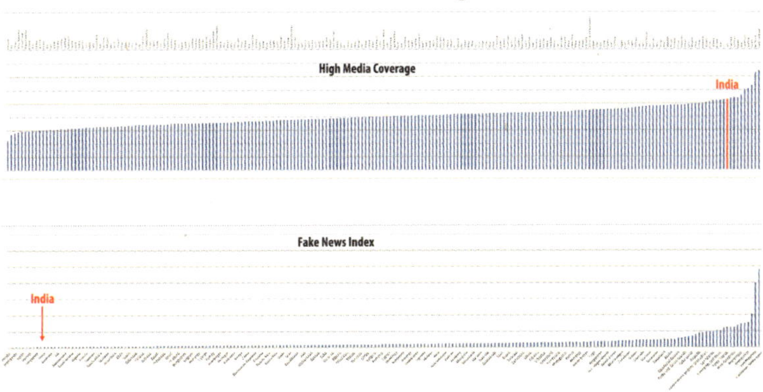

Mann Ki Baat Viewership

A unique aspect of the *Mann Ki Baat* viewership (*Figure 5*) on YouTube is a significant spike during the later run of the programme. For example, the episodes between Episodes 60 and 70 were the most viewed. The primary thrust of these episodes was on Jan Bhagidari.

In the Prime Minister's words, 'There have been times when we tried to establish a stronger emotional connect with our soldiers through the campaign Sandesh to Soldiers; we have also catapulted sales of khadi with Khadi for Nation-Khadi for Fashion. We internalised the mantra of Vocal for Local. Through Hum Fit Toh India Fit, we created awareness towards fitness. We turned sanitation into a mass movement through the endeavours of My Clean India or Statue Cleaning, #No to Drugs, #Bharat Ki Lakshmi, #Self for Society, #Stress free Exams, #Suraksha-Bandhan, #Digital Economy, #Road Safety ... Oh, the list is endless.'

FIGURE 5: *Mann Ki Baat* viewership on YouTube

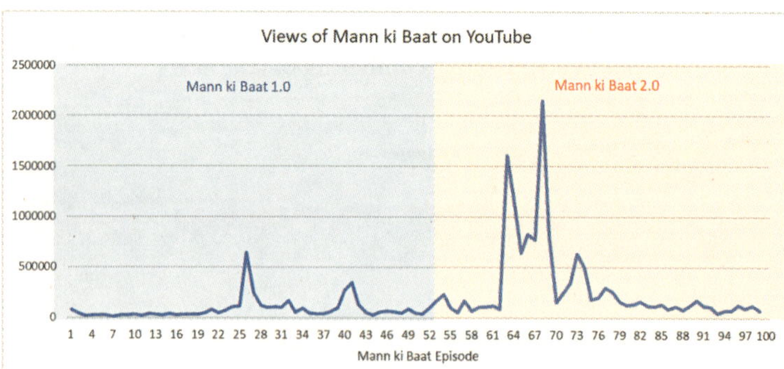

Source: YouTube on 14/04/2023; *Handle:* Narendra Modi

Word cloud – Key focus areas of *Mann Ki Baat*

The words that saw repeated mention in *Mann Ki Baat* over the 100 episodes, as per the word cloud (Figure 6), provide deep insight into the Prime Minister's intent and subsequent actions.

The repeated words show Prime Minister Modi's focus on certain themes. His focus has rarely deviated; it has always been centred on 'India', 'people', 'country', 'world', 'friends', 'women', 'water', 'teachers', 'farmers', 'khadi', 'yoga', 'daughters' and several other inclusive concepts, as can be seen from the associated word cloud map below.

FIGURE 6: Word cloud over 100 Episodes

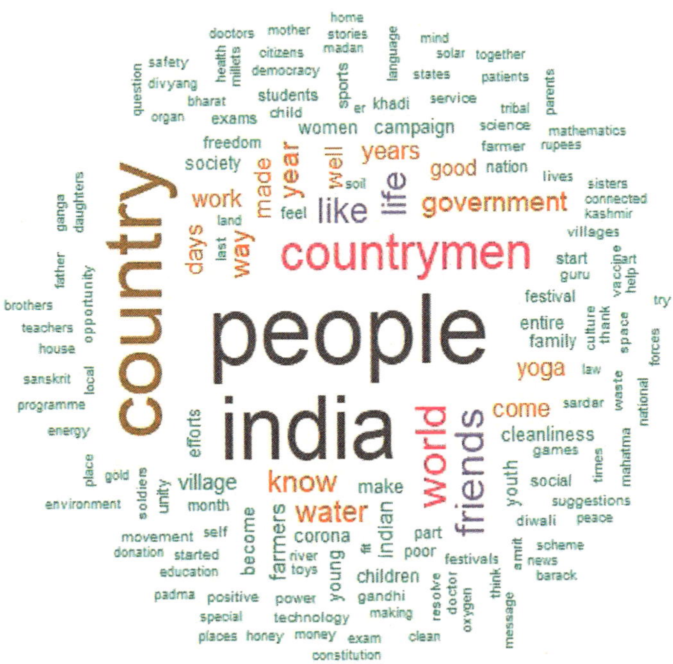

Sub-topics of *Mann Ki Baat*

Mann Ki Baat has had a profound impact on citizens' awareness of social issues such as the Khadi Story, Beti Bachao Beti Padhao programme or the construction of the Statue of Unity.

Each of these phrases registered significant hits on the internet. Figures 7a, 7b and 7c plot the search results of some of these phrases.

The most significant impact has been on the spread of awareness of the Beti Bachao Beti Padhao programme. We can see from Figure 7b that the baseline has fundamentally shifted upwards and there is more interest and curiosity in the concept and what it entails.

FIGURE 7a: Impact on search results for Statue of Unity after being mentioned on *Mann Ki Baat*

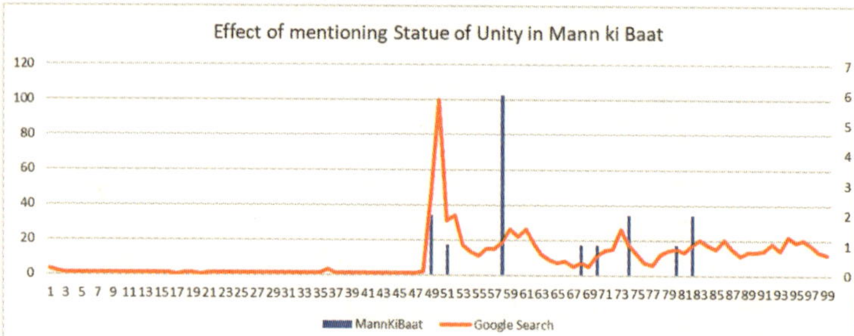

Mann Ki Baat has had a similar impact on startups. The various sub-charts in Figure 8 plot the registration of several types of firms and startups post-2014 and correlate them with the popularising and inspirational power of *Mann Ki Baat* supported by multiple government initiatives.

FIGURE 7b: Impact on search results for the Beti Bachao Beti Padhao programme after being mentioned on *Mann Ki Baat*

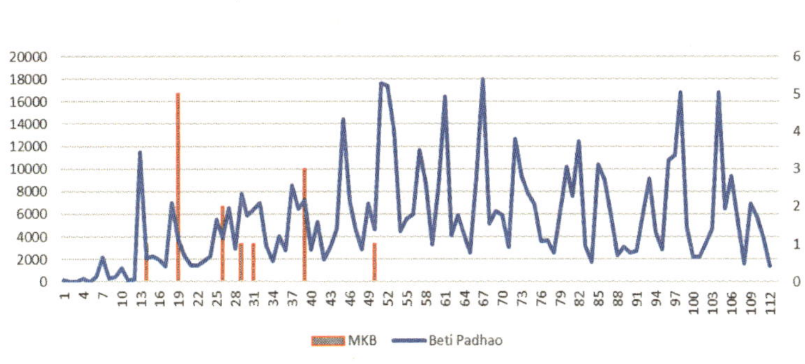

FIGURE 7c: Impact on search results for the Khadi Story after being mentioned on *Mann Ki Baat*

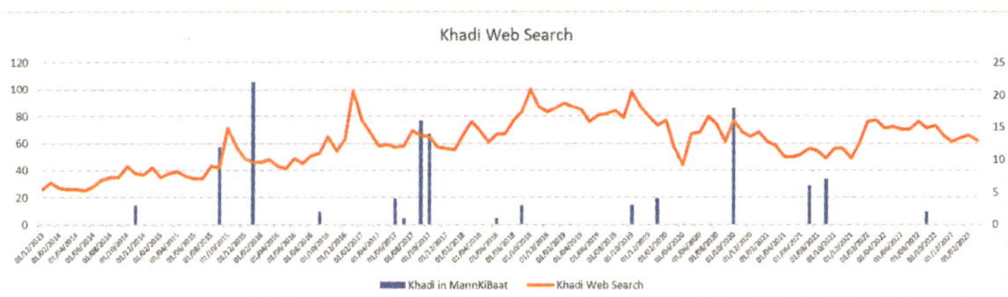

The registration of agri-startups in 2019 went up 2.4 times as compared to 2014 (*Figure 8a*). The registration of manufacturing firms in 2019 was 2.2 times more as compared to 2010 (*Figure 8b*). Registration of financial startups, in 2019 (before COVID-19), and startups in the education domain was 3.3 times more (*Figure 8c*) and 3.6 times (*Figure 8d*) more respectively.

Mann Ki Baat has highlighted several key thrusts that the nation has taken. Every time the PM mentions these, in isolation or as a part of the Jan Bhagidari initiatives, there is a multifield rise in the national conversations on these topics.

FIGURE 8a: Registration of Agri and Allied firms over the years

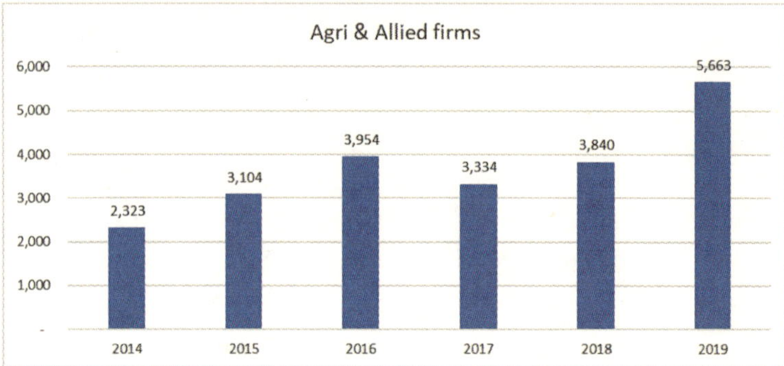

FIGURE 8b: Registration of Manufacturing firms over the years

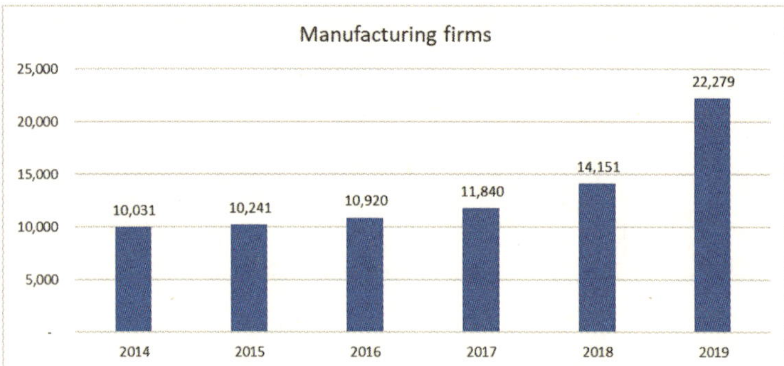

FIGURE 8c: Registration of Financial firms over the years

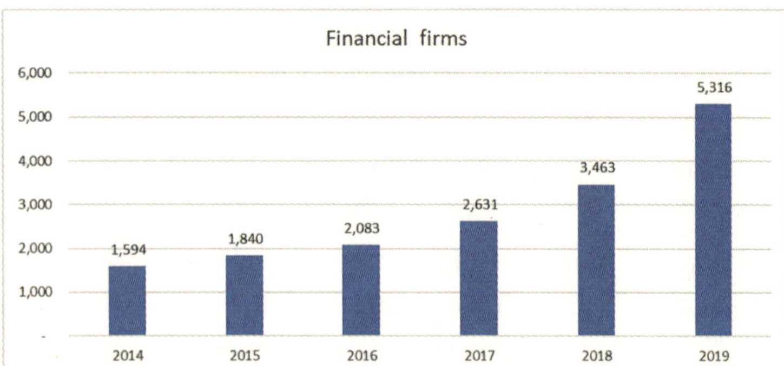

FIGURE 8d: Registration of firms in Education over the years

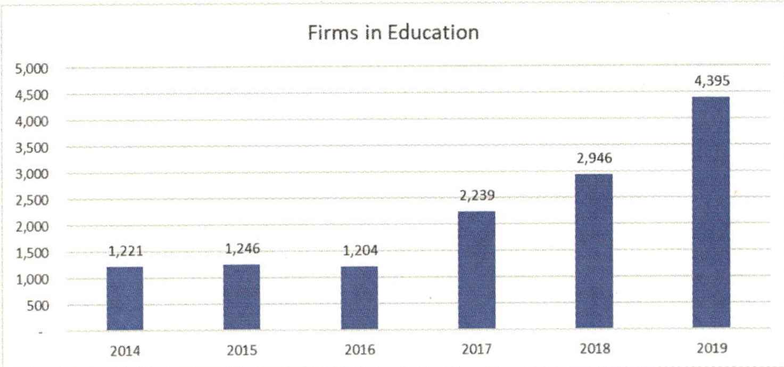

Eventually, these topics settle at a higher base and become a part of the usual routine or the new normal.

Be it the millets movement, the women empowerment initiatives, the push for yoga or tourism, the talking points have been many, and so have been the responses!

FIGURE 9: *Mann Ki Baat* mention triggers search for millets

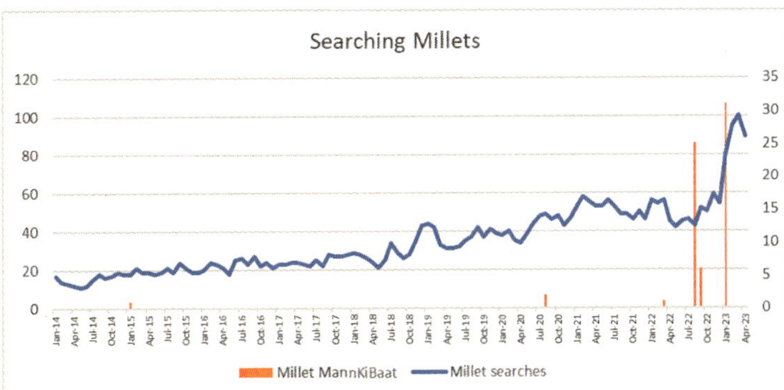

Searches on millets doubled after Prime Minister Modi focused on them in *Mann Ki Baat*! It averaged under 20 in Jan 2014 and jumped to nearly 30 in April 2023.

Regarding Nari Shakti, the profound impact of Prime Minister Modi's words on the national consciousness has been without parallel. The image below encapsulates the progress

FIGURE 10: Upward trend in Women Empowerment during Prime Minister Modi's tenure

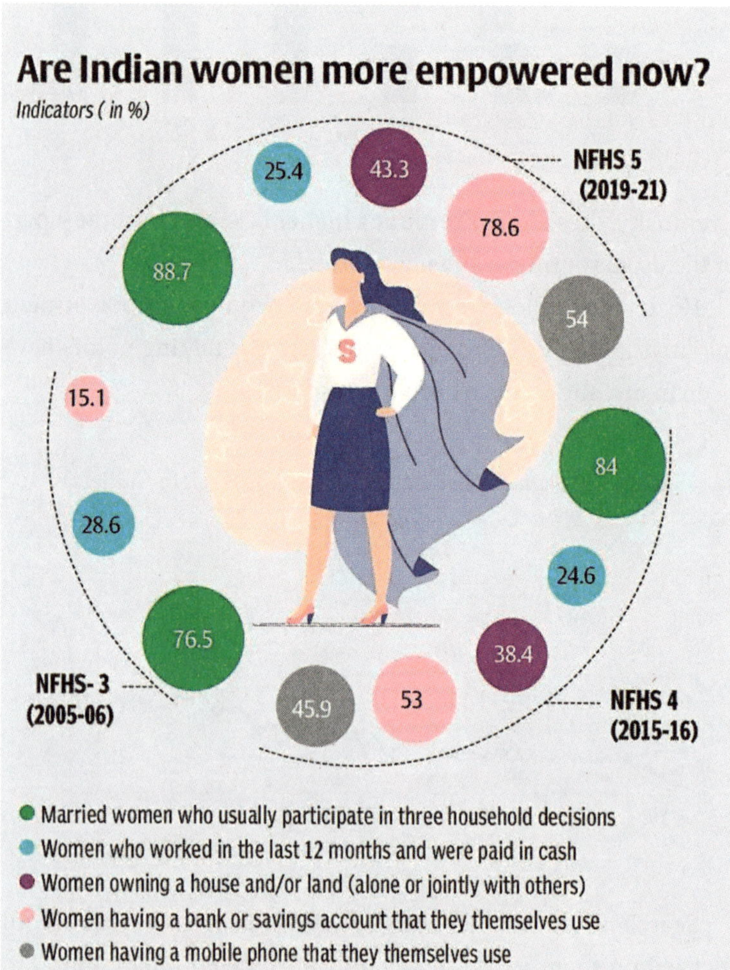

Source: National Family Health Surveys - 2015-16 & 2019-21

across five parameters, between NFHS-3 (2005-06 survey year) and NFHS-5 (2019-21). The jump from just 15.1 per cent in 2005 to over 78 per cent by 2019 in the number of women owning and operating their own bank accounts is just one of the many phenomenal transformations that have taken place. While the jump cannot be solely attributed to *Mann Ki Baat*, it cannot be denied that the constant championing of Nari Shakti on the programme has created a conducive national atmosphere for women to thrive and become equal partners in the national mainstream.

Searches about Yoga went up by 1.5 to 2.5 times after the Prime Minister spoke about it across various episode.

FIGURE 11: Impact of *Mann Ki Baat* on the number of searches on Yoga

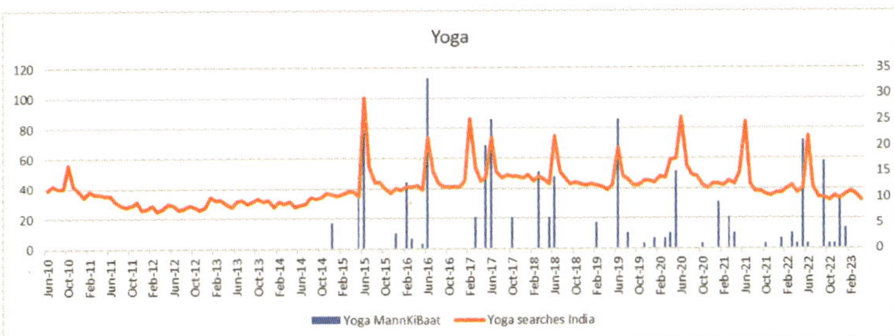

Incredible India—Prime Minister Narendra Modi's thrust on tourism—saw an expected spike when he mentioned it across several episodes. As an example, in 2019, domestic tourist visits were at an all-time high (before they declined in 2020 due to COVID-19 induced lockdowns) in line with the PM mentioning it on *Mann Ki Baat*.

Another extremely significant impact of the *Mann Ki Baat* messaging is the renewed honour that we have started feeling

FIGURE 12: *Mann Ki Baat's* impact on Domestic Tourism

FIGURE 13: India's rank in Tourism registering an upward trend

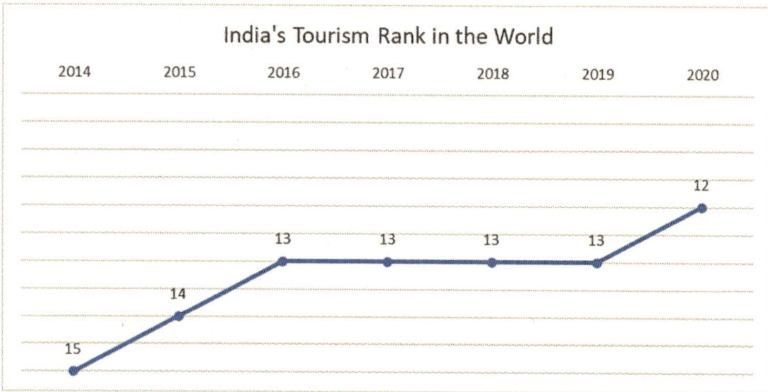

FIGURE 14: Correlation between *Mann Ki Baat* and searches on Swami Vivekanand

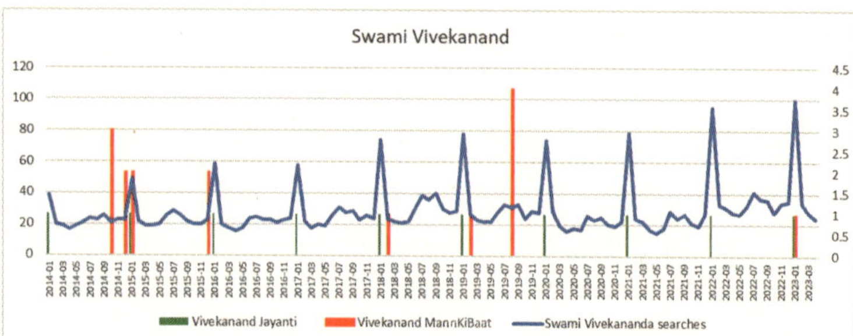

for our national heroes. The consistently positive reception has been incredible.

After the PM mentioned Swami Vivekananda on *Mann Ki Baat*, there was a 25 per cent increase in the average searches about Swami-ji:

Queries about the former Prime Minister Lal Bahadur Shastri have more than doubled in the last couple of years:

FIGURE 15: Correlation between *Mann Ki Baat* and searches on Lal Bahadur Shastri

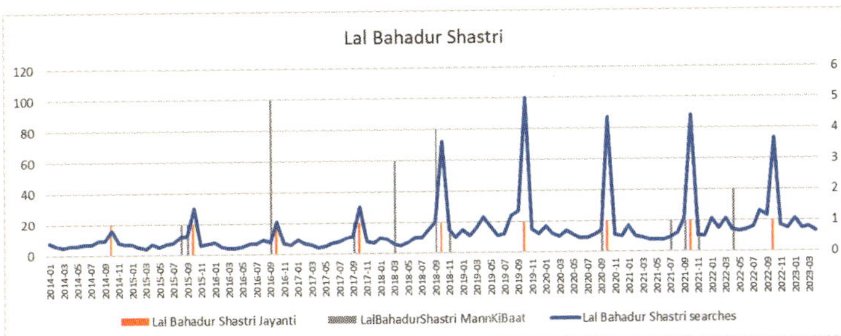

A 64 per cent increase in the average volume of searches on Dr Sarvepalli Radhakrishnan occurred, even though schools remained closed during the pandemic.

FIGURE 16: Correlation between *Mann Ki Baat* and searches on Dr S. Radhakrishnan

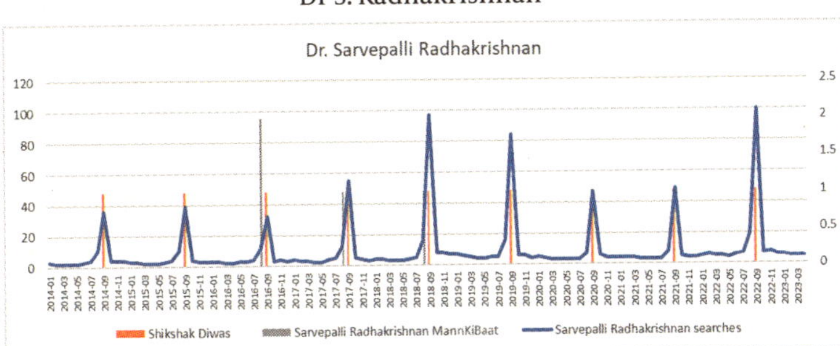

There has been an incredible rise of almost 75 per cent in searches about the Jallianwala Bagh in the last five years.

FIGURE 17: Corelation between *Mann Ki Baat* and searches on Jallianwala Bagh memorial

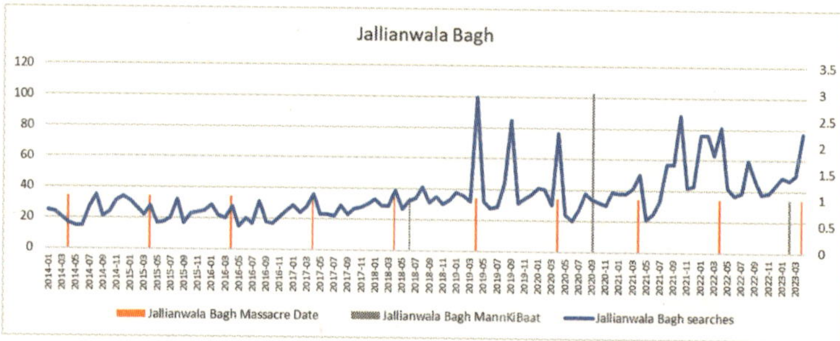

The above insights from the study by Prof. Bhuvanesh Pareek of IIM-Bangalore summarise the tremendous social impact of *Mann Ki Baat*.

2) INDIAN INSTITUTE OF MANAGEMENT, ROHTAK

Ahead of the 100th episode, an exhaustive study was also commissioned by Prasar Bharati and conducted by Indian Institute of Management, Rohtak. One of the key findings of the study was that *Mann Ki Baat* has reached 100 crore listeners at least once in their lives.

The report examined the reasons behind the popularity of the radio broadcast and listed out the most liked characteristics of the show that hook people to the broadcast.

An assertive and decisive leadership that seeks to establish an emotional connection with the audience emerged as a reason by those who follow the programme. The Prime Minister is seen as knowledgeable and empathetic in his approach of engaging with the citizens, directly. This is also a reason for the trust the programme has established. Gaurav Dwivedi, CEO, Prasar Bharati and Dheeraj P. Sharma, director, IIM Rohtak, presented the findings, 'Listener Feedback and Sentiment Analysis of *Mann Ki Baat*' via a press conference. Some other key takeaways were:

- *Mann Ki Baat* has 23 crore regular listeners, and 96 per cent of the Indian population knows the programme.
- *Mann Ki Baat* has influenced people's behaviour; 60 per cent have become interested in nation-building, 73 per cent have started feeling optimistic that the country will progress.
- 58 per cent of *Mann Ki Baat* listeners say their living conditions have improved since the airing of the programme, while 59 per cent have reported increased trust in the government.
- Most listeners of *Mann Ki Baat* (65 per cent) prefer listening to it in Hindi, while English comes in at the second place (18 per cent).
- *Mann Ki Baat* is broadcast in 22 Indian languages and 29 dialects, 11 foreign languages, excluding English, namely, French, Chinese, Indonesian, Tibetan, Burmese, Baluchi, Arabic, Pashtu, Persian, Dari and Swahili.
- *Mann Ki Baat* is broadcast by more than 500 broadcast centres of All India Radio (AIR).

3) INSTITUTE FOR COMPETITIVENESS, (IFC) SUPPORTED BY AXIS MY INDIA AND BILL AND MELINDA GATES FOUNDATION

The research by the Institute for Competitiveness took a closer look at the way *Mann Ki Baat* connected with people on certain topics:

a. Cleanliness and sanitation
b. Health
c. Wellness
d. Water conservation
e. Sustainable development

To quote the report, 'Just as *Mann ki Baat* speaks directly to ordinary people, it celebrates their achievements within—and beyond—their communities. The programme does not focus much on party politics or political news. Instead, it celebrates what Prime Minister Modi calls "grassroots level change makers". For instance, it emphasises the role of startups and small businesses in achieving a self-reliant India; encourages people of all ages to take action to promote the social and environmental causes that matter most to them; and spreads the word about government policies, programs, and initiatives aimed at economic, social and sustainable development.

'Our research finds that *Mann Ki Baat* has focused in particular on five thematic areas—cleanliness and sanitation, health, wellness, water conservation, and sustainability. The program highlights government action and citizen action in these priority areas. This, in turn, can encourage listeners to establish or participate in "change-making" initiatives in their own communities. All this can have a lasting and sustainable impact on lives of people and for the country.'

This report was released one episode shy of Episode 100 and focuses on sanitation, financial inclusion and digital banking, sports, environment, tourism, access to the job market, and more. The report celebrates grassroots-level change-makers in these key areas, as called by Prime Minister Modi, just as the radio show does. Using qualitative and quantitative data, including WordStat text-mining analysis, to show how *Mann Ki Baat* has addressed the five priority areas, it concludes that, '... it is fair to assume that such a widely popular broadcast influences listeners' behaviour. After each episode, public interest in the topics the Prime Minister mentions spikes. For instance, according to one study of post-broadcast Google searches, online interest in Teacher's Day increased up to 2,500 times in subsequent weeks'.

The crucial findings of the report on *Mann Ki Baat* are that it is inclusive, accessible, conversational and aimed at bringing social and economic change.

The timelines of the study show various topics and themes covered overall within a given year, or typically, within 12 episodes of the show:

While the 2015 episodes (*Figure 18*) show a slew of mentions by the PM of the various national unsung heroes and patriots alongside issues of welfare—farmers, sports, tourism, festivals—the episodes of 2020 were centred on how well the nation countered the COVID-19 pandemic. (*Figure 19*)

This concurs with IIM Bangalore's study on how well *Mann Ki Baat* managed to keep panic at bay because of the PM's direct communication with the nation.

The themes identified had further subthemes that furthered the PM's message. (*Figure 20*)

FIGURE 18: Timeline of Issues raised in *Mann Ki Baat* in 2015

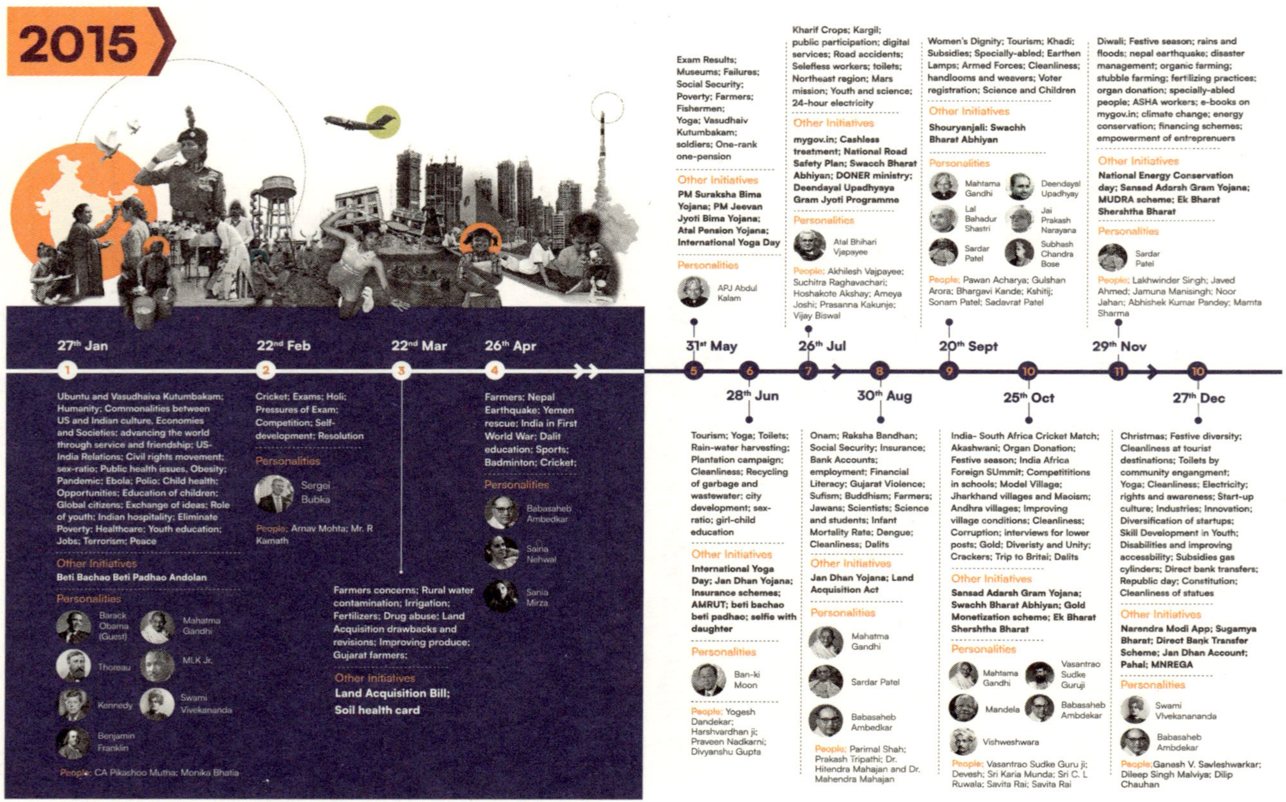

FIGURE 19: Timeline of Issues raised in *Mann Ki Baat* in 2020

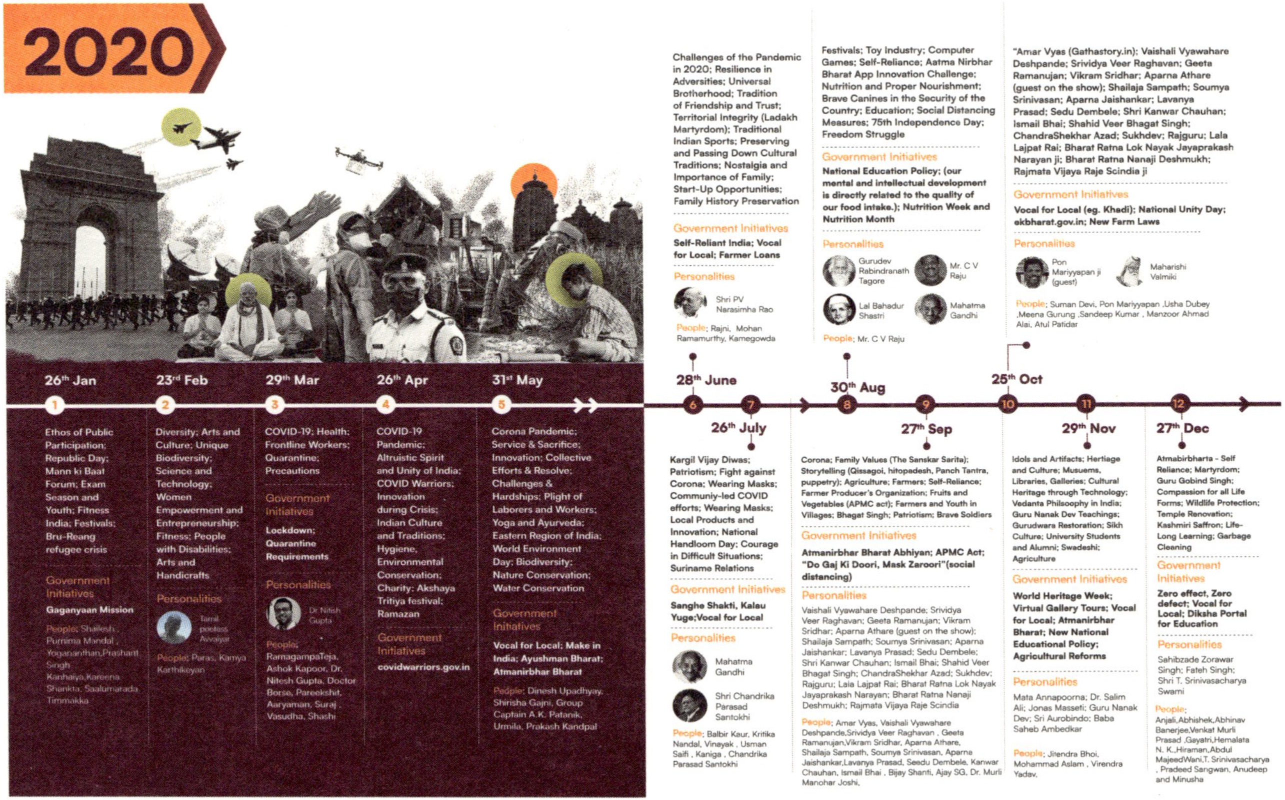

FIGURE 20: Themes raised on *Mann Ki Baat*

The dendrogram (*Figure 21*) also shows similar patterns. For example, the words 'water' and 'conservation' seem highly associated, suggesting that they often appear together.

FIGURE 21: Dendrograms depicting co-occurrence of topics

04 Hierarchical Clustering Analysis (Dendrograms)

WordStat allows users to apply graphic tools, known as hierarchical cluster analysis and co-occurrence analysis, to identify and categorize related words. (See Appendix: Methodology) It then produces dendrogram graphs that show the words most strongly associated with one another.

The following is a dendrogram generated from all the 99 transcripts from 2014 and 2023 depicting the co-occurrence of topics. Refer to Appendix: Methodology for year-wise dendrograms generated from the Mann Ki Baat transcripts for the years 2015-2022.

How to Read a Dendrogram?

Each branch of the dendrogram is called a clade. The arrangement of clades is based on their degree of similarity or dissimilarity. Clades that are positioned at similar heights are considered similar to each other, whereas those at different heights are dissimilar. The extent of dissimilarity increases with the difference in their heights.

Figure 2

Dendrogram representing 99 episodes of Mann ki Baat broadcast between 2014 and 2023

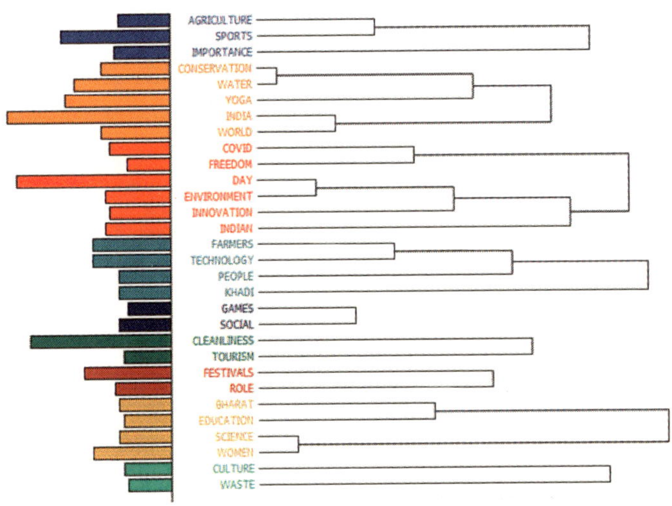

The Sankey diagram (*Figure 22*), another tool employed by this study, shows interesting patterns across the 99 episodes. This diagram also shows how themes flow into and relate to one another within each episode.

Quoting from the report, 'The linkages shown represent the co-occurrence of certain themes. The thickness of the linkage represents the frequency of their co-occurrence. For example, discussions around "cleanliness" invoked sub-themes

FIGURE 22: The Sankey Diagrams of 99 episodes of *Mann Ki Baat*

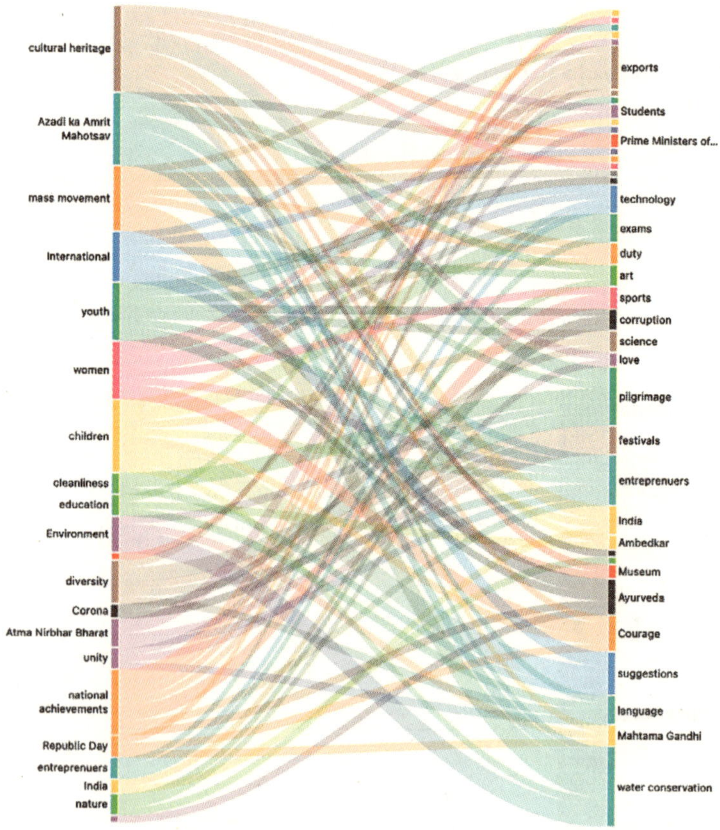

like "mass movement", "children", "women", "environment", and "Swacchta Abhiyan". Hence, using this an understanding can be gained about the context in which any given theme is discussed in the broadcast. Similarly, international discussion pertained to sports, national achievement, yoga, Ayurveda, and awards, representing the topics with an international component to them as discussed in the broadcast. Every theme on the left had linkages with multiple topics on the right, illustrating the holistic nature of the discussions on the programme. For example, the discussion around women covered diverse sub-topics such as UPI, Skill India, technology, sports, entrepreneurs and courage.'

The topical analysis of the five themes—cleanliness and sanitation, health, wellness, water conservation and sustainable development—is undertaken through case studies that depict the before (as is state) and after (transformed space) positions pictorially. From changemakers to collective actions tied to government initiatives, all are woven together to show how *Mann Ki Baat* enmeshed it all.

Having focused on a similar structure for all the topics, the study concluded that *Mann Ki Baat* is a unique radio programme that engages both rural and urban populations in India in a two-way conversation with Prime Minister Modi's government. Citizens can listen and learn about government initiatives and local and individual activism on some of the most important issues facing the country. They can give feedback and ask questions via letter, telephone, and social-media comments. As the analysis shows, the program focuses on five primary topics—sanitation, health care, wellness, water conservation, and sustainability—and highlights the accomplishments of ordinary

Illustration 1:

CASE STUDY 2

Waste Management by Champa Devi

The vision behind Swachh Bharat Abhiyan is that when citizens become active participants in cleanliness activities across the nation, the dream of a 'Clean India' once seen by Mahatma Gandhi is beginning to take shape. In the Mann ki Baat program in May 2022, PM Modi gave the example of Champa Devi from village Devar, Uttarakhand, who, he said, "through sheer hard work has created a forest full of greenery."

Starting almost 40 years ago, Champa Devi planted trees in the barren lands surrounding her village. Along with hundreds of her neighbours, she collects garbage door-to-door every day and tends to her trees twice a week. Over time, they have planted more than 100,000 trees, raising a completely new forest. As a result, water levels are rising, animal fodder is plentiful, and fuel is more easily available. As Champa Devi says, *"The forest is our life. If there is no forest, then we are not here. If there is no forest, then we cannot get oxygen. There is no water. There are many animals, and birds, and they all live in the forest. They all have their own food. When the trees dry, we have wood from them. When the leaves fall, we have manure from them. We have nothing without forests. Our life is dependent on the trees. These trees are like my son. When a tree is cut it is the saddest moment of my life."*

Champa Devi has become an inspiration and a hero to women across neighbouring villages.

Story in images

Champa Devi and her team planted hundreds of trees and created a forest of greenery.

The village where Champa Devi resides is filled with vast fields of green.

Champa Devi was inspired her to change the barren land behind her into a green-filled paradise with the help of the women of the village.

Illustration 2:

CASE STUDY 4

Subko Vaccine, Muft Vaccine in Dulariya, Betul

In 2021, after PM Modi made the COVID-19 vaccine free all over the country, many people in some areas, like the village of Dulariya, Betul, were hesitant to receive it because they worried about the harm it might cause.

A few residents, including Anil Kumar and Kishorilal, contacted PM Modi regarding the situation. Through Mann ki Baat, he got on a call with the whole village, addressed people's fears, and advised them to take the vaccine. PM Modi said not only was it safe, but getting the vaccine would help protect the entire community from disease. The village achieved a 100 percent vaccination rate, and villagers are now more willing to seek prevention and treatment services for a wide range of health conditions.

Story in images

The men responsible for spreading awareness about the effectiveness of the COVID-19 vaccine in their village

The clinic where the whole village went to get vaccinated

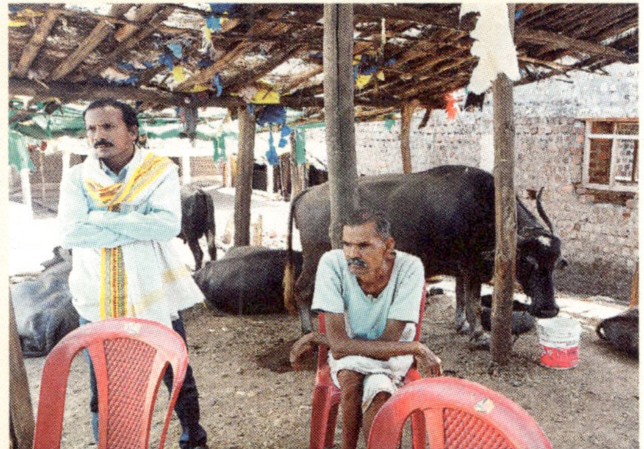

A few villagers who got vaccinated after listening to PM Modi talking about the vaccine on the Mann ki Baat program.

Dulariya, Betul and environs

people and communities, possibly inspiring listeners to become changemakers.

4) INDIAN INSTITUTE OF MASS COMMUNICATION (IIMC)

A special study conducted by the esteemed Indian Institute of Mass Communication, where a total of 890 respondents—media persons, media faculty, media students and media researchers from 116 academic institutions/universities and media houses from across the country—were interviewed, came up with the following big takeaways:

- Majority of the respondents (66 per cent) in the age group of 18-25 years listen to *Mann ki Baat.*
- 'Knowing about the country' and 'the Prime Minister's vision about the country' are the two prominent reasons which motivate audience to listen to the programme.
- 76 per cent of the respondents felt that *Mann Ki Baat* had initiated a trend where the awareness and appreciation for things in other parts of India has grown.
- 75 per cent of the respondents opined that *Mann Ki Baat* has emerged as a platform where people are introduced to trendsetters working selflessly to bring about meaningful change.
- 76 per cent of the respondents felt they were participating in the democratic process by listening to the PM on different issues on *Mann Ki Baat.*
- Education and grassroots innovators were the two most influential topics the respondents could recall.
- Most respondents shared their thoughts with their family members (32 per cent) or peers (29 per cent) regarding the topics discussed on *Mann Ki Baat.*

Out of the total 890 respondents, 583 (66 per cent) were in the age group of 18-25 years, 127 (14 per cent) were aged between 26 to 35 years, 84 (9 per cent) were 36 to 45 years old, 65 (7 per cent) were between 46-55 years and 31 (4 per cent) were 56 years and above. (See Figure 23)

FIGURE 23: Demographic of the survey respondents of IIM-C study

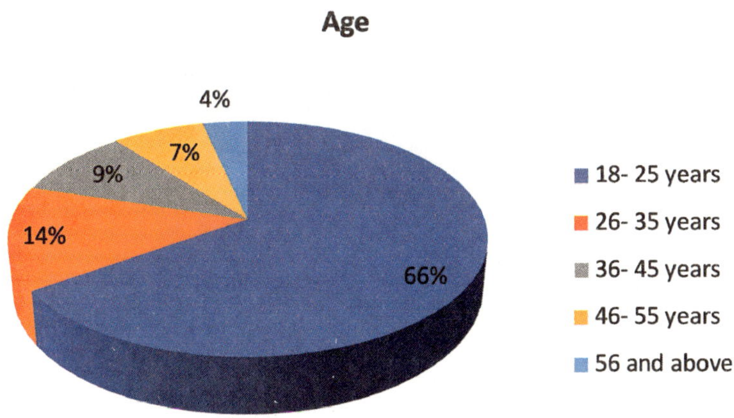

Some interesting insights came to the fore through some of the specific questions asked in the survey.

Responding to whether they listen to *Mann Ki Baat*, out of 890 respondents from the media industry, 760 (85 per cent) said yes that they heard the programme *Mann Ki Baat*. (Figure 24)

To the question as to why they listened to *Mann Ki Baat* (among those who answered yes), the reasons were informative as well as instructive (Figure 25)

When asked 'if *Mann Ki Baat* had initiated a trend where we were now more aware of things in other parts of India and had started appreciating them more', over 76 per cent people agreed or strongly agreed with the proposition (Figure 26).

FIGURE 24: Response on how many among the media fraternity listen to *Mann Ki Baat*

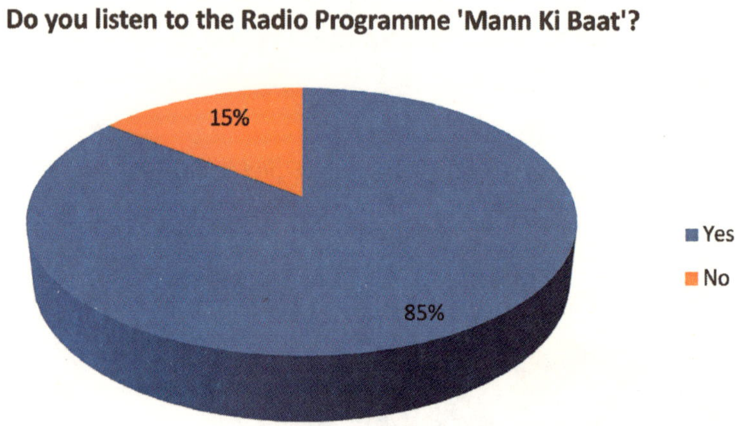

FIGURE 25: Reasons for listening to *Mann Ki Baat*

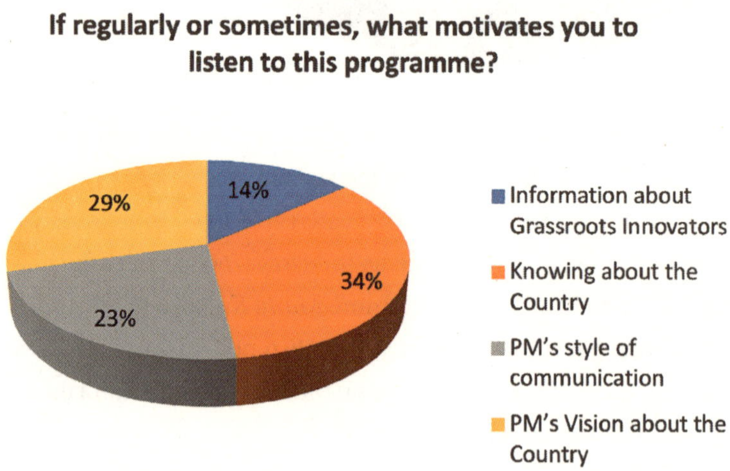

FIGURE 26: Has *Mann Ki Baat* made people more aware of their own country?

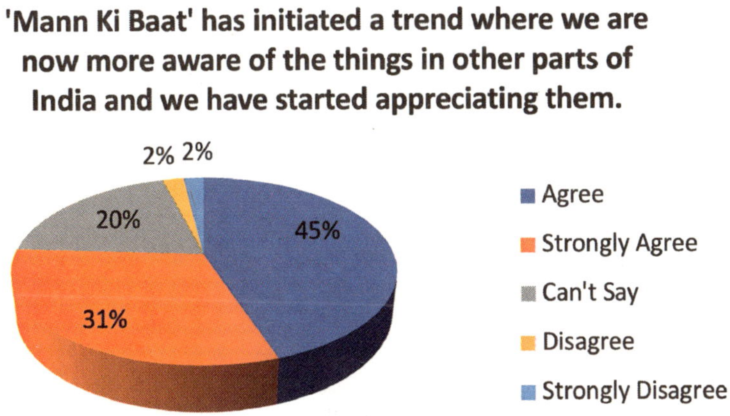

Regarding 'how *Mann Ki Baat* has emerged as a platform where people are introduced to trendsetters who are working selflessly to bring about a meaningful change in the lives of people', 75 per cent agreed that one of the great successes of *Mann Ki Baat* was that it identified and mainstreamed in the national consciousness, selfless trendsetters working for a social cause (Figure 27).

An important question to the respondents in the survey was, 'Which issue of national importance discussed on *Mann Ki Baat* had influenced their individual life'. (Figure 28)

In a supplementary question, which was optional and related to the previous question, the respondents were asked to specify if any other issue highlighted on *Mann Ki Baat* had influenced them. The respondents mentioned a lot of issues, such as the impressive style of the PM discussing contemporary issues—health & hygiene, heritage, foreign policy, education,

FIGURE 27: Does *Mann Ki Baat* identify and mainstream selfless work?

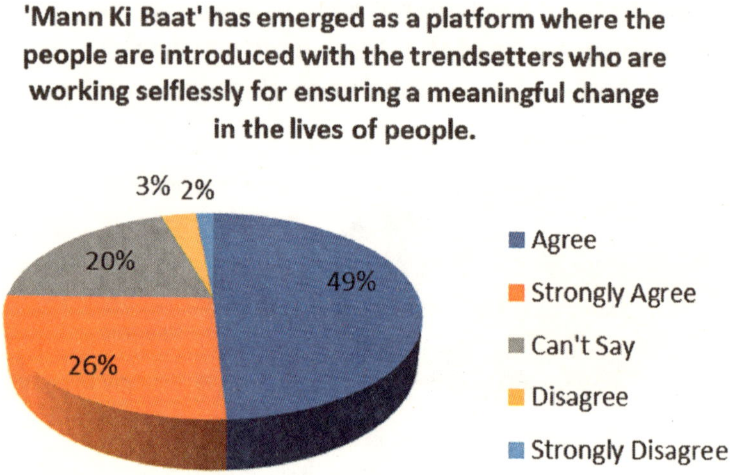

FIGURE 28: Issues on *Mann Ki Baat* that impacted the respondent's life

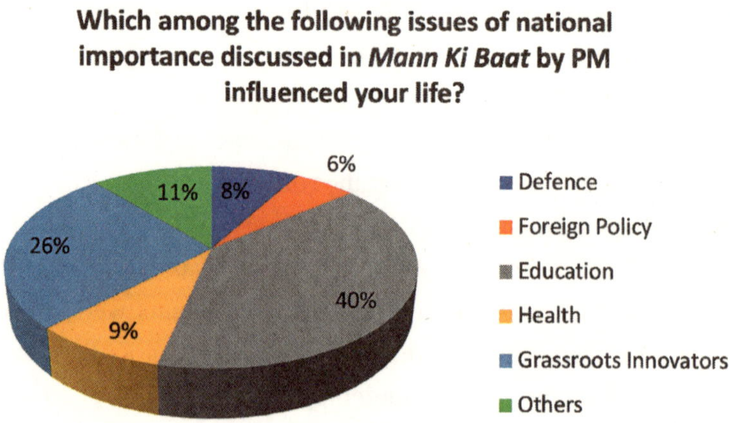

employment, agriculture and social enterprises, grassroots innovators, progress of the country, direct communication of the Prime Minister with the nation, Jan Dhan Yojana, the 1965 war, the amazing work by Indian scientists, Swachh Bharat, economic policy, connecting with the youth, information about the people who are working for social transformation, language and literature, etc.—in a simple manner and connecting them to the masses.

Respondents also spoke about topics like the Vocal for Local mission, use of bio-fertilisers, water conservation, the CRPF women battalion, labourers who built Kartavya Path, e-waste recycling, tribal upliftment, protecting and educating daughters, Har Ghar Tiranga, work done by health workers during the COVID-19 pandemic, lauding farmers for strengthening the country's agriculture sector, innovative ideas for farmers, Janta Curfew, recognising artists from rural areas, healthy lifestyle, millets, use of bamboo products, etc.

When asked, 'Do you discuss the issues addressed in *Mann Ki Baat* with your peers, family members or community after listening? If yes, with whom?' a surprising result came (*Figure 29*). Family and peers came first and together accounted for 61 per cent, while social media accounted for only 14 per cent. This finding established that *Mann Ki Baat* has a multiplier impact in real life, among friends and families, and is not limited to just social media. That *Mann Ki Baat* ignites conversations among people who know each other is perhaps also the reason why *Mann Ki Baat* has been so effective in bringing about social change and having a multiplier effect, in igniting the collective goodness of the nation.

FIGURE 29: Where do you discuss the issues raised in *Mann Ki Baat*?

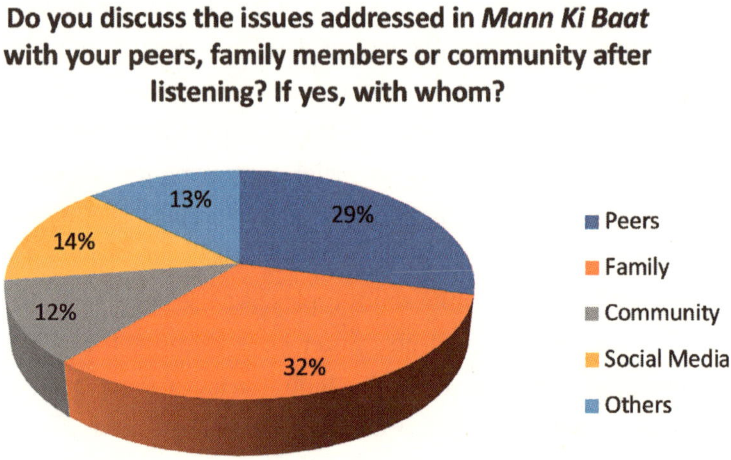

The last few responses were perhaps the most important in the survey on the question of 'whether *Mann Ki Baat* created an impact in people's lives' (Figure 30).

FIGURE 30: Has *Mann Ki Baat* created an impact in people's lives?

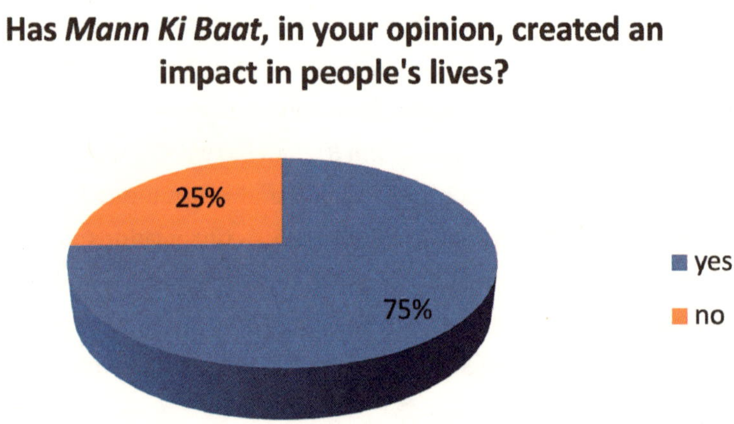

Out of 890 respondents, 665 (75 per cent) believe *Mann Ki Baat* has impacted people's lives, while 225 (25 per cent) feel it has not.

FIGURE 31: Does *Mann Ki Baat* make people feel like participants in democracy or ignite Jan Bhagidari?

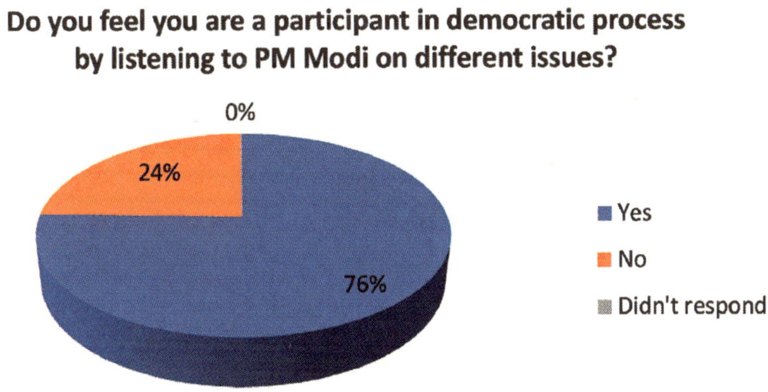

When asked if the respondents feel like participants in the democratic process after listening to Prime Minister Modi on different issues (Figure 31), out of the total of 890 respondents, 672 (76 per cent) said yes, 217 (24 per cent) said no, and 1 (less than 1 per cent) didn't answer.

An important subjective question was posed in the IIM-C survey to understand whether the respondents were following any particular advice given by the PM in *Mann Ki Baat* in their professional lives. The responses included that they now follow credible media outlets, promote local talent, check the sources of news, focus on grassroots innovators, have pledged for organ donation and cleanliness, have become aware that India is the mother of democracy, cover stories that make a positive impact on society, remain truthful, cover Indian historical temples, support vocal for local, have an optimistic approach in coverage of news, follow Har Ghar Tiranga, follow Rashtrahit Sarvopari, judiciously use social media for the development of society, have become their own trendsetters, work towards saving the girl child and gender equality, think innovatively about sanitation and cleanliness, use of, support Aatmanirbhar Bharat, have put the tricolour on their social media profile, save water, call disabled people 'divyang' and not 'viklang', spend time with their families, support Do Gaj Doori, Mask Hai Jaroori, manage time better, etc.

These four research studies are only symbolic of a larger attitudinal shift taking place in the minds and hearts of the ordinary citizens of India. The credit for that goes to Prime Minister Narendra Modi, especially because he gives credit for the success of *Mann Ki Baat* to all of us. Indeed,

> जब प्रेरणा को मिले प्रोत्साहन का साथ,
> तब होती है, आपकी, हमारी, सब के मन की बात!